Money
The Great Deception

"None are more hopelessly enslaved than those who falsely believe they are free." (Johann Wolfgang von Goethe, 1749-1832, German poet, novelist, playwright, natural philosopher, diplomat)

Then you will know the truth, and the truth will set you free.
(John 8:32)

Gottfried Hetzer

Money ... The Great Deception

Copyright

© 2018 Gottfried Hetzer

https://hetzer.jimdo.com

No rights reserved

Money … The Great Deception

Table Of Contents

Introduction	8
Whom Do We Serve?	9
PART A – How The World Financial System Works	11
01. Money	12
02. Interest	16
03. Banks	20
04. Inflation	22
05. Deflation	23
06. Summary	25
PART B – Destructive Effects Of The World Financial System	26
Introduction	27
07. Artificial Money Creation	27
(fiat money, fractional reserve banking, interest)	
08. Corrupted Banks	31
(legalised theft, limited liability, gambling with time)	
09. Skyrocketing Interest	32
10. Debt Madness	34
11. Disreputable Rating Agents	35
12. Governments Voiding Justice System	36
13. Growth Compulsion	37
14. Corporate Sector Fighting For Survival	39
15. Ailing Governments And Public Sectors	40
16. Overdevelopment Monetary Assets	41
17. Speculation Lunacy	42
18. Inflation	43
19. Income Without Performance	44
20. Interest Inflated Price Reduce Income	45
21. Growing Income Disparity	45
22. Climbing Unemployment	46
23. Ecological Exploitation And Ruination	47

24.	War And Capital Destruction	48
25.	Summary	49

PART C – Babylon   52

26.	Time To Leave	53

PART D – Looking For A Way Out   55

Introduction   56

27.	Back To Gold?	56
28.	Debt Relief?	57
29.	Tried Systems, Possible Solutions	59
30.	Opposition	64
31.	No Other Way	65

PART E – Changing The Paradigm   68

Introduction   69

32.	Egypt ≠ Canaan	69
33.	World System ≠ Kingdom Of God	72
34.	Ownership ≠ Setwardship	75
35.	Money Impacts Spiritual State	77
36.	Here And Now ≠ Eternity	80
37.	Summary	83

PART F – Kingdom Economy   85

Introduction   86

Principles   88

38.	Money	89
39.	Banking	90
40.	Borrowing And Lending	91
41.	Interest	107
42.	Collateral (guarantee, pledge, security, surety)	110
43.	Limited Liability	112
44.	Bankruptcy, Insolvency	114
45.	Partnerships	115
46.	Planning (His way)	117

47.	Investment	123
48.	Land, Buildings	126
49.	Payment Terms	129
50.	Pricing	130
51.	Marketing, Advertising	132
52.	Competitions	134
53.	Get-Rich-Quick Schemes	137
54.	Fear Factors (insurances, retirement/pension, security systems)	139
55.	Giving (tithe, offerings, generous lifestyle)	150
56.	Refund, Restitution	160
57.	Inheritance	163
58.	Taxes	165

Character — **166**

59.	Accountability	167
60.	Corruption (general)	169
61.	Bribery	171
62.	Integrity, Transparency	174
63.	Honesty (lying, fraud/cheating/swindling, theft, extortion, exploitation)	179
64.	Motivation	185
65.	Greed	190
66.	Work Attitude	194
67.	Relationships	199

PART G - Plan And Purpose — **204**

Introduction

There are diverse reasons for and approaches to writing a book on money. This one intends to shed light on a rarely considered perspective to it.

Systems are supposed to serve people and not vice versa. The Sabbath is but one example, where Jesus made that clear *(Mark 2:27)*. When people are forced to serve a system, something is obviously wrong, especially if the system is unjust, enslaving and destructive.

The world financial system is such an unjust, enslaving and destructive system. It should therefore be replaced by a just, liberating and constructive approach to handling money that does not enslave. This will only be possible in the context of the Kingdom of God.

At the highest level, the Bible is divided into the Old and New Testament. People often don't like to read the OT, for to them it seems boring and outdated. But unless we do so we are unlikely to fully understand and embrace the NT message. Similarly in this book, I'd like to describe our current money system and its all around negative effects first, even if it may not be the most thrilling story. However without reading it, the biblical alternative to this may not be fully understood, appreciated and embraced.

This book is written for those unfamiliar with the financial lingo, the common man if you like. My aim is to explain things in a normal, short and understandable way. I want to be as brief as possible avoiding overload and complicated detail. However, the information provided will be sufficient to get a good grasp of the secular money system and God's alternative to it.

Please note:
- Unless stated otherwise all Scriptures taken from the *NIV 2011*
- There are also a few references to the apocryphal book of *Sirach (NRSV)*

Whom Do We Serve?

From time to time, the media feeds us with the latest facts about the ever-increasing economic inequality in this world. Here are the most recent ones from early 2018:

- The six richest people are together wealthier than the bottom half of the world's population (= 3.7 billion people).
- In 2017, 82% of all capital gains went to the richest 1% of the world's population. 18% went to the other 49% of the top half. The wealth of the bottom half didn't grow at all.
- The top 1% of the world's population have more money than the bottom 99%.
- 15% of the world's population struggle to survive on less than $1.25 a day.
- 40% of the world's population (= 3 billion people) own next to nothing.
- By contrast, the world's corrupt elites, oligarchs and anachronistic monarchies spend countless billions on the most absurd luxuries.
- To avoid paying their fair share of taxes, the world's wealthiest people and largest corporations stash their money in offshore tax havens. The Tax Justice Network estimates that to be at least $21-$32 trillion.
- Even in the developed world countless millions of people are working longer hours for lower wages now than people did 40 years ago.
- The global economy rewards those at the top at the expense of everyone else. The powerful feed on the powerless.

Clearly, money 'rules' this world and the vast majority of mankind serves money. Most people would probably never say it that way, but that's exactly the way it is. It's an age old issue.

The Bible records Satan's failed attempt to overthrow God and usurp His place *(Is 14:12-14)*. For that reason he was banished from God's presence and will in time be thrown down to earth *(Ezek 28:17; Luke 10:18, Rev 12:9)*. His ultimate fate (eternal hellfire) is also sealed *(Rev 20:1-6)*. In his fury about losing his privileged place in heaven, the devil is out to take revenge. Powerless to win against God Himself, he targets God's image (mankind) instead.

The last paragraph looks a bit out of place in the context of money. But it gives, in a nutshell, the spiritual backdrop for the current unjust, enslaving and destructive monetary system. How come?

God is omniscient, omnipresent and almighty. The devil isn't. He is an angelic being. He doesn't know everything, can't be everywhere simultaneously and has only limited power. So, unlike God, Satan depends on a centralised, enslaving top-down approach with him at the top to stay in control of things on earth. Expressions of this are the push for a one-world government, a progressively globally connected or single market economy, or the already existing world financial system. As outrageous as this might sound, all this is designed to enslave and in the end destroy mankind, God's image. Jesus left no doubt that the works of the world are evil *(John 7:7)*. Money is Satan's most effective tool to force people into complete dependency and servitude *(Rev 13:16-17)*. He knows that man's bondage to money in the end will also cost their place in heaven *(see e.g. Matt 6:24; 1 Tim 6:10)*.

More than 2,000 years ago Jesus stated,

> *No one can serve two masters. Either he will hate the one and love the other, or he will be devoted to the one and despise the other.* **You cannot serve both God and money**. *(Matt 6:24, emphasis added)*

Remember, creation has delivered its own Creator to the cross for a ridiculous 30 silver coins *(Matt 26:15)*! Isn't it disturbing that the image of God (here the man Judas) has delivered God Himself for a pittance to die innocently?

How can money have such a destructive influence on humans? How is it possible that our money system can force its rule on us? To understand this we need at least a rough understanding of how the world financial system works. This system is no accident, but a planned, sophisticated construct. It serves the world system, whose ruler is Satan, the prince of this world *(John 12:31, 14:30; Rev 12:9)*. Its complexity is used to disguise its true intention.

In Part A we will, thus, avoid that complexity and rather focus on the important basics. This will still be sufficient to understand the evil intent behind this system.

Part A

How The World Financial System Works

1. Money

"The study of money, above all other fields in economics, is one in which complexity is used to disguise truth or to evade truth, not to reveal it." (John Kenneth Galbraith, 1908-2006, Canadian-American economist and author)

That says it all, doesn't it? It's impossible to condense all the ins and outs relating to money into a few book pages. However, looking at a few key issues of money will already help us to get a good understanding of how the world's financial system works. Which is exactly what we need here.

What Is Money?

Money is a symbol for wealth, security and independence, which is why everyone wants to have it. It's mostly received for work and spent for living. Money is taken for granted and appreciated as a useful tool in everyday life. With it you can buy and have almost anything.

Without money, buying and selling is limited to trading goods and services for other goods and services. This can be a very time-consuming and complicated exercise. Money, therefore, is a service tool that simplifies economic exchange. When goods and services receive price tags, people can more easily compare value for money. This helps to decide what to buy, how much, where and when.

Money has no inherent value like clothes, tools, food or something. It only gets its value, because it is publicly acknowledged, received and handed on as money. Today's market economies wouldn't work without it. It plays a very central role.

What people commonly call money does in fact relate to the technical term 'monetary assets', which are two distinct items. The one is physical/tangible the other one not. They are:

- CASH, which are physical coins and notes.
- CREDIT ITEMS or book money, which are 'claims on cash' stored up in accounts (current, checking, savings, time accounts, etc.) or other deposits (e.g. shares), hence intangible items.

Does this distinction matter? To most people it probably doesn't as they are not interested in how money works. They just use it. To the others it should matter.

The creation of cash is a monopoly of central banks. They bring cash into as well as retracting it from circulation in our economies. The actual amount of cash in circulation is fairly stable. The creation of credit items, on the other hand, is open to anyone and can increase indefinitely.

The primary function of cash is to pay for goods and services. When we deposit our cash with our bank, we convert it into a credit item (book money). We no longer have the cash as the bank has it now. We only have a claim on cash. When we pay for our goods and services electronically from our bank account, we simply transfer our credit item (claim on cash) to somebody else.

There are a some interesting phenomena associated with cash, which should be briefly mentioned here:

- Although the physical notes and coins are state property, nobody ever gets prosecuted for abusing or even destroying them.

- Law forces people to accept money as payment. But it doesn't force people to spend it to bring it back into circulation.

- Money never gets 'used up'. A person might run out of money by spending it all. But the cash itself doesn't vanish. It just passes on from one person to others and can be reused repeatedly as exchange medium.

- If we have goods but no cash, we need to sell first to be able to buy stuff. If we have no goods and no cash, we need to offer service for pay to be able to buy stuff. If we have cash, we can buy straight away. Therefore, cash has a 'liquidity advantage' over goods and services.

- Food perishes and goods fall apart over time, but the equivalent in cash stays unchanged. Services become obsolete, but the equivalent in cash never does. Consequently, money (the exchange medium for goods and services) is in no way equal, but much superior to goods and labor.

- Weight, volume and distance measures never change. One kilogram always has 1,000 gram, one meter always 100 centimetre, and so forth. Thankfully, this makes dealings in those measures predictable, even over extended time periods. But for some reason the measuring unit money constantly changes. Today the 'purchasing power' of $1 might be 100 Cent, tomorrow just 90. This transforms the economy into an unpredictable game of chance.

Credit/Loans And Debt

Remember, what we commonly call money is actually monetary assets, a mix of cash and credit items (claims on cash in accounts). When we lend our monetary assets to someone, they still remain monetary assets to us. To the borrower they are debts. However, two things are different for us now: (1) The availability of our monetary assets has changed. (2) If we lent cash, then it is now converted into a credit item (claim on cash) for us.

Loans/credits and debts always balance. When A gives a $500 loan to B, this loan is balanced by the $500 debt that B owes A. Even within the economy as a whole the total amount of loans/credits equates to the total amount of debts.

Because we can lend and borrow the same cash and credit items (claims on cash) over and over again, lending and borrowing is not limited by the amount of cash that is circulating in an economy. The increase and decrease of loans/credits and its corresponding debts depends entirely on the participants of an economy. They are mere book entries.

Problems Associated With Money

Cash can be produced in any given size and denomination. It's fairly small and handy so easy to transport and store. Cash is extremely durable, goes never out of style, doesn't create storage fees, and doesn't rust, age or go to waste. It can be used and reused by anyone, anywhere, anytime for almost anything.

These are all advantages over goods and services that make money a trailblazing invention. Logically they mask the erratic change of money's purchasing power caused by inflation. And so, money plays a pivotal role in our economies.

To fulfil its vital function as exchange medium, money must circulate continually. In other words, it needs to be spent. If the circulation process is interrupted, problems will arise. Lets illustrate this very simply based on a single $100 bill:

- Employee A gets $100 for his work and spends it on food at Grocer B.
- Grocer B uses the $100 to buy clothes at Clothing Store C.
- The owner of Clothing Store C uses the $100 to pay Supplier D.
- Supplier D uses the $100 to pay Electrician E who fixed his alarm system.
- Electrician E uses the bill to pay his $100 debt in the local Pub F.
- The owner of Pub F uses the $100 to buy more supply at Brewery G.
- Brewery G uses the $100 to pay Employee A.

In this example seven parties benefit from a single $100 bill just being passed on. And that is exactly how money circulation works. If, however, Employee A decides not to spend the $100 he receives, the other six parties in the succession line suffer. Then they won't have an income and the economic process breaks down. In the end even A won't receive an income anymore. That's precisely why money needs to keep circulating.

The next illustration adds another dimension to this fact. As long as the income flows 100% back into the demand and production cycle, i.e., the economy, all is fine. The circulation is steady. However, when spending is reduced to save up, banks play a vital role to ensure ongoing circulation. When people deposit their money with them for longer periods, banks need to release those savings as credits/loans back into the circulation process.

Simplified Money Circulation Model

Deposits		Credit
50	after 5th cycle	50
40	after 4th cycle	40
30	after 3rd cycle	30
20	after 2nd cycle	20
10	after 1st cycle	10

Each amount available for but withheld from circulation (e.g., savings at home; banks not giving loans) decreases the demand within an economy. Decreased demand leads to lower production and supply. Lower production and supply ends up in personnel layoffs and higher unemployment. Thus the income base shrinks. This will reduce the demand even further. And so the destructive cycle continues.

The illustration also highlights the problem coming from deposits (credit items). In our example 100 money units are circulating in cash. In each cycle 10 money units are deposited at the bank and passed on as credit to others to keep the circulation going. Should the depositor now decide to withdraw his deposits (50 money units) all at once, then the bank would have a major problem. It can't meet this demand. All 100 money units are circulating and used elsewhere. Organising the cash is a near impossible task. The bank is likely to collapse.

Let's state it again: keeping money in circulation simply means spending it! But here lies the conflict. Due to its superiority, people want to save as much money for as long as possible. Which is the exact opposite of keeping it in circulation! The solution to this conflict appears to be interest, which is described next.

In conclusion, money carries the potential of being a blessing (circulation) and a curse (interrupted circulation) to mankind at the same time. Jesus' statement indicating and encouraging circulation might appear in a new light now:

> *Give, and it will be given to you. A good measure, pressed down, shaken together and running over, will be poured into your lap. For with the measure you use, it will be measured to you. (Luke 6:38)*

2. Interest

Money keeps circulating in two ways: First, by its original trading function for buying goods and services. This is motivated by satisfying needs and wants. Second, by lending it. This is motivated by interest.

What Is Interest?

Interest is the price for giving up the advantage of immediate availability of cash or credit items. The one who borrows (the debtor) pays interest (supposedly a user fee or rent) for money that others own.

To the lender interest becomes an income without work. He might have worked for the money he lent. But the interest he receives on it is by default an income without work. He has not worked for it. The borrower or debtor has.

If the money owner doesn't want to lend his surplus money, it can't be used in the economy. The vital money circulation is now impeded. Hence, the interest must be high enough to encourage him to change his mind and lend.

Lending for interest sounds like a good idea to keep the money circulation going. But it does swiftly turn into bizarre and tricky scenarios. Here's an example:

- A borrows $1,000 and agrees to pay it back after one year with 10% interest. That is an additional $100. A spends the $1,000 the same morning on a PC. The money is gone but A still carries a whole year's cost (10% interest = $100) for making use of the loan.
- The PC store deposits the $1,000 from A at noon with the same bank that A borrowed it from.
- In the afternoon the bank lends the very $1,000 to B at identical conditions it had lend them to A in the morning.
- By being lent twice on the same day, one and the same $1,000 gain twice as much interest for the same year. Now both A and B pay 10% utilisation cost each (2x $100 = $200) for the same full year for the identical $1,000 of cash.
- And the very $1,000 will go that same route time and again, day in day out. This will create countless interest payments.

This scenario sounds unreal, yet it is exercised in similar fashion day by day all over the world on a much larger scale.

Through mediation (accepting savings and giving loans) banks play a vital role in maintaining the money circulation. Thus they are a hub for interest flows. They receive the debtors' interest payments, which they keep partly for themselves before passing the rest on to the savers.

But think of it. When you lend, for example, a specific equipment worth $1,000, you can generate income (rent) only once for a set period of time. For being able to lend the equivalent $1,000 in cash time and again, the bank generates multiple incomes (interest = 'rent') on it for a set period of time. Where's the logic?

> "Money was established for exchange, but interest causes it to be reproduced by itself. Therefore this way of earning money is greatly in conflict with the natural law." (Aristotle, 384-322 BC, ancient Greek philosopher and scientist)

Interest creates money out of money and thus turns the economic process on its head. Lending for interest first establishes how much money has to be created anew (interest), which then needs to be backed up by production and services.

Interest means an income without work for the lender. The borrower works for it. Interest causes those who are rich enough to lend to become even richer without doing anything for it. It is an advantage for them. Those who need to borrow get poorer despite having to work harder to repay the loan plus interest. To them interest is a disadvantage (unless they can pass their burden on to others).

Strictly speaking, lending for interest means a risk-free investment to the lender. The borrower carries the whole risk of earning the borrowed money plus interest back. The lender is not involved at all.

Interest is not only paid by debtors. Even those who never borrow pay it. How so? Almost all manufacturers and service providers borrow to invest in their operations. Consequently, interest factors in their production and service costs and is passed on to the consumer. Today it is not uncommon that a 10% share of a selling price represents interest payments. In extreme cases even 80% shares have been found. The general rule is that the higher the proportion of debt in a company's capital employed, the more inflated their prices are due to interest.

Simple Interest

Simple interest is the method in which the original amount lent (the 'principal') grows linearly with time. That's why it's also called linear interest. In each period the total balance grows by a fixed percentage of the principal. For example, if you put $1,000 on a savings account at 6% you gain $60 interest for every full year. Simple/linear interest is rarely used nowadays.

Compound Interest

What is commonly used instead today is compound interest. It is calculated on the combined total of (a) the principal and (b) all the interest that has already accrued. For example, if you put $1,000 on a savings account at 6% compounded, you gain $60 interest only for the first full year. The second full year will the yield $63.60 interest, which is 6% on $1,060 ($1,000 principal + $60 interest 1st year). Thus every year the interest gained will increase more.

Compound interest results in exponential money growth. A rate of 1% doubles money artificially in 72 years, 3% in 24 years, 6% in only 12 years and 12% in just 6 years. Like cancer, the money growth starts slowly and barely noticeable, only to develop into a sheer unstoppable force over time.

Compound interest makes it difficult to keep any economy healthy and the value of money stable. To ensure both, the economic output must keep up with the artificial and exponential money growth. We will soon see that this is impossible.

Take a look at the chart below that helps to illustrate the madness of compound interest growth. Let's imagine someone had put $1 at Jesus' birth on an interest bearing savings account. The table shows into what fortune this single dollar would have developed over the centuries based on different compound interest rates. Since the numbers in $ are far too large to display, they are converted into weights of solid gold. The rate used is from May 2017.

$1,180/ounce	1% interest in solid gold	2% interest in solid gold	3% interest in solid gold	4% interest in solid gold	5% interest in solid gold
1529 AD	106 kg	371,000 tons	1.1 trillion tons	2.9 quintillion tons	1x Earth' weight
2016 AD	14 tons	5.7 billion tons	2.0 quintillion tons	87x Earth' weight	21 billion x Earth' weight
2016 AD Simple Interest	$20.16	$40.32	$60.48	$80.64	$100.80

Incredible, isn't it? Evidently, a continual payment of compound interest is clearly impossible. Just look at the negligible results of simple interest in comparison. We can state: the compound interest mechanism creates an unhealthy driving force for chronic economic growth. It works like a hidden redistribution device that takes from the poor to give to the rich. It works everywhere at all levels.

> "Everybody, who believes that exponential growth in a finite world can continue forever is either crazy or an economist." (K.E. Boulding, 1910-1993, US economist)

To be fair, nobody works with saving and lending periods of 2,000+ years and for such tiny amounts. However, today we do talk about trillions $ and decades of terms in our economies. This also renders devastating effects as we will later see. Even simple interest causes substantial problems in those scenarios.

3. Banks

Despite many businesses and organisations offering bank-like credit facilities only two true types of banks exist. (1) Issuing or central banks and (2) Commercial or business banks. They play different roles in our economies.

(1) Central Banks (Issuing Banks)

According to economic textbooks, central banks (CBs) have three main functions:

- Organising the money supply to the economy;
- Ensuring the stability of the national currency;
- Regulating the basic interest rates at which money can be borrowed.

CBs are the bank for governments and commercial banks. As a 'Lender of Last Resort' they bail commercial banks out of trouble. CBs can also have supervisory powers to ensure that commercial banks and financial institutions do not behave recklessly or fraudulently. CBs, therefore, should fulfil a task of public law. Their success in this task depends on the tools available and rights granted to them as well as the veto-interference of governments.

For that reason independent CBs operating in national interest should be preferred. But they are hard to find today. Most CBs are either state-owned (e.g. China, Russia) or privately owned (e.g. USA, England). Both versions create a conflict of interests. The first group tends to focus on what benefits the government. The second one on what benefits its private shareholders. Neither one has first and foremost the national interest at heart.

(2) Commercial Or Business Banks

Commercial/business banks deal with individuals, businesses and organisations. They administrate their clients' funds and facilitate a host of transfers for them. For that they usually charge fixed or graduated fees to the account holders.

Business banks 'mediate' between lender/saver and borrower/debtor. In other words they lend what others have to spare to those who are in need of it. For this service they charge credit interest to the debtor (see following chart). Part of that credit interest, the bank margin, remains at the bank to cover their costs and profit. The rest is passed on as savings interest to the saver.

		Basic Interest
		(price for giving up liquidity advantage)
	+	Scarcity Surcharge
	=	Effective (Real) Interest of Saver
	+	Inflation Surcharge
		(to offset money devaluation)
1	=	**Interest for Savings**
		(bank paying to savers)
		Costs
		(personnel, equipment, building, credit risk, etc.)
	+	Profit before Tax
2	=	**Bank Margin**
1+2	=	**Credit Interest**
		(debtor's payment to the bank)

It is worrying that commercial banks use their short-term deposits for providing longterm loans, e.g. 15-30 year house mortgages, or other investment loans. Why is that? Because they don't know if they will have the money for these commitments. If a bank's short-term deposits are all withdrawn at the same time, will the bank be able to pay them out, since they are committed long-term? The bank can only hope for a constant flow of short-term deposits to cover this. This gamble is common practice today.

If banks could only lend out to the maximum cash amount deposited with them, loans would be restricted significantly. Indeed, the overall lending business of all banks worldwide would be limited to the maximum cash amount in circulation. That, however, is not the case anymore.

> "Banks lend by creating credit. They create the means of payment out of nothing." (Ralph M. Hawtry, 1878-1975, former Secretary to the UK Treasury)

> "The process by which banks create money is so simple that the mind is repelled." (John K. Galbraith, in 'Money: Whence it came, where it went', page 29)

Today business banks depend only to a fraction on cash deposits for their lending business. Based on fractional reserve banking they can create money effectively out of thin air. The next chart shows how it works. We assume a legally required reserve of 10% for the banks (in reality it varies between 2-10%, in China 15%).

- $1,000 cash are deposited at bank A. The bank keeps the required reserve of $100. The remaining $900 are loaned to a client who spends it at some store.
- The store deposits that $900 with bank B. The bank keeps the required reserve of $90. It lends the remaining $810 to a client who spends it at some store.
- The store deposits that $810 with bank C. The bank keeps the required reserve of $81. It lends the remaining $729 to a client who spends it at some store.
- The store deposits that $729 at bank D, etc. etc. We get the drift. And so this whole process can repeat itself umpteen times. And in reality it does.

	Deposit (paid in)	Reserve (10% kept)	Credit (lent out)
Bank A	$1,000	-$100	$900
Bank B	$900	-$90	$810
Bank C	$810	-$81	$729
Bank D	$729	-$73	$656
Bank E	$656	-$66	$590
Bank F	$590	-$59	$531
Bank G	$531	-$53	$478
Total	$5,217	-$522	$4,695

Please note that in our example only $1,000 in cash exists. All the banks involved taken together can, thus, only guarantee a maximum of $1,000. Here, the seven banks (A-G) guarantee $521.70 of that. Yet the fractional reserve banking allowed them to lend out a total of $4,695.33 at this stage already. This is a multiple of the existing $1,000 and is tantamount to phoney money creation, but can be spent. It's therefore safe to say that banks receive their greatest income from interest paid on an illusion (money they created from thin air).

4. Inflation

Frequently the media report about (consumer) inflation. But they are actually referring to the consumer price index (CPI), which is the 'rate at which prices increase or decrease' for products and services. These can have many reasons, but that should not be confused with real inflation.

The term 'inflation' in its genuine sense simply means that the amount of money in circulation is inflated compared to what the economy can bear. An increased amount of bank notes in circulation converts into more money being available to buy existing production. It denotes a shift in the healthy balance between supply and demand. Inflation, therefore, has two effects:

- The purchasing power of circulating money shrinks compared to the produced performance. A 10% inflation turns the value of 100 money units to 90.
- Based on the money in circulation, the general price level will rise. With a 10% inflation something that did cost 100 money units will now cost 110 instead.

The consumers' influence on creating an inflation is small. They would have to withhold money from the economic cycle purposely. And then release it after the CB has issued new money. For that to happen on any significant scale seems unlikely.

The root problem of inflation, therefore, lies with the CBs. They usually inject new money to encourage economic activity. Instead they should withdraw money from the circulation process. That would automatically lead to the vital circulation of the remainder. And it would increase the crucial circulation speed.

> "There is no other way but through inflation that so few people can become so rich and so many so poor in such a short period of time." (Fritz Leutwiler, 1925-1997, former President of Swiss National Bank)

Inflation always disadvantages the ordinary and needy people. They have neither the power nor means to compensate any loss of value in their earnings and savings. The rich are able to absorb inflation losses more easily. But as capital owners they use their power to protect their interests. Inflation losses are passed on in prices and better interest rates demanded for their long-term deposits. And so are better returns on investments, and so forth.

Inflation leads to a wealth transfer from labour (the poor) to capital (the rich).

5. Deflation

With inflation money loses its value over time. With deflation it's the opposite as money gains in value. Deflation is commonly considered to be the result of a combination of four factors:

(1) The supply of money goes down.
(2) The supply of other goods goes up.
(3) The demand for money goes up.
(4) The demand for other goods goes down.

When the supply of goods and services grows faster than the supply of money we get a deflation. Such scenario is consistent with these four factors. It also has negative consequences. As the overproduction must be reversed and production costs reduced, personnel will be laid off. Rising unemployment results. Moreover, in the race to sell production, price levels will sink. Eventually, companies will be happy to at least cover their fixed costs.

The scary part is that a deflationary crisis nurtures itself:

- Falling demand results in falling price levels. Eventually prices don't even cover a company's financing costs anymore.
- This leads to the liquidation of businesses that have become unprofitable.
- Business liquidation causes further personal layoffs. More unemployment means less income, which reduces the demand level even more.
- Moreover, the assets of liquidated businesses are now returned to the banks at lower value compared to the time when they were financed on debt.
- The attempt of banks to sell those assets to recover some of their loss leads to an oversupply.
- This oversupply causes another round of price decreases, resulting in more businesses going bankrupt.
- In this downward spiral, rising unemployment leads to the increase of the social burden.

That's why governments fear deflation more than inflation. To fend off any danger of deflation, government rather put up with an inflationary environment. They allow CBs to pump new money into the economic cycle in the hope of reviving economic activity.

6. Summary

So here is a brief summary of how the world financial system works:

- Money simplifies the trade of goods and services.
- Money must circulate all the time to ensure a healthy economy. This means it must be spent.
- As money has superior qualities to the goods and services it needs to help to trade, it tends to be saved whenever and wherever possible.
- Saving money, though, means an interruption of its critical circulation.
- To maintain a constant money flow, people are offered interest (more money) to lend their savings.
- Here commercial banks act as application agent. For one thing they administer the savings. At the same time they find parties who need that money and are willing to pay interest for its usage.
- But interest creates money out of money. Thus, by trying to keep the existing money circulating, the amount of money grows artificially bigger.
- Since we mainly work with compound interest, the amount of money grows exponentially.
- Moreover, commercial banks create money out of nothing (fractional reserve banking). This allows them to lend what does not exist for even more interest. This interest is 100% income to them.
- For a healthy economy, the purchasing power of money needs to stay stable.
- To achieve that, the economy must grow in step with the exponential money growth.
- Continual exponential growth with limited resources is impossible.
- CBs should regulate the amount of money circulating in an economy at a healthy level.
- However this is a very complex and difficult task to master. It means there is a constant danger of inflation (too much money circulating) or deflation (too little money circulating).

Part B

Destructive Effects Of The World Financial System

Introduction

> "The few who could understand the system will either be so interested in its profits, or so dependent on its favours, that there will be no opposition from that class, while on the other hand, the great body of the people mentally incapable of comprehending the tremendous advantage that capital derives from the system, will bear its burdens without complaint, and perhaps without even suspecting that the system is inimical [harmful; GH] to their interests." (The Rothschilds in a letter to associates, London 1863)

> "It is difficult to get a man to understand something when his salary depends upon his not understanding it." (Upton Sinclair, 1878-1968, American author)

In 'Part A' we looked briefly at key components of our financial system: money, interest, banks, inflation and deflation. And then summarised how that money system works. This should give us a good base to move on.

This 'Part B' now gives a synopsis of disastrous outcomes stemming from that apparatus. God willing, this will create a strong awareness of the wicked nature of the finance system God calls all believers to leave *(Rev 18:4)*.

> *My people have committed two sins: They have forsaken me, the spring of living water, and have dug their own cisterns, broken cisterns that cannot hold water. (Jer 2:13)*

The root cause of all described in this 'Part B' is swiftly outlined. It's man's refusal to embrace God's just economic approach. And it is man's utter failure to set up his own just economic system as a replacement. Or, as Jesus summarised it,

> *... the works of the world are evil. (John 7:7)*

7. Artificial Money Creation

Fiat Money

> "Gold is money, everything else is credit." (J.P. Morgan, 1837-1913, US American banker and one of the architects of the Federal Reserve System)

> "We are in danger of being overwhelmed with irredeemable paper, mere paper, representing not gold nor silver; no sir, representing nothing but broken promises, bad faith, bankrupt corporations, cheated creditors and a ruined people." (Daniel Webster, 1782-1852, 14th and 19th US Secretary of State)

What is fiat money? Unlike a gold-backed currency, fiat money is not backed by anything. It has no value whatsoever. It only receives value because of the faith people who use it place in it. The moment people lose that faith fiat money holds no value anymore. This is typically seen in inflationary environments.

A fiat monetary system is usually the upshot of too much public debt. When a government struggles to repay all its debt in gold or silver it risks default. The easiest way to avoid this is to remove the physical backing of the currency. By doing this, the government accomplishes two things:

- Pulling out all stops on artificial money creation;
- Getting rid of its obligation to repay its debts in real assets or commodities.

Removing the physical backing of money opens the sluice gates for unlimited credit creation. Hyperinflation is the logical terminal stage of any fiat money.

The word 'fiat' is Latin for 'it shall be' or 'let it be done' in the sense of a divine act to create something out of nothing. Since only God can do that, one wonders if that term is not deliberately chosen to mock God. That would be no surprise.

Since it's not backed by anything, fiat money is created out of thin air. How so? Well, anyone who borrows substantially from a commercial bank must provide a real, physical asset as collateral. But when governments borrow from CBs, which is also substantial, they don't. They simply give bonds (debts) as collateral for their debts. Debts are no assets. It's an obligation to pay what was borrowed plus interest back after an agreed period of time. So governments offer CBs a not yet existing collateral in exchange for not yet existing money. Put plainly, CBs create new money in exchange for nothing but a promise, i.e., from thin air!

Any fiat monetary system leads to debt slavery. There is no reason to be prudent in spending, instead deficit spending is encouraged. In the end someone has to pay the vast amounts of debts accumulated. This is usually the ordinary, hard working, tax paying citizen.

Moreover any fiat money system leads to inflation. Initially people don't realise the resulting subtle expropriation of their wealth. But later, in its terminal stage of hyperinflation, the outright wealth transfer from labor to capital shows openly.

> "Our whole monetary system is dishonest, as it is debt-based […] We did not vote for it. It grew upon us gradually but markedly since 1971 when the commodity-based system was abandoned." (Malcom Sinclair, The Earl of Caithness, addressing the UK House of Lords, 1997)

Fractional Reserve Banking

> "Banking was conceived in iniquity and born in sin […] Bankers own the world. Take it away from them, but leave them the power to create money […] and with the flick of a pen, they will create enough money to buy it back again […] Take this great power away from bankers, and all great fortunes like mine will disappear, and they ought to disappear, because this would then be a better and happier world to live in […] But if you want to continue to be the slaves of bankers, and pay the cost of your own slavery, let them continue to create (your) money." (attributed to Sir Josiah Stamp, 1880-1941, former president of the Bank of England)

Commercial banks are constantly wooing new and current clients into the slavery of debt. Why? Because fractional reserve banking provides them with almost unlimited resources to lend, hence prospective revenue increase.

By law, banks are only requested to keep a fraction of their deposits as a reserve. The rest can be lent multiple times. The chart in Part A under '03. Banks' reveals how it works. Conversely, this means that considering a full deposit (say $1,000) to be the required reserve (say 10%), a not yet existing $9,000 can be created with the stroke of a pen. What prevents banks from doing so? This artificially created money then can be lend for interest, constituting a 100% Bank profit.

These vast profits are based on illusions, if you like. They represent a silent, subtle wealth transfer from society to the banks. And it's legal.

> "By this means (fractional reserve banking) government may secretly and unobserved, confiscate the wealth of the people, and not one man in a million will detect the theft." (John Maynard Keynes, 'The Economic Consequences of the Peace', 1920)

> "Bank robbery is an initiative of amateurs. The true professional [robbers] start a bank." (Berthold Brecht, 1896-1956, influential German poet and playwright)

Think it over. When we borrow from a commercial bank we have to provide a physical asset as collateral. The bank provides us with an illusion (credit that has been created from thin air) in return. This in itself is a unjust deal. However, with every single instalment the bank receives our honest, real and hard-earned wealth in exchange for a mirage. In the end there is only one winner, the bank. Financing a house shows how.

For the 'privilege' of working with a loan the bank creates from thin air, the debtor pays a multiple of the house value back to the bank. In that deal only a fraction (the house itself) of what the debtor rightfully earns throughout those years stays with him. If the debtor cannot pay his debt (the non-existing money plus interest), the bank simply takes his asset (the real house) away. Just like that.

> "Keeping slaves required accommodation, food, medicine, hospitalisation [...] The employed serf ('wage-slave') can be dismissed at will, works for a pittance under duress, feeds and clothes his family, will happily pay us three times for a mortgaged house over a generation, and will be totally dependent upon the 'Owners of Capital' for his continued mutual survival." (Author unknown)

By acting in true financial prudence (living within our means and stop borrowing), banks would be straight away deprived of an evil, unethical way to

- enrich themselves excessively,
- enslave their clientele financially,
- subtly transfer their customers' wealth to the bank.

As unpleasant as it sounds, we are unwitting participants in this financial stratagem today.

Interest

Interest creates money from money. Today this is especially demonstrated by the wide use of exponentially growing compound interest. Remember, a compound interest rate of 1% leads to the artificial doubling of money in 72 years, at 3% it takes 24 years, at 6% only 12 years and at 12% we talk about a mere 6 years.

Compound interest makes it difficult to keep any economy healthy and the value of money stable. To ensure both, the economic output must keep up with the artificial and exponential money growth, which is virtually impossible.

8. Corrupted Banks

Legalised Theft

When we deposit our money in a bank it is still our money. We don't transfer ownership. We just park or store it there for safekeeping, similar to storing goods in a third-party storehouse. Our money remains an asset in our personal balance sheet, as it were.

But surprisingly, the bank now records our deposits as its own assets, too. But assets can have only one owner at any given time, not two. Because our money is owned by us, it cannot be owned by the bank. So technically the bank is stealing our assets. Granted, it does document its responsibility to us as a liability. But, by the stroke of a pen, the bank's accounting converts our strong position as owner into the weakened position of a creditor. We did not sell our money to the bank so we did not transfer ownership. We only transferred possession. But the bank accounting records an ownership transfer. Thus, this accounting amounts to theft.

The bank should not be able to treat our assets as its own and use it as it pleases. But it does. Without claiming other people's assets as their own, they could not engage in artificial money creation through fractional reserve banking. All in all, banks use what they 'stole' (client's deposits) to create something that does not exist (money created from thin air) to enrich themselves (lending for interest).

Just to be clear, we are stealing if we use something that belongs to someone else without asking the owner. We are liable to prosecution. So, our bank needs our permission to make use of our assets. If it doesn't ask, it steals our money and should be prosecuted for it. But banks never are, even though this is their daily business. Why? Because against all logic, modern law has ruled that a bank is entitled to record the deposits as its own assets on its balance sheet. And it can now do with it as it pleases. This is legalised theft. Clearly, the bank lobby has done a 'great' job here. Today's well-accepted double-entry bookkeeping might even give a legal looking touch to the whole shenanigan.

Limited Liability

Banks used to be partnerships. Bankers were liable with their own wealth for bad loans and poor investment decisions. It was therefore essential for bankers to be part of the social fabric and commercial development of their communities. Good personal relationship with their clientele and insight into the challenges, possibilities and opportunities they faced, allowed bankers to make wise, healthy and profitable decisions. They partnered with their clients in economic progress.

Today most banks are limited liability entities. The directors and managers have become distant from their customers and rarely partner with them for the economic progress of the community they are part of. Instead, clients have become to the banks a mere means for self-enrichment. Since the bank is no longer fully liable when deals turn sour, the threshold for taking risks has been almost entirely removed. While the bankers walk away with huge bonuses, the price for losses are borne by the customers and, in case of bailouts, taxpayers. (See also '43. Limited Liability')

Limited liability laws have transformed the commercial landscape drastically. This affects both the banking industry and other companies. Limited liability laws sound magic, but they don't let liabilities disappear. They just limit them for the perpetrators of the mess at the expense of those who had no say in it in the first place. This is morally very questionable.

Limited liability laws minimise the responsibility for making bad decisions, taking excessive risks and short-term profit making. They thus inhibit good stewardship.

Gambling With Time

'Borrowing short and lending long' is how an acquaintance termed the modern banks' gambling with time. Most deposits are short-term and therefore likely to be withdrawn within weeks or a few months. So it is difficult to understand why banks are tying these funds longterm somewhere else. They obviously bank on a constant flow of short-term deposits to sufficiently serve withdrawals. But it's a dangerous gamble with other people's assets. A collective withdrawal of short-term deposits for whatever reason (bank-run) will likely result in a bank collapse. The price for the bank's gamble with time is not paid by the bank (see 'Limited Liability' above and '43. Limited Liability'), but by their clients and, in case of a bailout through government, by all taxpayers.

9. Skyrocketing Interest

"Compound interest is the eighth wonder of the world. He who understands it earns it […] he who doesn't […] pays it." (Author unknown)

Let's do a quick calculation based on 2017 numbers.

- The current worldwide debt is roughly $233 trillion.
- For this debt, interest has to be paid. If we assume a low average rate of 3.5% across the globe, then the interest payment equals $8.2 trillion/year.
- This interest has to be recovered through the sale of products and services.
- The world's annual GDP (products and services) stands at $75.4 trillion.
- Thus the interest amounts to roughly 11% of the world's annual productivity.
- Consequently, the worldwide workforce has to spend 11 in every 100 hours of paid work just for covering interest payments.
- Put differently, on average every labourer needs to spend 11% of his paid work time to enrich the capital owners (individuals, banks) even further. And they themselves don't contribute anything productive for it.

"Interest is a tribute, which the labourer, from industrial workers right up to farmers and entrepreneurs, has to pay to the money lender in order to enable work at all. [...] It is a heavy burden for the vast majority and an effortless source of income for a small portion of the population. Interest is income without labor and therefore ethically unjustifiable." (Hansjürg Weder, member of the National Council of Switzerland, 1990)

Part A '2. Interest' revealed the absurd exponential growth pattern of compound interest. $1 put down for interest over 2,000 years leads to stratospheric interest amounts. Of course, no-one does that. But the world pays compound interest for hundreds of trillions in debts, which also leads to catastrophic results.

So let's stay with our above calculation.

- This year's interest averaged at 3.5% for the worldwide debt ($233 trillion) equates to $8.2 trillion.
- If this can't be paid the debt needs to be refinanced (increased) to cover this.
- As a result the worldwide debt will rise to $241.2 trillion for the next year.
- The applicable interest then increases to $8.45 trillion for that year, provided the applied average rate doesn't change from 3.5%.
- If we carry on like this for just five years, the current debt of $233 trillion will have accumulated interest to the tune of $43.8 trillion!
- In ten years it is already $95.7 trillion! That exceeds the annual productivity of the whole world.

This is all down to compound interest. It's pretty obvious that, regardless of how we cut it, compound interest leads to skyrocketing interest burdens. These vast interest amounts are an effortless income for capital owners. But for the workers, they are becoming an ever heavier burden.

10. Debt Madness

"Every economy is based on the credit system, which means it is based on the erroneous assumption that the other party will pay borrowed money back." (Kurt Tucholsky, 1890-1935, German-Jewish journalist and writer)

"After the $700 billion bailout, the trillion-dollar stimulus, and the massive budget bill with over 9,000 earmarks, many of you implored Washington to please stop spending money we don't have. But, instead of cutting, we saw an unprecedented explosion of government spending and debt, unlike anything we have seen in the history of our country." (Michele Bachmann, American politician, 2011)

"Blessed are the young, for they will inherit all the debt." (Herbert Hoover, 1874-1964, 31st US President)

Debt is not simply a problem of modern time. It has always been around since some form of economic activity exists. But the destructive and enslaving force of the debt development of especially the past 50 years is unrivalled in all history. Never before has the world been dominated and enslaved by debt as it is today.

There is hardly a nation, a state, a community, a company, an institution or a person without debts on this planet. All over the world borrowing has generally been accepted and embraced as state-of-the art financing method. During the last few decades, the explosion of debt, fuelled by especially compound interest, is a sad but logical consequence. The results are devastating.

The current worldwide debt stands $233 trillion (2017). To understand the weight of this number let's put it into context. The world's annual GDP is just about $75.4 trillion. Thus, the world's cumulative debt is 310% of the global productive performance. Put another way, just to repay the current debt, the whole world would have to work three years and one month free of charge. An impossible task. So racking up such debt levels is pure and outright financial madness.

It would seem logic that Low Income Countries (LIC) are indebted the most. Truth is that most debt is piled up in the industrial world. 'Economical powerhouses' like the USA, Japan, Germany, the UK, etc. drown in liabilities. Their debt levels (corporate, public, private) are multiples of their annual productive performance.

A few years ago a German professor for economics was interviewed on national TV. He was asked how Germany could manage to get out of its unmanageable debts. In all seriousness he suggested to borrow even more. He was convinced that the economy had to be stimulated to grow. With that people would earn more so government could tax them more. And with more tax income the debt repayment could start. Going more into debt to get out of it sounds like bad advise. You don't inject more cancer to get rid of cancer, do you?

Buying on tick was frowned on just a couple of generations ago. Today you are considered a fool if you don't borrow. But compound interest makes debt levels unsustainable. Remember, a compound rate of 3% doubles debt in 24 years, 6% in 12 years and 12% in just 6 years.

Wether we borrow privately, corporately or nationally is irrelevant. In any case, our income must grow enormously to cover at least the exponentially growing interest of our debt. And that's by and large a daunting task.

11. Disreputable Rating Agencies

Private credit rating agencies (Standards & Poor, Moody's or Fitch) play a major role in the financial system. They claim to provide sound assessments on, e.g., trustworthy debtors. Based on their publications, debtors pay low(er) or high(er) interest rates on their borrowings.

By definition a good debtor is (a) somebody who has shown financial prudence (never borrowed), or (b) somebody who has a proven record of repaying his debt swiftly and faithfully. That is logic.

Yet, those agencies give all their top ratings to governments with a long-standing record of never paying back anything at all! Their only faithfulness is to increase their indebtedness year after year. Germany and the USA, e.g., have never ever paid a single cent of their continually growing public debt back in at least 50 years. They have long reached a point of unmanageable debts. How is it possible that they still receive top ratings for being trustworthy debtors?

The track record of those rating agencies is terrible on a fairly consistent level. Yet they wield enormous influence on worldwide top financial levels. They also have no qualms resorting to blackmail and pushing whole nations into deeper debt slavery. One example should suffice here:

At the end of 2011 the US government had $14.3 trillion public debt. With that it reached the debt ceiling enshrined in its constitution. So unless Congress approved to raise this upper limit yet again (they did it 78 times since 1960), the US government wouldn't have been able to pay its obligations any more.

It was then that these private credit rating agencies started their move. They threatened to downgrade the US rating if they refused to go deeper into debt. That's blackmail. And it is ridiculous and shows how insane and upside-down things have become. If anything, they should have challenged and later rewarded the US for taking hard but truly sound fiscal actions to get their national budget in order. But they threatened to penalise them with costly downgrading, resulting in higher interest rates and thus even more debt, if they don't go deeper into debt. How bizarre is that? Needless to say that Congress approved raising the debt ceiling for the 79th time. And, since then, it has been raised regularly to now $20.5 trillion at the end of 2017! A 46% increase in only 6 years.

Just to put the agency's threat into plain words – Go deeper into even more unmanageable debt and we reward you with a good rating as a reliable debtor. That allows you to borrow more for lower interest. Should you decide to get out of debt (a good debtor's attitude), we rate you as a bad or questionable debtor. This will result in higher interest rates for you, so that you have a hard time resolving your debt-problem. It is hard to find words for this. This is criminal. It's just appalling and reminiscent of God's frustration as expressed in Isaiah,

> *Woe to those who call evil good and good evil, who substitute darkness for light and light for darkness, who substitute bitter for sweet and sweet for bitter. (Is 5:20, HCSBS)*

12. Governments Voiding Justice System

"Compound interest not only creates an impetus for pathological economic growth, it also works against the constitutional rights of the individual in most countries. If a constitution guarantees every citizen equal access to government services – and money may be defined as such – then it is illegal to have a system in which a small minority continually receive more of that service than they pay for at the expense of the vast majority of the people who receive less than they pay for." (Dr. Dieter Suhr, 1939-1990, German Professor for Constitutional Law and former Judge)

That's legalese, complex, complicated, and hard to understand. But the upshot of it is this: By allowing the interest-driven money system to be the basis for the economy, most governments break their own constitution they swore to uphold.

A constitution pledges all citizens equal access to government services. Money is such service, i.e., an exchange tool to simplify trading. So, when a government tolerates a money system that makes the rich richer at the expense of the poor, it acts against its own constitution. And thus opens the floodgates for injustice.

That's a big pill to swallow. If this law expert was correct in his assessment, then we mustn't be surprised by the ever so increasing lawlessness in our nations. And by the judicial power's failure to deal with it adequately and timely. Why is that? Because by definition, somebody who is corrupt cannot uphold or bring justice. That's a spiritual law. So if a country's leaders (wittingly or unwittingly) set an example of how to circumvent constitutional law, they lose both their (spiritual) authority and right to ask their citizens to adhere to it.

> *Do not exploit the poor because they are poor [...] for the LORD will take up their case and will exact life for life. (Prov 22:22-23)*

> *A ruler who oppresses the poor is like a driving rain that leaves no crops. Those who forsake the law praise the wicked, but those who keep the law resist them. Evil men do not understand justice, but those who seek the LORD understand it fully. (Prov 28:3-5)*

> *By justice a king gives a country stability, [...]. (Prov 29:4a)*

13. Growth Compulsion

> "Everybody, who believes that exponential growth in a finite world can continue forever is either crazy or an economist." (K.E. Boulding, 1910-1993, US economist)

The following illustration shows the three well-known basic forms of growth. The natural curve displays the growth pattern of life. The linear curve the typical production process. The exponential curve is a pattern that, in the physical realm, only occurs in connection with sicknesses, e.g., cancer. It ends with the death of the host and the organism on which the sickness feeds.

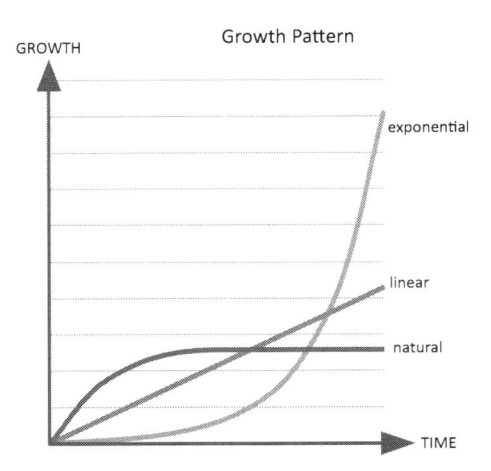

Growth Pattern — exponential, linear, natural (GROWTH vs TIME)

We are probably also aware of the four universal growth rules:

1. Unlimited growth in a confined area is impossible.
2. Every healthy and natural growth has an optimal limit.
3. In their development all organism parts must orient themselves at the whole.
4. All developments that disregard natural principles are condemned to crash.

The original purpose of economic activity is to provide for human needs. This follows the natural growth pattern. No matter how different the needs and desires of people are, at some stage a saturation effect takes place.

We know now that monetary assets (cash and claims on cash) grow exponentially due to compound interest. In order to make room for this increasing financial pressure, economic activity had to be redefined. It changed from providing for human needs to creating wants to pave the road for further growth. Most of these wants are increasingly questionable. Still, we encourage people to buy stuff they don't need with money they don't have to impress people they don't like.

Quietly, man, who used to be the defining subject of economies, has now been turned into its object.

Think it over. Do you know of a corporation, entity or government being content with the status quo? Aren't they all aiming for growth, year in year out? They have to, for their financial obligations demand this. But yearly growth rates work exponential, because the base on which they apply grows every year. So we are trapped in this upward spiral of incessant growth with exponential pattern. Let's put it into the context of the four universal growth rules.

1. Our planet and it's resources are limited. The unlimited growth our financial system demands, therefore, cannot be accommodated.
2. The optimal limit of a healthy and natural growth has long been crossed.
3. Money, a service tool with no inherent value, dictates the exploitation and destruction of everything that has value. There is no healthy balance.
4. Because the world's financial system disregards all natural principles, it is set to crash fatally.

14. Corporate Sector Fighting For Survival

Every business invests to either maintain, improve or expand its operation. To do that most of them borrow. Exponential growth due to compound interest makes this debt burden increase substantially. A business factors its debt service into its product or service prices. But consumers are price sensitive and shop around for best deals. So there is a limit to what a business can pass on to its customers. When the cost pressure gets too high, the business needs to act. Here are the typical options:

- Produce to full capacity and try to sell entire production. This leads to price battles for market shares, thus might be counterproductive.
- Exploit own workforce. More and more companies dismiss their staff only to give them the option of re-employment on worse conditions. In time it erodes the demand base, i.e., the money available to spend.
- Cutting costs in the operation. This happens quickest by laying off personnel. Can backfire too as higher unemployment tends to erode the demand base.
- Produce more efficient by replacing people with machines. Same result as the above. Also increases investment demands leading to more debt.
- Produce abroad, a subtle unethical way of exploitation. While keeping its high-income customer base at home, the business capitalises on the low-wage structure of the host country. Might gain a few years.

All the above options are shortsighted fixes that only postpone further trouble. Still other factors worsen the battle for survival in a debt-based setup even more:

- The increasing and ruthless focus on company's shareholder value. The payout of maximum profits jeopardises financial prudence even further.
- Management's conflict of interest: Streamline the operation and fire people to achieve goals that guarantee high pay and bonuses? Or discard personal monetary incentives and focus on a healthy, prudent, financial progress?
- Informal labor or clandestine employment (not usually free neighbourly help). Because most people have less and less means available, more and more jobs are given to moonlighters. But every job done by the informal sector harms the formal economy, no matter how good the justification.

15. Ailing Governments And Public Sectors

"Nothing is easier than the expenditure of public money. It doesn't appear to belong to anyone. The temptation is overwhelming to bestow it on somebody."
(John Calvin Coolidge, 1872-1933, 30th US President)

A nation's public debt is inflicted by its government on national, state, district and community levels. Even the seemingly strong economies of industrial countries show appalling levels of public debt. Anything between 70% and 250% of the respective GDP seems to be normal.

Across the world governments and their communities must face the question of how to get out of their debt. It is a tough ask as compound interest increases the debt burden exponentially, which in turn empties their treasury fast. Even a supposedly rich nation like Germany must pay almost $100 billion annually on interest alone. That is just about the amount it receives on income tax.

So Germany and every other government must become really inventive to reduce their deficits. But the financial leeway is restricted and options are limited:

- Increase inflation by pumping more money into circulation than the economy can bear. This will devalue monetary assets and debts alike, thus close the deficit gap. Will boomerang as it disadvantages especially the poor. Will result in an increased social burden for the government and communities.

- Cut spending. Sounds wise and prudent. But carries loads of challenges and dangers. Our current financial system requires constant economical growth and not stagnation. So the emphasis is usually on spending, not saving.
- More debt to (a) pay off the old one, (b) service the ever so increasing interest burden and (c) possibly even boost economic growth. Short-lived as an even higher interest burden will eventually eat up all generated extra income.
- Higher taxes, tributes and levies. Might become a too heavy burden for employers. Personnel layoff with social tension might be the consequence, counteracting much needed growth.

It doesn't really matter which option or combination of options governments chose. The ordinary worker is always hit harder than the owners of monetary assets, whose income continues to increase.

16. Overdevelopment Of Monetary Assets

> "When the Babylonian civilisation collapsed, three percent of the people owned all the wealth. When old Persia went down to destruction two percent of the people owned all the wealth. When ancient Greece went down to ruin one-half of one percent of the people owned all the wealth. When the Roman Empire fell by the wayside, two thousand people owned the wealth of the civilised world [...] It is said at this time less than two percent (2%) of the people control ninety percent of the wealth of America." (from 'Lincoln Money Martyred', CPA Books, 1998, first published 1934)

Just to refresh our minds. Today, more than 80 years after the above statement was made, things look even more gloomy: The six richest people in the world are wealthier than the bottom half of the world's population. The top 1% of the world's population has more money than the bottom 99%.

Monetary assets (cash and claims on cash) are most of all increased through interest. Compound interest is today's commonly used method and causes them to double in regular intervals. 72 divided by the interest rate tells us the number of years in which monetary assets double.

Let's, therefore, look at some current numbers we used already and calculate:

- Global debt = $233 trillion; worldwide average interest rate = 3.5%.

- Since monetary assets are balanced by an equal debt, a $233 trillion debt is balanced by $233 trillion in monetary assets.
- Let's follow the above formula and divide 72 by our interest rate of 3.5%. This equals 20.5 years.
- In other words, the current $233 trillion in monetary assets will grow to $466 trillion in just 20.5 years. This means a simply unsustainable overdevelopment of monetary assets.

Don't forget: every interest-driven money system shifts the income progressively from labor to capital, i.e., from those who work to those who don't. In other words, those who work must work double as hard during the next 20.5 years to make those who don't work double as rich. This is a simple mathematical reality. And it happens at an accelerating speed with arithmetical regularity.

17. Speculation Lunacy

In the past, company shares were treated as a life insurance or retirement fund. Their public listing was a way of attracting and securing investments. The value of company shares was based on productive capacity, performance and profitability.

All this changed in the 90s. Under Thatcher and Reagan, the governments of the UK and the USA deregulated the financial markets. Since then stock markets have become a playground for speculation and murky financial products. It's now all about making money fast, preferably with money. A subtly spread rumour can be more powerful in influencing a company's share values than productive capacity, performance and profitability. Here's just one example of frequent dealings:

'Shorting' or 'short selling', which works like this: A trader borrows shares (stocks) for a fee, but sells them! He then spreads a relevant rumour aimed at making the price of those shares fall. As soon as they have dropped in value, he buys back what he sold, only for less. The difference he cashes in as profit. And then he returns what he borrowed to its rightful owners. Sounds clever but is a dodgy deal for profit. Firstly, he makes money with stuff that doesn't belong to him. Secondly, his speculative transaction destroys the value of the shares, which he had borrowed and abused for his own financial gain. More bluntly, he enriches himself by deliberately destroying other people's possession! Ethically you can't get any lower. But it's legal, so who cares?

'Making use of unknown variables for your own benefit by manipulating information'. That's what speculation is. And it is applied to company shares; countless murky financial products; bets on interest rates; currency exchange rates; precious metal, commodities and food price developments; on forward purchases, and many more. It is all played out at financial markets.

Financial markets have grown much more important and bigger today than the real (production/service based) economy. The current global volume of financial transactions is about 70 times the world's GDP ($75.4 trillion). This equates to a staggering $5,278 trillion that are being shovelled around the globe in a year. And that with almost no relevance to real productivity (GDP) whatsoever. What's more, all the gold and currency reserves in the world just cover about 0.25% (= 22 hrs) of this annual monstrous trading volume. There is a tsunami lingering with no-one and nothing being able to mitigate financial collapse.

18. Inflation

> "Inflation means defrauding the people." (Karl Blessing, 1900-1971, former President of the German Federal Bank)

> "Inflation is taxation without legislation." (Milton Friedman, 1912-2006, American Nobel Laureate in Economics 1976)

> "By a continuing process of inflation, government can confiscate, secretly and unobserved, an important part of the wealth of their citizens." (John Maynard Keynes, 1883-1946, British Economist, Politician and Mathematician)

Inflation is a way governments (via CBs) readily employ to close the widening gap between their own income and debt. By issuing more money than the economy can bear, the purchasing power of it decreases. And so does the value of debt.

Manufacturers and service providers usually offset inflation losses by increasing the prices for their goods and services. At least to some extent. Chain stores and shops will follow suit. Capital owners will insist on higher interest rates and better returns on investments to cover their losses. Public service providers will increase their tariffs. But the end consumer has no way of compensating inflation losses.

Inflation simply makes the poor a loser. Their financial position is just too weak to fight for compensation. Thus inflation erodes their incomes and modest saving, if they have any. By chipping away at the anyway modest supply base of the poor, the social burden will increase. By employing inflation to reduce their debts, governments create consequently trouble for themselves in the long run.

19. Income Without Performance

Doctors, actors, sport stars, singers, politicians, CEO's, bank managers, celebrities, TV personalities, ... Such people we tend to associate with excessive incomes.

Why should, e.g., a gifted soccer player earn a salary of $0.5 million or more – per week!? This equates the annual salary of 16 NHS nurses in the UK. Or 100 workers in South Africa. Or 850 workers in any poor Low Income Country. Or why can a gifted actress command a $15 million pay per movie? The reasons for granting such disproportionate payments might be manifold.

Whatever they are, fact is that it is easier for people with such high earnings to bring large portions of it to the bank. There it doubles through interest in just a decade or so without any work involved from its depositor. It is the borrower who works for the interest the lender receives. And so, the borrower works hard for the rich soccer player's or actress's non-performance-based income. Even if they never ever watch them perform. Put more bluntly: the poor must work to create income for the rich who don't need to work anymore.

Income without performance is so much more unjust than widely differing incomes based on some kind of work. This is especially so, because the former is often a multiple higher than the latter. Somebody depositing $1 million at a bank for interest receives from it the salary of a well-paid employee, just without work.

Ultimately interest isn't only income without work. It also embodies an unethical, effortless wealth transfer from society to capital owners and banks. And that for two reasons:

- The borrower has to take from his own wealth production to pay the interest.
- If the debtor fails to pay, banks have no scruples to seize any assets serving as collateral against loans.

20. Interest-Inflated Prices Reduce Income

Every business invests to either maintain, improve or expand its operation. To that end they usually borrow for compound interest. A business factors its debt service into its product or service prices. The higher the debt-based capital cost part of a manufacturing process, the more inflated the product prices are due to interest. As mentioned before, 10% are common, while extreme cases show even up to 80% interest share. As a result products or services are overpriced.

Hence, the consumers buying these products or services pay more than needed. It leaves them with a smaller disposable income, which punishes the already struggling small income groups.

> "I have written extensively about interest being the major cause of rising prices now since it is buried in the price of all that we buy, but this idea, though true, is not well accepted. $9 trillion in domestic U.S. debt, at 10% interest, is $900 billion paid in rising prices and this equates the current 4% rise in prices experts perceive to be inflation. I have always believed the compounding interest to be an invisible wrecking machine, and it is hard at work right now." (American economic historian John L. King, 1988)

21. Growing Income Disparity

An analysis of the income development from 1950 to 1990 in Germany revealed an unpleasant truth. The income of employed people increased 16-fold while that of self-employed people increased 33-fold. This reinforces an increasingly unjust income distribution, certainly holding for most industrial nations.

The reason for that is simple. Business owners can pass virtually any cost increases on to their customers. This holds for rising debt services, levies, tributes and taxes, but also for any disadvantage inflation might cause in their private pockets. Business owners or self-employed people might not always do that or only in part. But at least they have the option, which an employee and end-consumer never has.

The disparity in income-development in Low Income Countries is likely to be much bigger. Much more than in the western world, it is reinforced through and fuelled by exploitation, corruption and nepotism.

22. Climbing Unemployment

Hundreds of millions of people are unemployed, not because there is not enough work, but because there is no money to pay them. The money available is simply distributed unfairly and amassed in the wrong places (capital owners, rich elite).

Full employment is always possible if the available work and the associated pay is flexibly distributed among those willing to work. When the total available work decreases work hours per worker should be reduced instead of the number of workers. But such solution is a non-issue in our economies. This is due to the increasing debt levels of businesses caused by compound interest.

> "Money interest artificially pushes the profitability threshold of businesses up, thus creates an additional rationalisation pressure, which causes the destruction of workplaces." (Catholic Family Association, Archdiocese Vienna/Austria, 1990)

A business has three distinctive options to absorb the exponentially growing interest burden (or any mixture of it):

- Increase sales – potential price war for market shares; price reductions mean lower profits; lower profits create new cost pressures; thus might backfire
- Increase prices – lose customers who shop cheaper elsewhere; less sales lead to new cost pressures; boomerangs
- Reduce costs – quickest measure is personnel layoff; reduces demand base

Each option leads to financial problems for the business. It's a catch-22 situation most businesses can't resolve. The end-result is always higher unemployment.

> "Our economy is not set for slow or even 'zero growth'. Growth stagnation means mass unemployment and consequently a catastrophic economical crash of the Federal Republic of Germany." (Hans Matthöfer, 1925-2009, Ex-Finance Minister)

Mr. Matthöfer understood that our financial system forces economies to grow or die. In reality economies can't and don't always grow. Therefore, it's impossible to stop unemployment growth let alone reduce the rate in the long run.

According to the CIA's World Factbook the worldwide unemployment rate is 30%. The world population stands at 7.4 billion. If only 1 billion of them is considered a potential workforce, then we are talking about 300 million unemployed people globally. And most of them have families to provide for. Not to mention the 1.1 billion people who must survive on less than $1.25 a day. All this means a huge financial burden to be ultimately covered by those still employed.

In the final analysis, the economies bear the costs of the ever-growing army of unemployed. Without the exponentially growing debt burden through compound interest there would be much more leeway to deal with it. At the end of the day it's very simple: interest (income without performance) causes unemployment (available performance without income).

23. Ecological Exploitation And Ruination

The world's economies are set up for permanent growth. This growth compulsion leads to heavy exploitation of the available natural resources. Today we use up our resources 1.7 times faster than we can replenish them. That's scary. Imagine only polluted air to breath, if there is still oxygen left. Or deserts instead of forests. Undrinkable water due to oil, chemical, or nuclear waste pollution. We are well on the way for this.

The third rule of growth states: An organism can only remain stable if all parts develop synchronously with the whole. If one part grow faster than the others, then the organism experiences tensions and complications until it eventually collapses. There are only two options to relieve this:

- Stop the overdevelopment of this specific part.
- Try to adjust the development of all other parts to the fast growing one.

The second option is exactly what the world is doing. The economies are forced to grow to catch up with the ever-growing monetary assets invested for interest. This, we know by now, is impossible. Yet the mayhem cannot be stopped to avoid a social collapse, the price of which is ecological collapse.

Every growth in economic performance requires the same growth in resource consumption. The result is more and larger rubbish dumps that are increasingly burdening people's health. Environmental and health protection is usually disregarded when it impedes promising economic growth and financial profits.

The fight to preserve this planet, its natural beauty and natural resources as an inheritance for generations to come and working against ecological destruction can become quite frustrating in an environment filled with ignorance.

"99 percent of the people don't see the money problem. Science doesn't see it, the economy theory doesn't see it, and the latter even declares it to be 'nonexistent'. But as long as we don't see the money economy as a problem, there is no prospect of an ecological transformation of our society." (H.C. Binswanger, Swiss economist)

24. War And Capital Destruction

Earlier we saw that our economic system doesn't follow the natural growth pattern. Otherwise it would be satisfied with providing for needs. Instead, it follows the exponential growth curve due to its compound interest base. It thus demands a continual productivity increase to postpone economical collapse. So the focus is on creating wants to accommodate this growth. But consumers can only consume so much. At some point in time the markets are saturated. Hence other, usually foreign markets are targeted and exploited. Sometimes by force. Infrastructural projects (roads, hospitals, airports, government buildings, etc.) are created. Armament and weapon exports get high on the agenda. Whatever is possible will be exploited for more growth.

It sounds preposterous but one way to postpone the inevitable collapse is war and capital destruction. If there is no way to grow anymore, we need to destroy to be able to rebuild again. Ergo, wars are much more suited to postpone the collapse than any economic measure would ever be. Armament and war are extremely effective tools to secure vital economic growth.

> "War is the most generous and effective 'cleansing crisis to get rid of over-investment'. It opens enormous possibilities of new additional capital investments and ensures that all accumulated stocks in goods and capital are thoroughly consumed and worn, much faster and more drastically even than any common depression with the strongest artificial support would accomplish. Thus […] war is the best means to postpone the ultimate catastrophe of our capitalistic economic system." (Dr. Ernst Winkler, 'Theory Of The Natural Economic Order', 1952)

That's both a stunning and shocking statement at the same time. As if to prove this statement to be correct, scandalous practices in connection with the gulf-wars have been uncovered. Nations supplying war machinery, started bargaining for their share in rebuilding what their weapons helped destroy. How sick is that?

History shows that as long as the economy is busy with rebuilding what wars destroyed, there is little interest in manufacturing and supplying weapons. But once the rebuilding processes are finished and consumer needs are more than satisfied, armament becomes a promising market again. Even to the extent of proliferation. You can kill your enemy only once. Yet today the world's weapon production has grown to such an extent that each living person can easily be killed thousands of times over.

> "Every weapon that is produced, every warship that is launched, every missile that is deployed, basically embodies a theft from those who hunger and aren't fed or those who shiver and aren't clothed." (Dwight D. Eisenhower, 1890-1969, 34th US President, in his speech 'Chance for Peace' on 16 April 1953)

The above statement points at the social tensions and potential conflicts that are connected to armament even without war. The 'dividends' coming from weapon production already cause harm during times of peace, to say nothing of the victims once those weapons are used.

25. Summary

Look at the next illustration, which is used with permission.

It is from the book 'Das Geld-Syndrom' (The Money Syndrome) used by economic analyst Helmut Creutz. This illustrated synopsis reveals our monetary system's problems, and displays the intertwined, interlocked dependencies brilliantly.

(1) The productive performance cannot keep up with the demand that money capital has on the economy. The exponentially growing compound interest makes money grow much faster.

(2) As a result the income part left for the work force is persistently shrinking. Profits (business) go down and wages/salaries (employees) decrease.

(3) This leads to a regression in demand and investment as people have less to spend. Bankruptcies and higher unemployment looms. The longer it takes the higher the social tensions with possibilities of strikes, turmoil, crime, violence, and even the danger of war (6) become.

(4) Therefore, its crucial to avoid income declines for those who work. But with our system that is only possible by increasing the GDP year after year.

Higher interest burden for the economy — **1**

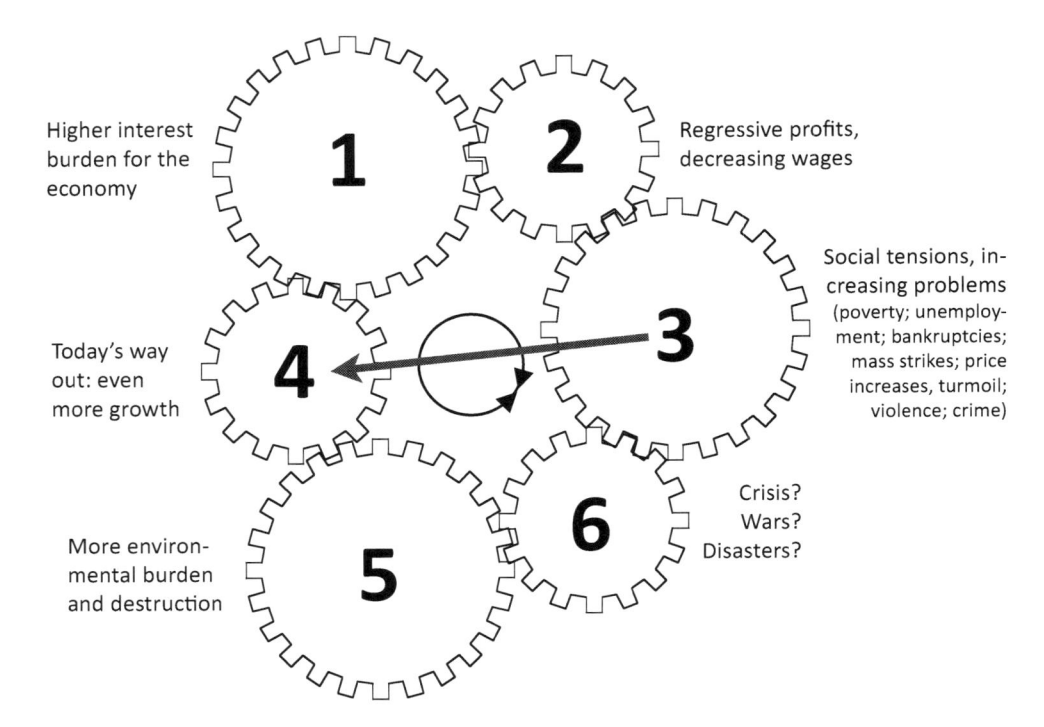

2 — Regressive profits, decreasing wages

3 — Social tensions, increasing problems (poverty; unemployment; bankruptcies; mass strikes; price increases, turmoil; violence; crime)

Today's way out: even more growth — **4**

More environmental burden and destruction — **5**

6 — Crisis? Wars? Disasters?

(5) Yet any performance increase requires more resources. This leads to an accelerated exploitation of natural wealth and to environmental destruction.

(6) Hence the way out of today's economic-social dilemma leads straight into an ecological one. We intensify the threat of environmental disasters and of violent disputes over natural resources.

Let's round this chapter off by summarising. The world's money system is

- driven by constant money devaluation (inflation)
- because of artificial and unchecked money creation (fiat money, fractional reserve banking)
- and huge growth compulsion due to compound interest.

On balance this system proves to be enslaving and destructive. It feeds a tiny minority at the expense of the vast majority of the world's population. It is unjust and destroys the livelihood of especially the poor and needy. It thrives on fear, anxiety and worry, and has no escape button.

> "The essence of all slavery consists in taking the product of another's labor by force. It is immaterial whether this force be founded upon ownership of the

slave or ownership of the money that he must get to live." (L.N.Tolstoy, 1828-1910, Russian moral thinker, novelist and philosopher)

We are forced to serve money, thus cannot serve God, at least not fully.

No one can serve two masters. Either he will hate the one and love the other, or he will be devoted to the one and despise the other. You cannot serve both God and money. (Matt 6:24)

So what's the solution?

Part C

Babylon

26. Time To Leave

Everything that has been outlined in Part A and B embodies the biblical picture of Babylon. Babylon represents open rebellion against God and His good order, and is the epitome of the secular financial system. Here is why.

> *By your wisdom and understanding you have gained wealth for yourself and amassed gold and silver in your treasuries. By your great skill in trading you have increased your wealth, and because of your wealth your heart has grown proud. (Ezek 28:4-5)*

All but the last ten words of the above Scripture read like a portrait of an astute but greedy business man of today. Yet it is part of a dual prophecy against the King of Tyre and Satan. Discontent with the splendour that God had bestowed on him, Satan used already in Eden unrighteous trading methods for self-enrichment *(Ezek 28:12-18)*. That, besides his beauty, made him become proud, thinking he'd be like a god *(Ezek 28:1-2, 17)*. That in turn led to Satan's rebellion against his Creator where he tried to take God's place *(Is 14:14)*.

Today's idolisation of wealth and beauty is still rebellion against God. Satan's most potent weapon to ensure and mislead man has always been a composite of money, lies and deception. Money seems to be the strongest element.

But what does that have to do with Babylon? We need to go back to *Genesis* to see the connection.

Nimrod was the first man recorded in the Bible to build a kingdom for himself *(Gen 10:8-10)*. This kingdom was located in Shinar, which is Babylonia. Right there the world united to build a city for themselves – Babylon, and in that city the tower of Babel was erected *(Gen 11:1-4)*. The Bible records this as man's effort to make a name for himself and avoid being scattered across the earth, a direct violation of God's command to fill it *(Gen 1:28; 9:1+7)*. Trying to build such a high tower was man's attempt to access God's (spiritual) realm on his own terms.

This Babylonian project undoubtedly underpins the true character of Satan. It is a rebellious self-serving scheme of control and arrogance. In the Bible, we read only once that the Trinity descends to earth to intervene. It was here at Babel *(Gen 11:5-7)*. It shows the gravity of man's evil plan to build that tower, an act clearly inspired by the devil. Interestingly, the European Parliament building in Strasbourg was deliberately modelled on the Colosseum in Rome and is also depicted on an official EU poster alluding to the famous picture of the unfinished Tower of Babel by Bruegel. Both of which are a clear sign that Satan still entices man to finish this project?

Though the project was never completed then, the adulterous Babylonian spirit behind it is at work ever since. It has become the driving force of the world's commercial activities *(Is 47, Jer 50+51, Rev 17+18)*. Today's world financial system clearly demonstrates Satan's unrighteous methods of self-enrichment.

Furious about losing his privileged place in heaven, Satan is out to take revenge. Unable to win against God Himself, he targets God's image (mankind) instead. Satan works tirelessly to enslave people through his vicious system, knowing that this serfdom will eventually cost them their place in heaven, too *(Matt 6:24; 1Tim 6:10)*.

In Eden everything was made available for the common good. God's system of grace and trusting relationship was at work. But the Babylonian system does not know grace and trust-relationships. To the contrary, it feeds our selfishness all the time and is therefore competitive, ruthless and destructive. It works like poison.

The Bible calls Babylon (Babylonian system) the 'great prostitute' and 'mother of prostitutes' *(Rev 17:1+5)*. These names are a reference to the system's deception and betrayal to God. They express their opposition to God's righteous ways for man's coexistence.

Rev 18:9-23 shows how this system penetrates and influences all spheres of economics, commerce and the financial industry. By employing debt, interest, unjust weights and measures, as well as fictitious money, it fuels selfishness, greed, fear, worry, exploitation, slavery, oppression, destruction and wars. In a word, everything we looked at in Part A and B. Logically, it thus opposes God's every command. No wonder it has so far destroyed the lives of individuals, entire communities and nations and will continue to do so as long as it exists.

This is precisely the reason why God urges believers to leave Babylon,

> *Come out of her, my people, so that you will not share in her sins, so that you will not receive any of her plagues; (Rev 18:4; see also Jer 51:45)*

Part D

Looking For A Way Out

Introduction

Although most people notice the effects of the Babylonian system, many don't really know what's going on and certainly don't see any negative spiritual force at work here.

So it is mostly left to financial/economic experts to at least analyse the obvious destructive nature of the system and think about solutions. Some of them proved not only theoretically but also in practice how advantageous a system change can be, but then they were cut down to size by higher authorities. In this Part D we'll have a brief look at some of the suggested answers to the current mess.

27. Back To Gold?

The US Dollar has only been backed by gold for 60% of the 230+ years since its inception. During its early days $1 equaled 0.048 Troy ounce of gold, and the death penalty was pronounced on the debasement of those coins. The American constitution allows only gold and silver coins as real money, not paper. It also has given the power of coinage (creating real money) only to Congress. However, the constitution became useless when the private Fed obtained fraudulently the right to print paper as (Fiat) money. In 1971 the gold-standard was abandoned last to allow a Fed-driven unhindered money creation. It shows that considering gold-backed currencies is no guarantee for lasting success.

Gold-standard means that the currency is pegged to gold with a fixed value set per ounce. Hence, the creation of new money can only happen in step with gold production. This has great advantages. It prevents artificial money creation (fiat money; fractional reserve banking), which in turn enforces financial prudence. On all levels (private, corporate, public) people have to live within their means. Deficit spending (debt) is limited to the savings of others. Banks can only lend real money other people don't need and have deposited with them.

A gold standard is certainly not the philosopher's stone. It does not automatically abolish simple and compound interest. But it puts an end to the current unrestrained money creation from thin air. This in turn curbs the wealth transfer and expropriation from labor to capital owners, banks and government. It also limits exchange rate speculations. Finally, it also shuts the door on most wars, military conflicts and the resultant capital destruction. Why? Because history shows that most wars could only be financed when the currency was decoupled from the gold-standard that restrained money creation.

This all sounds pretty amazing, despite the shortcoming about interest. But there are also critical voices that argue:

- *Restricting money creation will stifle economic growth and prevent wealth creation.* – Money wealth creation would be limited to gold production, yes. Economic growth and physical wealth creation, however, have very little to do with money creation. They depend on the circulation speed of money.

- *Many nations will be disadvantaged, because they don't produce their own gold.* – Perhaps. But those nations could acquire gold reserves and use them to create their own gold-standard. In fact, a nation's currency could be pegged to anything valuable and scarce in supply. Any commodity-based currency is better than worthless fiat notes whose value depends solely on the faith and trust that people put in it.

- *A commodity-based currency will lead to great problems for the local economy when engaging in global markets.* – Admittedly, switching to such currency is no sure-fire success. But the important question is this: Do we rather want to go down with flags flying, clinging to a destructive monetary system? Maybe by using a commodity-based money system we don't need to engage in global markets, for there is less growth pressure.

Bottomline, a gold-standard or something similar isn't the be-all-and-end-all. But it promises to be a great start to reverse some of the evils that come with fiat currencies.

28. Debt Relief?

Debt relief, or debt forgiveness for poor nations is a recurrent topic. It is often seen as the solution to free them from their financial/economical problems. But there is a difference between state, bank, IMF and World Bank loans.

State Credit

If a government has given a loan it can relatively easily decide to forgive this debt. Simply put, debt forgiveness makes the lender poorer and the borrower richer. That's why it is doubtful if governments are genuinely prepared for this. It is more likely that taxes and other kinds of tributes are raised to make up for it. In other words, it wouldn't really be a debt relief or forgiveness. It would be a simple shift from one debtor (the poor nation) to others (its own citizens).

Bank Credit

With bank loans, debt relief is much more complicated, if possible at all. As mediators between savers and borrowers, banks are not the real owners of the money they lend (even if they can declare other people's deposits as their assets). The administrative correct way for a bank to forgive debts is by reducing the savings of its clients proportionally. This would be fair since, prior to this, clients benefited from the interest payments of those who suffered. But national laws generally prohibit this.

What about fractional reserve banking? How does debt forgiveness work in case of artificially created monetary assets being lent? With a stroke of a pen it would tear an immense hole in the bank's balance sheet. Banks will never agree to that.

Thus, the price for the 'cancellation' of bank credits is socialised, i.e., just like with state credits, all citizens have to shoulder it. Here, the vast majority gets punished although they never had any benefit from the interest income in the first place.

IMF And World Bank Loans

Incidentally the same holds for loans granted to poor nations by both the World Bank and the International Monetary Fund (IMF).

The IMF works with money provided by its member countries. According to their contributions, members have a right to say what happens with this money. The World Bank issues bonds (debt obligations = promises to pay back in the future) to raise money at the financial markets, which it then uses for loans. Both institutions work closely together. Both have very tight requirements for granting their interest-based loans.

When either one grants debt forgiveness it leaves the institution with depleted funds, which have to be replenished for future activities. And here lies the crux of the matter. That replenishment comes from the member countries. Again, the price for these 'generous' acts is shouldered by all citizens (taxes, levies, tributes). Most of them never benefitted from the interest income in the first place.

Barely Exists

True debt forgiveness hardly exists. Debts are shifted from old debtors to new ones, but never disappear. The owners of monetary assets remain the same. Thus the total indebtedness in the world continues to increase unhindered.

Bible

The biblical concept of canceling debt after seven years *(Deut 15)* refers to God's people only. In OT terms that was Israel, in NT terms it's believers of the Christian faith. This is the same for the year of jubilee *(Lev 25)*, where every 50 years the land is returned to the original owner amongst God's people (OT = Israel, NT = believers). This is not to say that others can't receive debt forgiveness, only it cannot be demanded on biblical grounds.

In Summary

It is unlikely that debt forgiveness alone does the trick anyway. There are plenty of examples in recent history where the forgiven debtor was swiftly back in the debt trap. Without a change of approach to money, any debt relief or forgiveness will only briefly postpone the inevitable.

29. Tried Systems, Possible Solutions

Here are some of the systems that have been tried, tested and successfully used in the past and present.

Brakteaten

'Brakteaten' was a currency used between the 12th and 15th century in Europe. It was usually issued by the respective towns, bishops and sovereigns. The purpose was (a) to help with the exchange of goods and services and (b) to create a means of collecting taxes. The coins were made from thin metal sheets of low metal value with a relatively short durability. Crucially, these coins were 'recalled' between one and four times a year, voided and then re-minted.

Generally, four old coins had to be exchanged for three new ones, equating a 25% taxation, if you like. Hence nobody wanted to keep this money, the very opposite of what we do today with ours. Instead, people kept it in constant circulation. As the recall of the coins wasn't on specific dates, they simply tried to avoid that potential exchange loss. So besides buying for daily needs people also invested in furniture, solidly built houses, artwork, etc. They actually invested into anything that promised to increase or at least keep its value.

During this time, some of the finest works of art and architecture were created through paid work, not slave labor. Hundreds of towns with solid stone houses were built in German-speaking areas alone. Since there was little chance to store monetary wealth, tangible wealth was created instead.

Without trying to glorify this currency, but the centuries during which it was used mark one of the cultural culmination points in European history. Artisans worked a five-day week. The so-called 'blue' Monday (a work free day) was introduced. And the general standard of living was comparatively high to what it was before. In addition, there were hardly any feuds or wars between the various dominions.

So it's rather surprising that, despite its positive effects, people started hating the Brakteaten. The substantial loss at originally fairly regular but few intervals might have been a reason. But the chief reason was probably the abuse of this money. Authorities played fast and lose with the coins by increasingly recalling them for self-enrichment. Chaos ensued because people became confused about which coins were the current valid money. And so, by the end of the 15th century, the 'eternal' penny was (re-)introduced, a currency no longer recalled. However, with it interest returned. And with the interest, the accumulation of financial assets in the hands of fewer and fewer people. The accompanying social and economic problems through accelerating impoverishment followed suit.

Work Certificates (Interest Free Money) – 'Miracle' Of Woergl

During the recession of the 1930s, economic activities slowed down drastically almost everywhere in Europe. Mr. Unterguggenberger, the mayor of the small Austrian town of Woergl, had learned about the importance of constant money circulation. He invested much time teaching his understanding to the community. As a result so-called 'Work Certificates' were introduced for the town in 1932/33. This was an interest-free money with a 'demurrage-fee', i.e., circulation incentive. Backed by an equivalent amount of Austrian shillings deposited in the bank, Woergl sent

5,490 such certificates into circulation. Every month this money lost 1% of its value. So in order to keep its value, a stamp worth 1% had to be glued to it. Amazingly, this caused the Work Certificates to circulate 463 times during the next 13.5 months. It created goods and services worth more than 2.5 million shillings (5,490 x 463), which was a remarkable economic boost. Here is what the mayor's measures brought about during the strong recession:

- Reduction of Woergl's unemployment rate by 25% within a year. (The rest of Europe suffered from rising unemployment.)
- Additionally, investments into public works increased by 220%.
- The income from local taxes rose by 35%.
- The circulation fee collected by the local administration, amounted to a scanty 659 shillings (12% of 5,490) for that year, but even this small fee was used for the common good and not for individual gain.

The 'economic miracle of Woergl' caused worldwide furore. But when several hundred mayors from Austria wanted to emulate the Woergl model, the Austrian National Bank put an end to it. It saw its own money monopoly jeopardised and thus prohibited the printing of this and any other local currency. A very promising attempt to revert to a more righteous money system was undone.

JAK-Member Bank System (Interest Free Savings And Loans)

JAK was started because its founders consider interest unethical and destructive to economies. Hence, JAK's ultimate goal is an interest-free economy. The bank has currently about 39,000 members and is run by annually elected directors. None of them can hold more than one share in the bank. JAK operates in Italy, Sweden, Denmark, and Germany. All its activities are outside the capital markets.

The main task is to provide members with interest-free 'savings loans', as they call it. JAK does not offer any interest on savings. Loans are financed exclusively by member savings. Administration and development costs are only a fraction of what is common elsewhere and are paid for by membership and loans.

JAK offers two products:

1. **A Balanced Savings Loan**, best suited for individuals. It is designed for people who are saving in order to get a loan for themselves, a relative or friend. A certain amount of 'savings points' that are borrowed have to be balanced out by an equal amount of 'saving points' that are saved. The saving can either be done before the loan is taken or during repayment. Bank and saver/borrower agree

that the balance will be reached three months after the payment of the last instalment. Then the money that was saved can be withdrawn. In this system the borrower also becomes the lender. There are no inflationary adjustments. The advantage of having a loan when money is worth more is balanced out by the fact that when the savings is paid out it is worth less.

2. **A Support Savings & Loan Tool**, designed for small companies and associations who can only afford to pay the fee and instalments but not the savings part. Since these loans also have to be balanced, a third party becoming responsible for the savings is included. In that sense the system doesn't differ from the current world system. Yet it works without interest and on different premises.

JAK works with official currencies that are still subject to world system influences. However, the JAK system guarantees much more financial justice. It cuts out risk premiums, liquidity premiums, interest for savings, and inflationary adjustments when granting a loan. The loan/savings premiums, therefore, can remain stable throughout the whole period. Only fees for administration and development are paid. These are, as mentioned before, significantly lower than commonly used.

Complementary Currencies

Complementary Currencies (CCs) look like the most feasible way of curbing the negative consequences of the interest driven system and economic globalisation. CCs are not a substitute for existing currencies, but rather a way of paying with a built-in goal. There are two types of CCs:

1. **Sectoral Currencies – serving a limited purposes (e.g. Saber, Fureai Kippu)**

   The 'Saber' (Spanish/Portuguese for 'knowledge'), e.g., was launched to solve the education problem in Brazil. Government put a 1% education surcharge on every mobile phone bill. The money collected from this was put in a fund to finance a voucher system (Saber). The Saber vouchers can only be redeemed for education and lose 20% value annually to avoid hoarding. The vouchers are handed to schools for their youngest pupils on the condition that they choose a mentor from the next grade up to strengthen a weaker subject. Those mentors in turn can use the Saber themselves to get tutored in weak subjects. Thus the currency is transferred step by step from the younger to the older students. Eventually a senior, who wants to go to university, can use it to pay part of the tuition. The Saber is estimated to achieve ten times more than what a direct allocation of money resources for education would accomplish.

There are major and very telling differences between sectoral and traditional currencies. Prof. Dr. Magrit Kennedy, expert for CCs, listed them:

- Use-oriented instead of profit-oriented.
- Aiming to connect under-utilised resources with unmet demands instead of making more money out of money.
- Useless for speculation on international financial markets.
- Useless for anything else than the purpose they were created for.
- Use a circulation incentive or demurrage mechanism to keep the money flowing; thus avoid all problems associated with an interest based system.
- May stop the drain of money to low-wage countries and tax havens; hence counteracts wealth loss and increasing unemployment of the nation.
- Create win-win situations; everybody involved benefits rather than just a few, as with interest based systems.

2. Regional Currencies – serving geographic areas (e.g. Chiemgauer, Roland)

The Chiemgauer circulates around the large Chiem lake in Southern Germany, for example. It is essentially a voucher system, designed to benefit all parties. 1 Chiemgauer equals 1 Euro. Regional associations can buy the Chiemgauer at a 3% discount. So they pay 97 Eurocents for 1 Chiemgauer worth 1 Euro. They then can sell it for 1 Euro to their members in turn. The members who bought the Chiemgauers to support their association can now spend this regional currency in several hundred participating shops. Similar to the Woergl model, buyers accept an annual fee of 8% to guarantee circulation. It means that four times a year a stamp worth 2% of the value of the voucher has to be attached to retain its nominal value.

Businesses that accept these vouchers can use them to pay other participating businesses at no extra fee. Or they can exchange them for Euros at a 5% fee. Most businesses accept the vouchers to cultivate customer loyalty and to strengthen the regional economy.

Prof. Dr. Margrit Kennedy cites some very good reasons why it pays to think about implementing a regional currency:

- They provide all the benefits of the Sectoral Currencies and are specifically designed to help the region, however that region may be defined.
- They allow partial decoupling from a globalised economy.

- They encourage an increased use of regional goods and services.
- Added value and surplus remain in the region.
- They help to strengthen regional identity.
- They help create new links between consumer and producer.
- They result in a reduced need for transport and energy.
- The community owns essential public utilities.

30. Opposition

Some options to counteract the major problems of our money system have been mentioned in this Part D. But of course, this is by no means an exhaustive list. Despite all efforts, nothing has been achieved to date in terms of lasting success. In fact, it looks like there is much opposition to fix, let alone replace this evil Babylonian system. The logical question, 'Why?', leads us immediately to vested interests.

> "The few who could understand the system will either be so interested in its profits, or so dependent on its favours, that there will be no opposition from that class, while on the other hand, the great body of the people mentally incapable of comprehending the tremendous advantage that capital derives from the system, will bear its burdens without complaint, and perhaps without even suspecting that the system is inimical (harmful; GH) to their interests." (The Rothschilds in a letter to associates, London, 1863)

This statement, although more than 150 years old, is more relevant than ever. Those who greatly benefit from the system still want no change. Those who make a living by working for the system are unlikely to challenge the hand that feeds them. The vast majority of people, however, have more likely no clue as to what's going on. The Rothschilds predicted this precisely. It is an evil plot.

> "Money is a new form of slavery, and distinguishable from the old simply by the fact that it is impersonal – that there is no human relations between master and slave." (L.N. Tolstoy, 1828-1910, Russian moral thinker, novelist and philosopher)

> "Debt is such a powerful tool, it is such a useful tool, it's much better than colonialism ever was, because you can keep control without having an army, without having a whole administration." (Susan George, American activist)

This yoke of slavery can be dismissed as an evil of man that can be fixed by man. Or it can be seen as a physical expression of a spiritual reality. A reality where Satan attempts to control and ultimately destroy God's image (mankind) through economical slavery.

> *It also forced all people, great and small, rich and poor, free and slave, to receive a mark on their right hands or on their foreheads, so that they could not buy or sell unless they had the mark, which is the name of the beast or the number of its name. (Rev 13:16-17)*

This Scripture speaks about economic control by and servitude to Satan. Which is why a mere system change can never be the complete answer.

31. No Other Way

Satan cannot outsmart and defeat God. But he can outsmart and defeat God's image (man), unless man resolves to submit to God. So the only successful approach to averting financial servitude is for man to return to God.

> *My people have committed two sins: They have forsaken me, the spring of living water, and have dug their own cisterns, broken cisterns that cannot hold water. (Jer 2:13)*

This indictment concerns Israel and we could, therefore, just as easily dismiss it as irrelevant for us today. Israel turned their back on God. And Israel created its own supply system. But Paul made clear that such things were written down as warnings for us today *(1Cor 10:11)*. So we are warned not to turn our back on God. And we are warned not to create our own provision system. Both leaves us open for a defeat by Satan. Cutting God out of the equation leads to a flawed and dysfunctional system. And this is exactly what we see today:

- As the economy's defining subject man used to be in charge of the system.
- Today the system is in charge of man. This is because the man-made debt-based, interest-driven money system has turned mankind into the mere object of economies. The system is forcing its rule on its maker.
- God instructed man to be a good and faithful steward of the entrusted natural resources and goods.

- But by today mankind has turned into a throwaway and consumerist society, disregarding what was entrusted to them.

Thus, the only way to establish something flawless and functional is by bringing God back into the equation. This means we need to be looking at the Kingdom of God. It is, however, incomparable and incompatible with the world system as we will see in more detail soon in Part E. A brief distinction should suffice here:

- In the (capitalistic) world system, money is at the heart of every decision and activity. It functions by imposed authority and produces economic slavery. Relationships are sacrificed for business profit and personal gain. The outlook is limited to man's lifetime on earth. The works of the world system are evil *(John 7:7)*.
- In God's Kingdom, God and people are at the heart of every decision and activity. It works on voluntary submission and leads to total freedom. Here, relationships are championed and have precedence over monetary goals. The outlook is eternal life. God's works are all good *(Gen 1-2; Eph 2:10; Phil 2:13)*.

So it is obvious that a life in the Kingdom of God requires radical rethinking. The goal posts have to be moved from our pursuit of business profit and personal gain to a focus on good and right relationships with God and our neighbours. God's economy works relationally and not on rules and laws based on the world financial system. The rule of money and the unholy trinity of 'me, myself and I' must make way for God to rule (again). If you feel up for the challenge keep reading on.

May your Kingdom come soon. May your will be done here on earth, just as it is in heaven. (Matt 6:10, NLT-SE)

We pray this prayer quite frequently, don't we? But do we really mean it? Do we truly believe that the King and His Kingdom are the answer for all problems? Are we convinced that our Creator knows best?

For in him all things were created: things in heaven and on earth, visible and invisible, whether thrones or powers or rulers or authorities; **all things have been created through him and for him.** *He is before all things, and* **in him all things hold together.** *(Col 1:16-17, emphasis added, see also Psa 33:6-9; Heb 11:3)*

All our lives we have been trained to assess things based on human logic. They must make sense to our human minds. But we are created beings, with limited understanding. We only know in part. We don't know the full picture our Creator knows. That's why it is futile to try and compress God's eternal plan and purposes into human comprehension. It's pointless to try and pull God down on our level to show Him our perspective. He already knows and has a better view on things. We should rather allow Him to lift us up on His level, so that we can see things from His perspective. It's more comprehensive. We need to allow the Holy Spirit to change our worldly, time limited paradigm (the common way of thinking about something or doing something) into God's eternal paradigm (again).

Part E

Changing The Paradigm

Introduction

"Instead of always accepting society's status quo, we should ask God to show us more biblical alternatives." (Randy Alcorn, 'Money, Possessions, And Eternity', page 347)

The change from our usual way of thinking about money or dealing with money (worldly paradigm) to God's eternal paradigm, begins with the startling revelation that God's priority is not money but relationships. As a relational being, God's prime concern is not economic growth but right relationships both between man and Himself, and between human beings.

The Bible uses various images that stand for the abuse and destruction of healthy relationships in favour of economic gain. In this Part E we look at some of these to highlight the necessity for a paradigm shift and the framework needed for a new paradigm.

32. Egypt ≠ Canaan

The Old Testament does not only provide the foundation for the New Testament but also foreshadows it in many ways. You cannot fully understand the NT unless you know the OT. Furthermore, many negative events and experiences of the OT were recorded as a warning to us today as Paul declared,

These things happened to them as examples and were written down as warnings for us [...]. (1Cor 10:11)

For everything that was written in the past was written to teach us, so that through endurance and the encouragement of the Scriptures we might have hope. (Rom 15:4)

And so the essential principles of Israel's Exodus account from Egyptian captivity *(Ex 1-19)* are as relevant to us today as they were then.

Instead of passing through the desert in just under a couple of weeks, Israel took forty years! Without knowing the story this sounds mind-boggling. 14,600 days instead of twelve, more than 1,200 times longer than needed! What makes a whole nation waste so much time, energy and promising future?

They were escaping countless years of horrible slavery and torture in Egypt. They just had enough provision for a short stay in the desert and God's promise to receive a land where milk and honey flow. So what in the world made them stay longer in the scorching desert heat? It was their rebellion and distrust in God. They wanted freedom on their own terms.

One might think that the traumatic period of slavery under a cruel world power had changed Israel. But that wasn't the case. Though they left Egypt, Egypt never left their hearts. Whenever things got difficult on their escape, they wanted to go back to what they knew. The awesome displays of God's power did not induce continued faith and trust in His promises, provision, protection, and abilities to conquer their enemies before them. Continually they broke their promise to follow Him wholeheartedly and rebelled.

Eventually God had had enough. Except faithful Joshua and Caleb, none of this obstinate, unyielding Israelite generation would enter the Promised Land. They were to die in the desert. Missing out on what God had in store for them must have been a complete shock to everyone. Abundance and unprecedented blessing were in sight, but inaccessible. Driven by fear they opted to return to pagan slavery when standing at the doorstep into God's promised inheritance. Voluntarily! Worry and fear can be very powerful. In the end the next generation, not born in slavery, got a new chance.

This picture of Egypt-Desert-Canaan is quite significant for today. God still wants His children to leave Egypt for Canaan by way through the desert. Only these three don't represent physical places anymore. Egypt is a picture of a nation ruled by the cruel, enslaving, destructive, yet temporal world system. The desert represents the transformation process that must take place to enjoy Canaan. And Canaan represents freedom from slavery, God's eternal rule, protection and provision. *Romans 12:2* describes this brilliantly:

Egypt – *Do not conform any longer to the pattern of this world,*

Desert – *but be transformed by the renewing of your mind.*

Canaan – *Then you will be able to test and approve what God's will is – his good, pleasing and perfect will.*

The desert is the critical place and time. Here our forced reliance on Satan's enslaving, temporal world system gets destroyed, while our voluntary reliance on God's freeing, eternal Kingdom gets established.

'Desert time' sounds like suffering, and it usually is. Yet the wilderness is God's chosen place of transformation and preparation. There we must learn to totally rely on Him. Abraham, Joseph, Moses, Elijah, John the Baptist, even Jesus Christ himself, Paul and many others had to go through it. And so must we. It's just a question of how long we'll dwell there. It is our choice. Until we die like that particular stubborn Israelite generation that never saw Canaan? Or will we swiftly move on?

Many Christians are not (yet) prepared, let alone wanting to wholeheartedly and uncompromisingly leave the world system. But there is an urgent call to do so.

Leaving Egypt and crossing the desert to enter Canaan sounds swift 'n easy but is easier said than done. Being raised in 'Egypt' and growing accustomed to the 'Babylonian system' makes it hard to imagine something entirely different. And besides, our daily handling of money makes sense and is logical, right? Of course, but only in the world system context, not in God's Kingdom. And since the world system is cruel and enslaving God's love provides us a way to leave. The decision, however, is ours.

The 'desert' route is not going to be a walk in the park. The devil wants us to stay in Egypt and tries by all means to frustrate our move. Our natural instincts and worldly mind hooked to the Babylonian system avoids going against the mainstream and into the desert like the plague, so we must expect difficulties, challenges, opposition, persecution, ridicule and the like. However, on that journey our reasoning and actions will change steadily into an eternity-based pattern although they won't make sense. Yet we can know that the tougher things get, the closer we are to Canaan.

God would love to welcome us in 'Canaan'. But if we refuse to learn His lessons we will never enter. Life in Canaan works on a completely different set of rules and principles to Egypt. It's relationship-based and not profit-driven. The true freedom of Canaan cannot be compared to the so-called freedom of Egypt, which only conceals slavery. So on balance it's worth enduring the relative hardships of the desert to enjoy the true freedom from slavery in Canaan.

Part of the transformation process that happens in the wilderness is learning and acknowledging that the world system and the Kingdom of God cannot function together let alone coexist. Let's have a look why.

33. World System ≠ Kingdom Of God

I have come into the world as a light, so that no one who believes in Me should stay in darkness. (John 12:46)

For he has rescued us from the dominion of darkness and brought us into the kingdom of the Son he loves. (Col 1:13)

Do not be yoked together with unbelievers. For what do righteousness and wickedness have in common. Or what fellowship can light have with darkness.[…] And no wonder, for Satan himself masquerades as angel of light. (2Cor 6:14; 11:14)

Have nothing to do with the fruitless deeds of darkness, but rather expose them. (Eph 5:11)

These Scriptures point to a massive conflict between two sides. The one is the dominion (Gk: *exousia*) of darkness, which is shrouded in obscurity and secrecy. We call it the world system. The biblical images of Babylon and Egypt are an expression of it.

The other is the Kingdom (Gk: *basileia*) of God's Son, which is operating and presenting itself in light, transparency and openness. It's the side every believer should be fighting for. Let us define these two a bit further.

World System

'Dominion of darkness', 'kingdom of darkness', 'evil world', 'this age', 'the world', or 'this world' are biblical expressions for the realm where the Lord is unwanted. They refer to authority, government, jurisdiction, sovereignty, mastery, control, command, power, sway, rule, that is completely opposing the God of the Bible. We are not talking merely about a physical territory but about a system. It is built and maintained by unbelievers, but hosted, encouraged and promoted by Satan.

The Holman Christian Standard Bible defines it as 'the organised Satanic system that is opposed to God and hostile to Jesus and His followers; it also refers to the non-Christian culture including governments, educational systems, and business.'

This system is supposed to manage and cater perfectly for all aspects of man's life without God's help and interference. Remember *Jer 2:13*?

> […] that ancient serpent called the devil, or Satan, who leads the whole world

astray. He was hurled to the earth, and his angels with him. (Rev 12:9)

Satan, who is the god of this world, has blinded the minds of those who don't believe. (2Cor 4:4a, NLT-SE)

For our struggle is not against flesh and blood, but against the rulers, against the authorities, against the powers of this dark world and against the spiritual forces of evil in the heavenly realm. (Eph 6:12)

In essence the world system is defined by everything that is run and done without God. As a result it is under the rule and influence of Satan. The world's financial system, therefore, is evil. Part A and B surely confirm that.

Kingdom of God

In *Matthew's Gospel* Jesus refers 31 times to the 'Kingdom of heaven'. Matthew's primarily Jewish readers knew this term from OT writings *(e.g. Dan 2:44)*. The other writers, addressing non-Jewish readers, used 'Kingdom of God'. In the four Gospels Jesus refers 121 times to Kingdom concepts. Undeniably, He had a clear Kingdom message at heart.

My Kingdom doesn't belong to this world. If my Kingdom belonged to this world, my followers would fight to keep me from being handed over to the Jews. My Kingdom doesn't have its origin on earth. (John 18:36, GWORD)

Our Father in heaven, hallowed (kept holy) be Your name. Your kingdom come, Your will be done on earth as it is in heaven. (Matt 6:9b-10)

There we go. God's Kingdom is not from this world. But by doing His will it will be increasingly demonstrated here.

During His lifetime on earth Jesus showed his audiences what this means and how it practically works. After His ascension, He sent the Holy Spirit to continue this work as a 'personal tutor' to every believer if you like. He teaches about the Kingdom of God and how it is practically lived out.

The Kingdom of God is everything that falls under the sovereign rule and reign of God. It is demonstrated on earth whenever and wherever people live in voluntary, faithful obedience to the King.

Incomparable And Incompatible

The world system and the Kingdom of God are totally opposite, i.e., like black and white or darkness and light. We cannot live in both realms concurrently, never mind trying to merge them as the comparison of the next table shows.

Please note, the world system looks like a war zone in itself, which is exactly what we witness today. However, it is also at war with God's Kingdom, with obvious results: competition instead of complementation; oppression instead of freedom; destruction instead of building up; dictating instead of serving; hate instead of love; hoarding instead of sharing, etc. You'll get the hang of it.

Logically, the world system (Satan's rule) and the Kingdom of God (God's rule) cannot truly coexist. It is not possible to serve both of them equally, let alone wholeheartedly, because they also work with different mindsets.

World System	Kingdom of God
Platform for forced rule of man and slavery of man	Platform for voluntary submission and freedom of man
• God and Satan are fantasies • No creation; existence by chance • Fight against others for survival • Very egocentric (all about 'me'), yet impersonal (no care for others) • Progress through selfishness • The least ones are failures • A person's chief occupation: work for man, making money • Economy's main end: create wants • Highest goal: profit maximisation (fading values – money) • Reliance on man's ability, wisdom, and common sense (all pretty limited) • Good life requires taking what we want, whenever and wherever we want it • System dictates to people how they and their lives have to look like • God unnecessary; man got it all worked out and under control	• God and Satan are real • Deliberate creation • God takes care of His children • Altruistic (care for others), yet very personal (God is interested in the 'me') • Progress through service and sacrifice • The least is the greatest • A person's chief occupation: work for God, building His Kingdom • Economy's main end: provide for needs • Highest goal: maximising heavenly treasures (eternal values – people) • Reliance on ability and wisdom of God Almighty (totally unlimited) • True fulfilment comes only by staying in God's will • Freedom for people to be the individual God created them to be • God is needed; man got nothing truly worked out or under control

34. Ownership ≠ Stewardship

The ownership-mentality is foundational for the world system. The concept of stewardship on the other hand is pivotal for the Kingdom of God.

Ownership

This way of thinking is rooted in evolution, so a just Creator-God doesn't feature in how things are seen and handled. Consequently,

- trust is put into the visible, physical realm;
- everything belongs to man; he can do with it whatever he wants;
- the earth' resources are limited;
- to ensure safety, security, supply and provision man has to own as much as possible; he needs to see that he gets his share of the cake;
- the operation mode is fear and mistrust.

Stewardship

> *The earth is the LORD's, and everything in the world and all who live in it. (Psa 24:1)*

> *For by him all things were created: things in heaven and on earth, visible and invisible, whether thrones or powers or rulers or authorities; all things have been created through him and for him. He is before all things, and in him all things hold together. (Col 1:16-17)*

Stewardship acknowledges the Lord as the Creator and owner of everything. His presence and involvement are essential to hold everything together. Put another way, Jesus needs to be in charge to keep everything going ok. Consequently, in the stewardship way of thinking,

- my trust is placed on God Almighty
- on the basis of my purpose, calling, character, maturity, etc. a portion of what belongs to God is entrusted to me;
- God created by speaking; He still can speak things into existence; I can tap into His unlimited resources;
- there will be always enough for everyone, even if I can't see it;
- the operation mode is faith and trust.

The term 'stewardship' is derived from the Greek word *oikonomos* and means 'steward, administrator, manager of a household, director, trustee'. The Holman Bible Dictionary defines stewardship as:

> "Utilising and managing all resources for the glory of God and the betterment of His creation."

When we make Jesus Christ the Lord of our lives, a few things in regards to our stewardship role become nonnegotiable.

1. Since God owns everything *(1Cor 10:26)* stewardship dispossesses us! Things in this world don't hold together because of us, but because of Jesus *(Col 1:17)*!

2. We come naked into this world and will depart naked *(1Chr 29:14b; Job 1:21)*. So everything we have between birth and death is a gift of God *(Eccl 3:13; 5:19)* and will be left behind for others *(Psa 49:10)*.

3. God has appointed us to be His stewards *(Gen 1:26; Matt 25:14+19)*. He gave us the mandate to rule over the earth and all that is in it, except man (!) *(Psa 8:6-8)*, thus equipped us to fulfil this task to its best.

4. We are accountable to God *(Eccl 12:14; Luke 16:2; Rom 14:12; Heb 4:13)* for the way we handle whatever He entrusted to us. This is not to scare us but for our own benefit and protection. As much as we would like others to treat and use 'our' things carefully, responsibly and faithfully, God expects the same of us *(Luke 6:31)*.

5. A good steward acts faithfully in his master's interest before his own *(Matt 24:45; Luke 16:12; 1Cor 4:2)*. To manage his master's property well is important to him *(Matt 25:14-30)*.

God gave each person seven distinct areas to steward, namely: (1) physical body; (2) time; (3) relationships; (4) natural and spiritual gifts; (5) environment (earth) and its natural resources; (6) material possessions and finances; (7) spiritual insight, understanding and revelation. They are all linked up. Consequently, good stewardship in one area has good influence on the others, and bad stewardship in one effects the other areas negatively. Which is why, generally, our stewardship needs to be solidly based and established on (a) biblical truth; (b) God-given revelation; and (c) the lead and guidance of the Holy Spirit.

Like Fire And Ice

It is pretty obvious that ownership and stewardship are two mutually exclusive mentalities. They must be, as they serve two opposing realms, the world system and the Kingdom of God.

As long as we are persuaded to be owners, we won't allow God, the true owner, to decide on things. The transition from economic slavery to economic freedom, therefore, only works if we are willing to let go of our ownership mentality and fully embrace stewardship. For this we need the help of the Holy Spirit.

The transformation period in the desert should also lead to a greater grasp of how much our dealing with money influences our spiritual state.

35. Money Impacts Spiritual State

To the person who pleases him, God gives wisdom, knowledge and happiness, but to the sinner he gives the task of gathering and storing up wealth to hand it over to the one who pleases God. [...] (Eccl 2:26)

What a Scripture! The sinners (the Hebrew *hātā* literally means 'those who do wrong, miss the way') WILL (not 'may' or 'might' or 'perhaps') gather and store up wealth, only to hand it over to Christians. Marvellous!

[...] the sinner's wealth is stored up for the righteous. (Prov 13:22b)

The righteous (Hebrew: *tzaddiq*) are 'those who are righteous, upright, just, innocent in accordance with a proper (i.e. God's) standard'.

Two well-known OT accounts provide scriptural backup for the above statements, thus showing the Bible's consistency:

- The first is about Joseph, who became Prime Minister in the pagan nation of Egypt. Encouraged by its ruler Pharaoh, Joseph provided to his family the very best this ungodly nation had to offer *(Gen 45:20)*.
- The second took place a few hundred years later. When Israel left the slavery of Egypt, the Egyptians actually provided them with silver, gold and clothing on their departure *(Ex 12:35-36)*.

Please note that both accounts involve Egypt, a representation of the cruel, enslaving world system. Both times, Egypt voluntarily hands over its wealth to God's people. The first account ends positively for God's people, the second one badly. Why was that? The key is quite likely training and qualification.

Training And Qualification

In the thirteen years of his enslavement and imprisonment, Joseph learned to be a very trustworthy and faithful steward. Whatever was delegated to him, he handled with absolute integrity. That qualified him for the position he received under Pharaoh (see also *Luke 16:10*). Handling that one faithfully and in total integrity led to the material blessing Pharaoh showered on Joseph's family. Joseph never lost faith in God and never made wealth his idol.

Before Israel left Egypt, they had lived there for many generations but ultimately as slaves. The prolonged time of oppression and mistreatment resulted in their submission to their fate. Unlike Joseph they had lost their zeal for God. When Egypt showered them with wealth on their departure, they had had no experience and training how to handle it. The dreadful consequences of turning this newly gained wealth literally into an idol is well documented. They made the Golden Calf their God.

As mentioned before, much of the OT was recorded for us today to learn from *(1Cor 10:11)*. So let's learn from this.

Without doubt most believers would love to see such biblical wealth transfer come true. The fact that this is rarely seen in our days must make us think. Are we sure we can handle wealth well in God's eyes? We would never entrust money to crooks, right? So why should God entrust money to people who have not been found trustworthy in His sight? You may feel offended by this remark. But handling money wisely in the world's eyes doesn't qualify here. Neither does simply giving tithes and offerings. We all need solid training on how to handle money in the Lord's eyes. Until then, God is likely to protect us from major problems and damage by not giving us more than we can handle at present.

Surprising Statistics

The NT contains about 215 verses on 'faith,' 218 on 'salvation,' but almost 2,100 on financial issues. That is more than any other single subject! It is, therefore, surprising that there is comparatively little teaching on this subject in Christian circles that goes beyond tithing and offerings.

John the Baptist prepared the way for Jesus' ministry on earth. When the people came to be baptised by John they were greeted with a pretty tough message about repentance *(Luke 3:7-9)*. The crowd wanted to know, *"What should we do then?" (Luke 3:10)*. John's answer was quite surprising: share with those in need; don't overcharge people; don't extort money but be content with your pay *(Luke 3:11-14)*. Some may prefer to dismiss it, but it was a clear message about restoring economic/financial justice. It embodies a practical application of God's command to love your neighbour as yourself *(Lev 19:18)*, which soon after was endorsed by Jesus *(Mark 12:30-31)*. And it reflected Jesus' later statement that no one can serve God and money at the same time.

Do not forget that the Lord Jesus Christ was delivered to the cross for money! Because money has a tremendous influence on peoples' lives, it is a bigger topic in the Bible than most believers want to believe or admit. The way we deal with money has massive impact on our spiritual condition.

Spiritual Condition

In *Luke 16:10-13* Jesus provides us with some substantial teaching on money. It is part of a more extensive address especially to the Pharisees *(Luke 15:11-16:13)*. It was precisely they, of all, who loved money *(Luke 16:14-15)*, and so it was of great import to put things into proper perspective for them. We want to focus first on *Luke 16:10-12*.

> *Whoever can be trusted with **very little** can also be trusted with **very much**, and whoever is dishonest with **very little** will also be dishonest with **very much**. So if you have not been trustworthy in handling **worldly wealth**, who will trust you with **true riches**? And if you have not been trustworthy with **someone else's property**, who will give you **property of your own**? (emphasis added)*

We can look at the three comparisons (see emphasised words) in three ways:

1. For each of the three comparisons the following applies: if you cannot even handle the lesser, you disqualify yourself for handling the bigger.
2. The first item in each of the three comparisons represent one and the same thing and so does the second. The first relates to the world system, the second to the Kingdom of God.
3. There is a progression, namely from quantity (very little – very much) to quality (worldly wealth – true riches) to property (someone else's – own).

All three interpretations may be valid. But since conjunctions are used to connect the comparisons, it seems most likely that the second one is intended. So what does it mean, then?

- The first equation is 'very little' = 'worldly wealth' = 'someone else's property'. This is what the world system offers in comparison to the Kingdom of God.
- The second equation is 'very much' = 'true riches' = 'property of your own'. That is what the Kingdom of God offers in comparison to the world system.

Worldly wealth is, by definition, temporary and very little in comparison to the fulness of true, eternal riches of the Kingdom. Worldly wealth is property that belongs to the world system, which is under control of the devil, who robs, steals and destroys. Worldly wealth can't be taken to our eternal home. True riches are spiritual insight, wisdom, understanding, revelation, authority, God's promises for eternity, a new body and a new home on a new earth in a new universe. All these are the believers' own property (rewards) for they are God's heirs *(Rom 8:17)*.

On balance *Luke 16:10-12* tells us that the way we handle worldly (unrighteous) wealth has bearing on our handling of spiritual (righteous) wealth. The 'handling' is measured by biblical standards, not by the world's. This is crucial because,

No one can serve two masters. Either you will hate the one and love the other, or you will be devoted to the one and despise the other. You cannot serve both God and money. (Luke 16:13)

To summarise, not only does our handling of worldly wealth influence how we will handle spiritual wealth. But we are also warned that we cannot serve worldly wealth and God concurrently. It is, therefore, no exaggeration to say that our dealing with money expresses our spiritual state.

36. Here And Now ≠ Eternity

"Our whole education tends to fix our minds on this world." (C.S. Lewis, 1898-1963, Irish novelist, scholar, broadcaster)

Throughout our lives, we are trained and conditioned to care and cater only for the here and now (short-term), but never for there being a time after (physical) death. Our entire life plan is confined to our limited time on this earth. No wonder we try to make the most of it. It's just being a nuisance that God had a different plan for us.

God created us in His image, as eternal beings. Our body is going to die one day, but our spirit and soul never will. Our decisions and how we spend our life on this planet will result either in resurrection to eternal life or to eternal damnation. Heaven or hell – that's the only biblical choice for us. Those who will be raised from the dead to eternal life will receive a new body at resurrection. And they will spend eternity well and alive in God's presence on a new earth in a new universe. For them life will continue on this, albeit renewed planet, where no evil, no curse, no bad is found anymore.

> *For this world is not our permanent home; we are looking forward to a home yet to come. (Heb 13:14, NLT-SE)*

> *We have been born into a new life which has an inheritance that can't be destroyed or corrupted and can't fade away. That inheritance is kept in heaven for you. (1Pet 1:4, GWORD)*

You don't establish your life in a place you are just passing through, right? Putting down roots doesn't make sense when you are moving on anyway. From God's vantage point we are just passing through. We leave this fallen planet anyhow. It is not our eternal home. New heaven and new earth are. Having eternity in sight should, therefore, influence the way we live our life here in the transition phase.

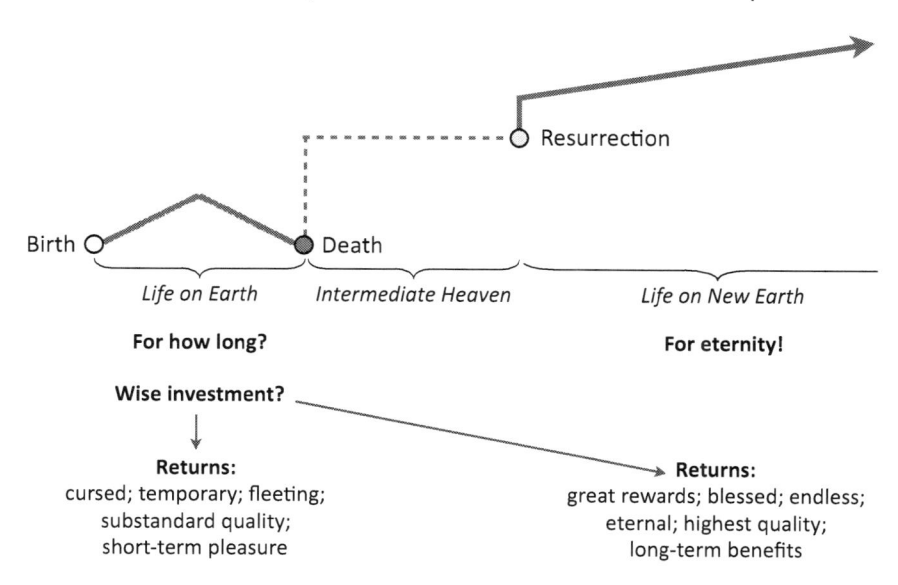

Birth ○ ──── ● Death ──────── ○ Resurrection ──→

Life on Earth | Intermediate Heaven | Life on New Earth

For how long? — **For eternity!**

Wise investment?

↓

Returns:
cursed; temporary; fleeting;
substandard quality;
short-term pleasure

Returns:
great rewards; blessed; endless;
eternal; highest quality;
long-term benefits

The illustration on the last page attempts to depict this. We don't know how long our time on earth will be. But what we can know is where we will spend the forever and ever. So the question is this: How do we best invest everything entrusted to us (time, resources, relationships, abilities, ...) during our time on earth? What kind of returns do we want? Short-term or eternal?

The world rejecting God has established its own framework for managing life on earth. Naturally, this framework is useless in our walk with Him.

> *Do not conform to the pattern of this world, but* **be transformed by the renewing of your mind**. *Then you will be able to test and approve what God's will is – his good, pleasing and perfect will (Rom 12:2, emphasis added)*

We can't transform ourselves. But we can stay open to be transformed. The key is to allow God to change our paradigms, our framework of thinking. If we do that we will discover that this will alter the way we interpret experiences and make decisions. If we can get a true perspective and understanding of eternity, we will stop trying to get the most out of theses few years on this planet. Instead we'll increasingly want to give all we can during life on earth to gain the eternal rewards awaiting us.

The illustration below is copied from the caricature 'Perspective' by Viuti from Argentina. Adding the arrows and labels, I have adapted it as it brings the message across beautifully. The stairway represents Earth. Though we are all living on the same planet, we don't necessarily have the same perspective. When our perspec-

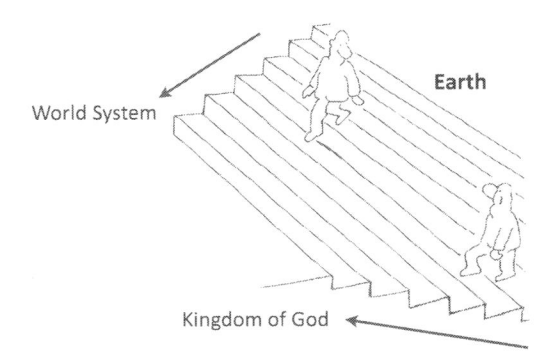

tive is fixed on the world system we will face the abyss, the eternal death. The way goes down to hell. With our perspective fixed on the Kingdom of God we head for eternal life in the presence of our Creator. The way goes up to heaven. Harsh? Just read:

The path of the wise leads upward to life, that he may avoid [the gloom] in the depths of Sheol (Hades, the place of the dead). (Prov 15:24, AMP)

And set your minds and keep them set on what is above (the higher things), not on the things that are on the earth. (Col 3:2, AMP)

The following Scriptures show us how fruitless it is to follow man's wisdom (the world system) anyhow.

For it is written: "I will destroy the wisdom of the wise; the intelligence of the intelligent I will frustrate." (1Cor 1:19)

For this world's wisdom is foolishness (absurdity and stupidity) with God, [...] He lays hold of the wise in their [own] craftiness; [...] The Lord knows the thoughts and reasonings of the [humanly] wise and recognises how futile they are. (1Cor 3:19-20, AMP)

No one can comprehend what goes on under the sun. Despite all their efforts to search it out, no one can discover its meaning. Even if the wise claim they know, they cannot really comprehend it. (Eccl 8:17)

There is no wisdom, no insight, no plan that can succeed against the Lord. (Prov 21:30, see also Prov 3:5+7a)

37. Summary

At the beginning of this book I boldly asserted that man serves money. Yet God states, that we can't serve money and Him concurrently.

Part A, therefore, looked at key components of the world's money system and how it works. The goal was to find out why the system demands man to serve it.

Part B then revealed a host of troubles caused by this system, evidencing its evil, destructive nature. It proved that man indeed serves the money system and not vice versa.

Part C revealed that all of this corresponds to the biblical image of Babylon, a wicked system of Satan that God's people ought to leave.

Part D provided a condensed overview of secular solutions to break free from the destructive financial system. It concluded that the framework of God's Kingdom is best suited for the much needed change. But God's Kingdom requires a new paradigm shift, something entirely different to our usual, worldly way of thinking about money or dealing with money.

And that's exactly what this Part E was all about.

- 'Egypt-Desert-Canaan' was Israel's route from slavery to freedom. Our today's corresponding path, 'World System-Desert-Kingdom of God', leads us from the Babylonian tyranny to freedom. The 'Desert' represents the transformation process where our paradigm gets changed.
- Part of that change is learning and acknowledging that the world system and the Kingdom of God can neither coexist nor function together.
- Another, that as God's children we are His stewards and no longer owners of what we have. We therefore manage everything in God's interest, not ours.
- Further, we must realise that the way we deal with money has major influence on our spiritual state.
- Last but not least, our perspective for decisions and actions must be extended from the here and now to eternity.

With all that in mind, we can now move on to the economic approach in God's Kingdom.

Part F

Kingdom Economy

Introduction

One of the many reasons why God chose Israel as a people for Himself was to show the difference of a nation living under His rule rather than under a secular government. The bedrock of Israel's society was life in extended families, where each household was provided with productive land. Hence families were rooted and solidarity strengthened. Several families formed close-knit communities. God gave basic laws relating to economics, finance, health care, justice, welfare, defence, religion, etc. for a healthy life within and between the communities. All aspects of life were relationship-based. In brief, there was no need and place for centralised welfare and social systems and government.

By and large, todays societies are very much the opposite of that divine blueprint. People's lives are mainly driven by money and all relationships are subjected to it. Most households don't have property, let alone productive land. Families are uprooted and disconnected from a place since the economy requires them to be mobile. Centralised impersonal welfare and social systems have replaced the duties of the healthy social fabric of close communities. Central governments, which are less and less in touch with reality on the ground, are progressively regulating the lives of their citizens through a complex system of regulations, laws, surveillance and taxes. The monetary interest of capital owners, large corporations and banks leads to the ruthless plundering of our planet's limited resources. By and large, a productive economy, serving people's needs, has lost its influence to the ever-increasing force of a non-productive financial industry.

If we look at the Kingdom economy as a solution to the Babylonian mess, it may be surprising that neither money nor economic growth is God's primary concern. As a relational being, His main focus is on healthy relationships (a) between man and Him and (b) between people. This makes sense, since only humans have an eternal future, whereas everything else on earth and the current earth itself are non-permanent. However, God knows that economic aspects play an important part in human relations. And so, right relationships form the basis of the Kingdom economy.

A host of Scriptures define what God-pleasing human behaviour looks like, for example as a family member, employer, employee or investor. This includes the care for widows, orphans and foreigners who are almost always disadvantaged in relational and financial terms *(Deut 10:18; James 1:27)*. Unsurprisingly God's relational principles regulate Kingdom economies (capital ownership, work incentives, finance, money system, taxes, welfare). They are not only equitable, efficient, and have eternal relevance. They also stand in stark contrast to the shortsighted materialistic vision of the world system, which shamelessly exploits and destroys the social fabric of society.

> *See to it that no one takes you captive through hollow and deceptive philosophy, which depends on human tradition and the basic principles of this world rather than on Christ. Since you died with Christ to the basic principles of this world, why, as though you still belonged to it, do you submit to its rules. (Col 2:8, 20, NIV 84)*

> *You have commanded that your guiding principles be carefully followed. (Psa 119:4, GWORD)*

Believers should follow God's guiding principles for life, for if they do that, they will also prosper economically *(Deut 28:1-14)*. But if they don't, they will face negative economic repercussions *(Deut 28:15-68)*. What exactly are these principles (laws, commands, decrees, statutes) that it is so important to follow?

Well, for a start, principles can't be invented. They are established right at the point of creation. A principle is 'The first law established by the manufacturer or creator of a thing.' Principles are normally laid down in a handbook to simplify the use of a thing and avoid problems through abuse.

Let's take a car for an example. When you buy a car, you have no authority to determine the principles on which it works. Your opinion or mood doesn't make the car run. Nor does your origin, history, background, present circumstances, culture, place of living, the weather, or anything else. Given that you want to make best use of the car you must give it what it needs. If you don't do it, you cause harm. Just because you can't smell petrol doesn't mean you can switch to milk or apple juice for fuel. If you do, the car may start and run for a short time, making you feel vindicated. But as soon as the residue of petrol in the system is used up and the engine exposed to 'unnatural' fuel, it will break.

God established perfect laws and principles for our lives when He created us. But we don't want to obey them, rather we do what we want. At the moment it may still look fine as there are still Christian residues in our 'system'. So we feel justified. But violating God's principles will eventually destroy. No one gets away with it. Principles have no respect for anyone.

> *The wise in heart accept commands, but a chattering fool comes to ruin. (Prov 10:8)*

God's principles for man are laid down in the Bible, the handbook for man's life. They aren't there to limit, but to protect. *'You shall not steal'* is not a restriction to what you can have. It is a protective law that denies you illegal access to what was entrusted to others. And it denies others illegal access to what was entrusted to you. Obeying this principle alone would make most of the laws and protection mechanisms of this world superfluous.

> *Jesus replied: 'Love the Lord your God with all your heart and with all your soul and with all your mind.' This is the first and greatest commandment. And the second is like it: 'Love your neighbour as yourself.' All the Law and the Prophets hang on these two commandments. (Matt 22:37-40)*

These two directives provide the bedrock of all right and healthy relationships of man to God and one another, which in turn form the foundation for all Kingdom economies. As we look at biblical principles for a host of financial/economical topics now, we must always keep the following two questions in mind:

- How does that affect my relationships with God?
- How does that affect my relationship with my neighbour?

We will probably find that more often than not both our relationship with God and our neighbour are affected in the same way. This makes sense because our relationship with other people reflects our relationship with our common Creator *(Matt 5:43-48; 1John 4:20-21)* and vice versa. Which is why it's so immensely important to,

> *Do to others as you would have them do to you. (Luke 6:31)*

Principles

"To accept the fact that all our dealings with money is to be governed by Kingdom principles is an extremely difficult challenge for folks raised in democratic, materialistic societies." (Wolfgang Simson, 'The Starfish Manifesto', page 374)

38. Money

People in power have almost always abused their power to tamper with money. What began with false weights and measures for means of payment in the old days, continued with the advent of money in debasing coins. Today, artificial, debt-based money creation (fiat currencies, fractional reserve banking) as well as inflation constitute money tampering. The object of all this has always been a disguised fraud and robbery, a cleverly veiled theft of other people's wealth.

Acting this way certainly doesn't please God since He detests the use of falsified means of payment *(Deut 25:13-16; Prov 11:1, 20:23; Mic 6:11)*. **They represent a theft and consequently violate His 8th commandment,** *'You shall not steal' (Deut 5:19; Mark 10:19; Rom 13:9)*.

If Christians are actively and knowingly involved in this type of theft, they rebel openly against God's good order. It shows their disrespect for Him. Participation in the theft of the wealth of others shows everything else but no love for your neighbour. It creates tension in the relationships.

If, as believers, we were to change the current money system into an honest one, it would need to be based on the biblical principle that theft is a crime. Any action that undermines the value of money is a theft. It takes wealth from others without their permission. Therefore, everyone creating false money should be treated as thieves and punished accordingly, regardless of who they are. The biblical penalty for this crime is twofold restitution *(Ex 22:7-9)*.

It is possible to create a money system that is less open to misuse, manipulation and exploitation than our current one. But the truth is that any system can be misused, no matter how good and righteously it is set up. All in all, it depends on the character, the honesty and the heart of its users, whether a system is just and helpful or not.

The overwhelming majority of believers will never be in a position to change the current money system. They are forced to get on with what is available. That is not to say that we shouldn't pursue change whenever and wherever we can. When Jesus came to earth He did not change the money system either. Jesus used the available currency Himself. However, He was sad and angry to see how people had diverged from God's righteous ways in handling money and wealth. They'd become slaves to an evil economic system. Hence Jesus taught to follow God's principles from a right heart attitude. Much of it is contained in this book.

39. Banking

Secular banks only care about themselves. Customers are subjected to the bank's selfish interests to increase profits. Overall banks show very little honest concern for the financial wellbeing or economic progress of their clients, unless, of course, it serves the bank's own interests. Rather than serving in the truest sense of the word, the banking sector dictates to the productive economy what can and can't be done.

In *John 10:11-13* Jesus speaks about the difference between a shepherd and a hired hand. The shepherd is very concerned about his sheep and protects them against dangers. The hired hand just does a job and abandons the sheep in the face of danger. Various meanings can be drawn from this comparison taken from the animal husbandry, a typical economic setup of that time. This comparison also reflects todays general banking approach, where bankers act as hired hands. With most banks having limited liabilities today there is no need for true concern and care, let alone protection against 'wolves' (see also '8. Corrupted Banks' and '43. Limited Liabilities').

This type of banking approach does not find the approval of God for it is distant, cold, calculating, dictating, and exploitative. It leaves clients (neighbours) out in the rain rather than offering true help when they are in difficulty. It certainly is no platform for a loving relationship with neighbours (clients), as they are feeling used and potentially abused. Surely, bankers and their employees would hate to be treated like that, so why do they then treat others this way *(see Luke 6:31)*?

Banks in the Kingdom economy must be different. Bankers need to become like 'shepherds' again that show true commitment and concern. They should not encourage and lure their customers into dangerous and questionable dealings, exposing them to 'wolves'. Their sole task should be to support and promote healthy economic progress of the community they belong to. Bankers must again become part of the social fabric of the community they serve. They must act as honest and transparent service agents, who have the financial wellbeing of their customers at heart. That would surely please God and their clients alike.

A Kingdom bank, therefore, cannot

- report deposits as its own assets in its balance sheet
- engage in fractional reserve banking
- use short-term deposits for longterm loans (futures)

- use their customers' money to speculate and invest in financial products on their own account
- use interest
- overcharge for its services

Why? Because these are forms of fraud, theft, dishonesty, and exploitation. The Bible doesn't justify any of this, but strongly warns against it (see '63 Honesty').

A Kingdom bank can

- administer their clients' money, and do financial transactions on their behalf
- charge fairly for its services
- make interest-free loans; only with money that was made available for that purpose (no deposits on call), whereas the loan terms must match the terms of deposits; loan terms should not exceed seven years *(e.g. Deut 15:1-2)*

There is no inherent fraud, theft, dishonesty and exploitation in this. If executed with a proper Kingdom mindset, this kind of service can easily become a catalyst for economic progress within a community.

40. Borrowing And Lending

Debt is almost as old as mankind. But never in all history has the population of this planet been financially indebted as it is today. On average, every single living citizen on earth, regardless of age, has a debt of $31,500. That's quite a burden. Nowadays it's hard to find a nation, a business, an organisation, an institution, or even an individual that is debt-free.

Different Point Of View

Debt is the world's way of financing something that would otherwise not be possible. In the world, debts are perceived to be opening up opportunities. They are seen as a catalyst for economic progress. Hence, creating debt is normally considered wise and therefore encouraged and in many ways officially supported.

The Kingdom of God presents an entirely different view. Since the world's wisdom is foolishness in God's eyes *(1Cor 1:19, 3:19)*, believers are not to act as the world does *(Rom 12:2)*. Debt is seen as enslaving and thus a catalyst for destruction.

[…] the borrower is slave to the lender. (Proverbs 22:7)

A slave has no say. He can't choose what to do and what not, but has to obey his master. When we borrow, the lender becomes our master. We can't choose the terms, but must accept what our master dictates. We have become a financial slave to the lender. But since Jesus has bought our freedom *(Gal 5:1)*, God does not want us to become slaves of men again *(1Cor 7:23)*.

In *Deut 28*, God details blessings and curses for His people. Blessings are the result of obedience to God, curses the consequence of disobedience.. Part of the blessings is the ability to lend. There is no need to borrow. His people can act as the head *(verses 12-13)*. Part of the curse is the necessity to borrow. There is no ability to lend. His people will be the tail *(verse 44)*, i.e., slaves to the head.

Bear in mind that *Rev 13:16-17* discloses Satan's agenda to control and enslave man financially. The goal is man's destruction and debt is the tool for this. That's why we must avoid going into debt. The only debt we are really permitted to have, is the constant debt of love *(Rom 13:8)*. We should never cease to love one another, as Christ never ceases to love us. This is in line with God's two foundational laws of loving Him with all we are and have and our neighbour as ourselves *(Matt 22:37-40)*.

So if we get indebted or help other Christians creating debt, there is a break of trust in our (and their) relationship with God. We are disobedient and treat what He has done with contempt, hence expressing our independence from Him. The pressure of debt also negatively impacts our relationships. By helping others to get indebted we become guilty of putting their relationships at risk.

Please note, there's no biblical penalty for getting into debt. So it's entirely up to us to borrow or not. Some believers are convinced that making debt is a wise decision and God has no problem with it. This is especially true in connection with the purchase of a house or a flat, because the payment of a mortgage can be cheaper than rent. And why should they pay off the mortgage of somebody else, anyhow? Well, borrowing is not a sin and maybe everything goes well.

However, the Bible warns against the destructive consequences of debts. We will look at them more closely as we progress. As described above, debts are never God's preferred option for His children. Christians may be enslaved by debt for they are desperate, thoughtless, ignorant, or misjudging the effects of debt. Or they simply lack faith in God's ability.

Two Representative Examples

People are in debt for all sorts of reasons: to make a living; to finance studies and education; to go on vacation; to buy things; to acquire a house or other property; for gambling; to invest in their business or for the future; to pay for celebrations, weddings and anniversaries; to pay for medical visits, hospitalisation, property or equipment maintenance, and so on. The list is long.

Some people borrow out of despair. Others, because they are too impatient to wait until they can afford something. Others, to finance their addictions. Others, to outdo their neighbours, or simply show off with stuff. Others, because they are hoodwinked into it. And still others, because they know no better, or are taught or told that this is a wise thing to do.

Here, we will be using two examples from everyday life, which will help us understand the biblical approach to this topic. One looks at purchasing a consumer product, the other one investing into property.

1. **Example (Consumer Product)**

    Here is the situation. You want to buy a new TV but lack the money. Since you don't want to wait until you have it, you go to your bank to borrow. The bank offers you a loan at these terms: $2,000 at 10% interest, all repayable after one year (see financial scenario in table below). You are completely happy to save up $2,200 to pay to the bank in a years time just to buy a $2,000 TV now.

	Today	1 year later
Television Set	$2,000	
10% Interest/Year	$200	
Total (1)	$2,200	
Savings (2)	$1,905	$1,430
5% Interest/Year	$95	$70
Total	$2,000	$1,500
Difference (1) - (2)	$295	$770
in %	15.5%	53.8%

    If you'd wait patiently for this TV until you can afford it, you could save a year long to gain interest, say 5%. Getting interest is always less than paying it. So to buy the $2,000-TV in a year, you have to save $1,905.

Either way you'll have to save up. But your impatience does cost you $2,200-$1,905 = $295 or 15.5% more than if you were a bit patient. But there is more.

A year from now the same TV is likely to cost less, say $1,500, since newer models hit the market. So to get the TV you laid your eyes on you'd only need to save up $1,430. In other words, your impatience actually costs you $2,200-$1,430 = $770 or 53.8% more than patience!

Borrowing money to buy consumer goods you can't afford right now is the order of the day. It is quite often a decision taken at short notice. Since the amounts are not too large, such borrowing is considered unproblematic and manageable. Whatever the reasons for such debts, the greatest driving force seems to be impatience.

2. Example (Property)

You want to settle down and have your own house or apartment but lack the funds to buy. A monthly rent and a monthly mortgage repayment don't seem to differ much currently, if anything, the rent seems more expensive. So you choose a mortgage to buy your own property rather than paying the mortgage of another person's property. In our example here we ignore rates, property tax and potential maintenance costs. A bank offers you the needed $200,000 at 5% annual interest over 25 years (see Table 1 below). The new property serves as collateral. Provided the interest rate remains the same for the next 25 years, your total repayment will amount to $350,900. That's 75.5% more than the asset value due to interest.

Table 1

	Total	% of Mortgage	⌀ Paym./Month
Term	25 years		
Mortgage	$200,000	100.0%	$667
Interest	$150,900	75.5%	$503
Total Debt	$350,900	175.5%	$1,170

Your obligation now is to pay 300 successive instalments (25 yrs x 12 mths) of $1,170 each to cover the total debt. The pressure is to keep these payments going without a single interruption. Any temporary default increases the total debt notably, and prolongs the repayment period. Each interest rate change alters the total repayment, too, sometimes positively but mostly negatively. If you fail to honour your contract you loose your property to the bank.

Your monthly instalment equates to 1/300 or 0.33% of the total debt. Yet, if you believe that both the mortgage and interest are reduced by the same percentage every month (as indicated in table 1), you err. Mortgages are set up in such a way that in the beginning you are paying proportionally more interest than for the asset itself. Table 2 on the next page exposes this imbalance clearly. Look for example at the status after ten years, which equals 40% of the mortgage term.

While your mortgage reduction is just about one quarter (26.1% = $52,130), you'll have already paid almost three-fifth (58.5% = $88,270) of the total interest due for 25 years. In other words, by then you will have paid the interest 2.2 times faster off than your asset.

Have a close look at Table 2 below and you'll see how unrighteous mortgages are set up.

Mortgage – actual repayment after 'x' years   **Table 2**

Duration		Mortgage		Interest		Total	
Years	Percent	Absolute	Percent	Absolute	Percent	Absolute	Percent
1 yrs	4.0%	$4,120	2.1%	$9,920	6.6%	$14,040	4.0%
5 yrs	20.0%	$22,830	11.4%	$47,370	31.4%	$70,200	20.0%
10 yrs	40.0%	$52,130	26.1%	$88,270	58.5%	$140,400	40.0%
15 yrs	60.0%	$89,750	44.9%	$120,850	80.0%	$210,600	60.0%
20 yrs	80.0%	$138,030	69.0%	$142,770	94.6%	$280,800	80.0%
25 yrs	100.0%	$200,000	100.0%	$150,900	100.0%	$350,900	100.0%

On balance you are working hard to mainly enrich the bank through interest first, before eventually acquiring your own asset. The bank does absolutely nothing productive here to deserve this income. All it does is giving you what isn't theirs (money) and holding on to 'your' property as collateral in case you default. Should you want to pay your debt off quicker, which is a good thing as you free yourself faster from the clutches of slavery, then you might even get punished with an overpayment penalty. That is absolute crazy and illogic.

In the final analysis, a mortgage is a very one-sided economic affair that only benefits the bank. You, however, are financially enslaved to the lender for a very very long time.

A rental, hire-purchase or income-share agreement are preferable options to consumer loans and mortgages for they share risk more fairly between consumer and financier.

If you borrow longterm to invest on a corporate level (e.g. into land, buildings, machinery, etc.) there is not much difference to how mortgages work. The interest might spread more evenly over the loan term, but it still constitutes an income without work for the lender. And you are still enslaved to the lender for a substantial period of time and are required to provide collateral in case you default. Regardless of how this turns out, the lender wins. The only difference to private borrowing is, that, although you make the decision, you are not really held accountable if it fails. The company carries the risk and it's customers the costs. Interest inflated prices are the result of corporate debts.

Borrowing money to invest is ordinarily a very deliberate decision and not taken lightly, as it affects your longterm cashflow. At the private level, the biggest driver is unquestionably to get your own property instead of financing someone else's property through rent. Independence from a landlord's dictate is a further big issue here. At corporate level, the main drivers are usually survival, competitiveness and profit maximisation.

Wise Financial Decision?

There are countless reasons to justify borrowing. But in the final analysis, debt simply remains a shortcut to finance what an individual, company, organisation, institution or government cannot afford at the moment.

As mentioned before, the Bible contains no laws prohibiting or punishing debt. However, God considers borrowing as extremely unwise, even destructive, due to its consequences. Perhaps that's penalty enough? It would be beneficial to check out and reflect on the following reasons:

- Generally believers should show great patience *(Col 1:11, 3:13; Heb 6:12)*. It also means patiently waiting until we can afford something. A healthy biblical wealth creation happens step by step, i.e. in moderation *(Prov 13:11, 16:8)*, and depends on a person's maturity *(Luke 16:10-12)*. Debt bypasses this.

- We cannot serve both God and money *(Matt 6:24; Luke 16:13)*. But when we borrow money we become a slave to the lender *(Prov 22:7)* and now serve money demands. We also jeopardise the freedom that Jesus has bought dearly for us *(Gal 5:1)*. Thus debts work against God's intention that we should never again become slaves to man *(1Cor 7:23)*.

- Since the borrower is slave to the lender, debt is the most likely tool for the devil to force his destructive economic control on us *(Rev 13:16-17)*.

- Debts tie us to the world's money system, hindering us to follow God's urgent call to leave it, i.e., 'Babylon' *(Jer 51:45; Rev 18:4)*.

- God prohibits charging interest amongst believers. Lending money for interest is a risk-free 'investment' for money lenders, but exploitation of those in need *(Lev 25:36-37; Neh 5:7-11)*. By implication we should avoid paying interest, as it embodies an exploitation of our (perceived) need.

- Economically, borrowing money is simply bad stewardship. Why? Because of interest, we pay considerably more for the object than its actual value. We are wasting entrusted resources that could be used elsewhere better.

- Our interest payments are an income without work for the money lenders and thus violate *2Th 3:10*. We are fuelling an unrighteous system.

- Interest withdraws resources from the Kingdom of God and gives them to the enslaving world financial system (banks, capital owners, money lenders). It's like weakening God's Kingdom financially to strengthen the enemy instead.

- God owns everything *(Psa 24:1)*. We are His steward and therefore should act faithfully in His interest with what He has entrusted to us *(Matt 24:45; Luke 16:12; 1Cor 4:2)*. By borrowing, we use future resources that we have not yet received from God and actually may never receive.

- Borrowing is manipulating God into our own agenda. We assume the role of the master (we make the loan decision) and demote God to be the obedient servant (He has to comply by providing us the means to pay it off).

- By borrowing, we consume now what should be at the disposal of the next generation. As a result and in violation of the 8th commandment, *'you shall not steal' (Ex 20:15; Matt 19:18; Rom 13:9)*, we are stealing from their future and leave them with a debt burden instead. We become responsible for our children's enslavement *(2Kings 4:1-7)*.

- By borrowing, we have to create extra room in our current cashflows for the related debt service. Therefore our financial leeway, which God may want to use, is markedly reduced.

- Only God knows the future *(James 4:13-16)*. We can well imagine what's coming, but we can't be sure that it actually happens. It's not in our hands. We can plan but God's purpose prevails *(Prov 19:21, Lam 3:37)*. Perhaps that is why God limited the planning horizon for debts for His people to just seven years *(Deut 15:1-2)*. At the end of it unpaid debts must be cancelled. So enslaving ourself to unbelieving money lenders and for longer periods, like with a mortgage, is a foolish thing.

- It seems inconsistent to trust God for constant mortgage payments, but not for regular rental payments or sufficient funds to buy without debt. Paul also rented *(Acts 28:30)*. You might say that he knew his time was now limited as he was facing trial before Caesar. But our time on earth is limited, too. We are just passing through *(Phil 3:20; Heb 13:14)*.

- Whether rented or bought, when we die we can't take anything with us *(Job 1:21; 1Tim 6:7)*. So we better know that it was part of God's plan for us to toil all our life to pay off what we leave behind anyway. We should be focused on eternal, not earthly things *(Phil 3:19; Col 3:2)*.

- God says that we do not need to borrow when we follow His commands faithfully *(Deut 28:12-13)*. We may not want to hear that, but being financially indebted is, therefore, above all a vote of no confidence against God. It's a declaration that the almighty, omniscient, omnipresent Creator of everything that exists is powerless to care for us.

That's a lot of reasons to reconsider the issue of debts. But there is still more.

Terrible Effects

Whatever the motive for getting into debt, most borrowers can testify to the immense pressure created by the need for regular debt service in their lives. The share of late payments or insolvency is continually rising in our time, making debt-collection services a booming industry.

Things really get bad once people get investigated for non-payment. For fear of debt-collection they often stop answering the door or phone. They withdraw from the public, pretend to be away and go into hiding. Often, lies are told to buy time, and to get rid of the unrelenting pressure, at least temporarily. In business, people are now merely seen as potential source of earnings. Each customer is screened regarding his prospective contribution to solving the financial shortage. Relationships to friends, acquaintances and colleagues are being put to the test. And especially family members now have to deal with increasing aggressive behaviour and dropping grace levels of the debtor.

Debts have terrible effects beyond the possible loss of all possessions. Debts work like a modern day slave master and the once enjoyed freedom is lost. Many relationships, families, churches, organisations and companies are destroyed because of indebtedness. Remember,

> *It is for freedom that Christ has set us free. Stand firm, then, and do not let yourselves be burdened again by a yoke of slavery. (Gal 5:1)*

These are terrible effects as long as we are still alive and able to deal with our debts in one way or another.

But what if we lose our job, struggle to get a new one, get disabled in an accident or die prematurely and leave our debts to our spouse and children? *2Kings 4:1-7* describes the dreadful circumstances in which the wife of a prophet and devout servant of the Lord found herself after his untimely death. We are not told why he died. But we are told that she inherited so much debt from her late husband that the creditor now demanded her two boys as slaves to pay up for it. Can it get any worse? What a picture of debt enslavement – you get into debt and your kids have to pay the price. If God had not stepped in with a miracle to pay off these obligations, life would have become a nightmare for her. But God doesn't always step in like that.

Obligation To Fulfil

When we borrow something, we make use of what belongs to somebody else. We use it for an agreed period of time and then return it in acceptable condition. Normally there is a fee for utilising other people's property. If we borrow money, we agree to repay the borrowed sum plus interest.

If loans were always repaid in time and to the full, debt collection agencies would be out of business. But the opposite is true as their trade is flourishing. That tells us something about the debtors' conduct, which also includes the unbiblical way of applying for insolvency (see '44. Bankruptcy, Insolvency') that punishes the lenders and suppliers.

> *Repay your neighbour when a loan falls due. […] If he cannot pay, the borrower has robbed the other of his money." (Sirach 29:2b, 6b, NRSV)*

> *The wicked borrow and do not repay, […] (Psalm 37:21)*

Certainly there are many reasons for default. Some are beyond people's control, but most aren't. Besides, there are cultural differences in how people interpret the agreed pay back arrangement. In Africa, for example, a loan is often repaid only when the creditor's need is greater than that of the debtor. And, since banks are perceived to always have money, debt-repayment is no matter of urgency. Scriptures like the two just mentioned make clear that there is no biblical basis for the borrower to decide when it is convenient for him to repay the lender.

To the western mind the above approach to debt repayments might sound odd. But even the West comes up with strange counsel on how to handle debts. A popular secular book amongst believers on how to achieve financial freedom advises debtors as follows: 'Only offer 50% of what you are able to repay per month, as the lender should be happy to be repaid anyway. Save the other 50% for yourself. In this way you build up your own fortune at the same rate as you pay off your debts.' That's very questionable advice. There is no scriptural basis for this. *Prov 3:28* and *Rom 13:8* require a contrary attitude.

God wants us to treat others the way we want to be treated *(Matt 7:12)*. If we do not want to be exploited by others for their enrichment, we should not do that to others. Once we agree borrowing terms and how debts are repaid, God expects us to honour the contract *(Prov 3:28; Rom 13:8; James 5:12)*.

Bad Advice – Good Advice

The author of the aforementioned bestseller strongly recommends using other people's money to invest in our business, but never our own. Honestly, how do we feel if others wanted to borrow money from us to finance their business ideas to avoid using their own money? Doesn't it convey a few simple messages?

- That person wants to get rich at our expense.
- The deal is probably bad and risky. Otherwise he would surely use his own means and not even tell us about such great opportunity.
- This person does not really want to do us any good.

I'd definitely feel hoodwinked and exploited. That is bad advice. Jesus gave some good solid advice by instructing us to treat others the way we want to be treated *(Luke 6:31)*. Hence, if you don't want to be exploited then don't exploit others.

Many claim that it is impossible to buy a piece of land, a house, a car, expensive equipment, etc. without getting into debt. No ordinary person has the required means available, they say. Does this argument justify the debt of a believer? Or is it not per se easier to get a loan (even if it's on unfair terms) from a bank (even if it's a corrupt institution) than to trust God? Jesus stated that we will receive everything we need, not necessarily what we want, if His hearts-desire is the driving force in our life *(Matt 6:33)*. That's a great and solid promise.

Buying our own property instead of renting is deemed a better use of resources, because our money benefits us rather than somebody else we usually don't even know. Also, we can do with our own property what you want and don't need to ask permission from the landlord. That sounds like wise, intelligent and logical worldly reasoning at its best. But is it God's reasoning?

Whether we build, buy or rent, for us as a believers, the owner is always God *(Ex 19:5; Psa 24:1; Col 1:16-17)*. And God expects us to steward His possession with great care, regardless of how we received it. In fact, God owns even the money He entrusts to us and thus needs to be consulted about its use, in this case whether to buy or to rent.

Perhaps God's intention is for us to show His amazing character by being a really good, faithful and honest tenant to your landlord? In the world, rental property is often returned to its owner in a rundown condition. In the Kingdom context we can't get away with this. If we don't handle responsibly what belongs to others, we disqualify ourselves for getting our own *(Luke 16:12)*. This procedure is superb. So a believing tenant must maintain the rental property at least in good condition. If he improves it, even better. It would be a powerful testimony to the landlord and for the Kingdom of God.

Another frequent argument for buying is that the house can simply be sold when running into financial difficulties. In reality a quick sale to cover debt rarely works out. In fact, the debt clock is ticking and potential buyers know it and are trying to exploit this by pushing the price down. What's more, due to the speculative nature of the real estate market, there is almost always the potential of a crash. Even if it doesn't turn out as bad as it was 2007 in the US, it will always be hard to sell without loss when it happens. And if you sell under pressure at a loss, is that a wise way to handle entrusted resources?

Maybe the conclusion here is the following: Since we don't know what happens to us tomorrow *(James 4:14)*, the best is to follow the advice and lead of The One who does know.

No Debt = No Investment?

We may appreciate that it is better to buy a consumer product only if we have the money for it available. So we are willing to change our habit and to save up in the future before we buy. That's one thing. But when it comes to investments, be it private or professional, that's different, isn't it? It would be really overkill to save up for that, right? After all, we're not talking about trifles here, but about big sums of money.

Well, whilst there is a need for investment into tangible assets in the Kingdom, the Bible doesn't nullify the reasons why debts are unwise and destructive for larger sums. So how can we get the money without borrowing?

Maybe the first step is to ask God if that investment is truly needed. What we consider crucial, God may see differently *(1Cor 1:20, 3:19)*.

> "Debt deprives God of the chance to say no or to provide through a better means." (Randy Alcorn, 'Money, Possessions, And Eternity', page 315)

> "Before you take matters into your own hands, God wants an opportunity either to provide your needs or to show you that they aren't really needs." (ibid, page 325)

If this investment is really necessary, then in a second step, we can consider other approaches to funding than simple borrowing. Hire-purchase or income-share agreements distribute the risk more fairly between borrower and lender.

Or, we simply allow God to be God. This may turn out to be a daunting challenge for us, as His ways and timing tend to differ from ours. Still, it's worthwhile since Scriptures are full of amazing accounts in which God provided large amounts of various resources to His people in His perfect timing and unique ways:

- Remember how Pharaoh voluntarily gave Joseph and his entire family the very best Egypt had to offer *(Gen 47:1-12)*. It was a massive resource injection into a large family business (livestock). Without it the family would not have survived the famine and could not have multiplied into the nation Israel.

- Or 430 years later, when Egypt, the slave master, handed its riches freely over to their Israelite slaves, when they let them finally leave *(Ex 12:31-36)*.

- Or God's 40-year free-of-charge food supply program for 2.4 million people in the desert. It's worthwhile to get a swift perspective on this sublime provision.

  Considering one nutritious meal/person/day at a mere $2/meal means a $4.8 million food bill per day, for 14,600 consecutive days, without fail. That's $70 billion in total just for food. Do you think Moses was worried?

If we were tasked with feeding these people, we would need to find a way to get approximately the following quantities into the desert, daily: 1,500 tons of food; 4,000 tons of firewood to cook the food; and 42 million litres of water for drinking and hygiene. That they crisscrossed the desert and camped at 42 sites during their 40 year stay doesn't make things easier, does it?

And then the camping ground. With a mere 10 m² space per person for living, sleeping, cooking, a walkway between tents, etc., a usable area of 24 km² is needed. How about that for a challenge?

Anyhow, the list of amazing provision reports is extensive. So let's just pick the greatest investment project ever undertaken by man for us to look at in a little bit more detail: the Temple and Solomon's palace in Jerusalem, built simultaneously over a period of 21 years.

The table on the next page is a summary of the quantifiable material and labor cost for this project. I recalculated it in early 2017 based on biblical information and current metal prices. Despite setting the wages for the workers to a very low level, the present-day value of this project is still nearly $187 billion! And everything was more or less paid in cash, except some of the wood, which was settled up with ten cities. So, quite obviously, whatever your investment needs are, they will look minute by comparison and really shouldn't pose a problem for the Lord.

Of course there are many lessons to learn from this account. Here are two.

First of all, God's blessing is of the essence. The table reveals that the funding for this extraordinary project was a mix of private and state resources saved for this purpose, voluntary private contributions and barter. But it only worked because God blessed it.

Second, timing and circumstances are of the essence. Even though it was King David's heart's desire to build this temple (not the palace though, which was his son's idea), God did not allow it. The reason being that David was a man of bloodshed and wars *(2Chr 22:8)*. Instead, God instructed him to prepare everything for his son Salomon, a man of peace, to carry out this huge project after David's death *(2Chr 22:9-10)*.

Provision for Temple and Palace Metal prices February 2017

① *1Chr 22:14* – saved up by David for this purpose

Gold	100,000	Talents	$148,914,800,000
Silver	1,000,000	Talents	$21,342,400,000
Bronze, Iron, Stone, Algum, Pine, Cedar			Immeasurable

② *1Chr 29:3-5* – David' private contribution

Gold	3,000	Talents	$4,467,400,000
Silver	7,000	Talents	$149,400,000

③ *1Chr 29:7-9* – private contributions of leaders, commanders, officials

Gold	5,000	Talents	$7,445,700,000
Gold	10,000	Darics	$3,300,000
Silver	10,000	Talents	$213,400,000
Bronze	18,000	Talents	$1,800,000
Iron	100,000	Talents	$2,400,000
Precious Stones			Unspecified

④ *1Chr 23:3-4* – paid by the state

Supervisors	24,000	Levites	$1,008,000,000
Artisans, Craftsmen, Carpenters, Masons			Unspecified

⑤ *2Chr 1:17-18* – paid by the state

Stonecutters	80,000	Foreigners	$1,680,000,000
Carriers	70,000	Foreigners	$1,470,000,000
Supervisors	3,600	Foreigners	$113,400,000

Total			**$186,812,000,000**

(Please note: During the time of the kings of Israel only silver was considered money. It's unclear how long it took to save up the mentioned amounts in silver. But a prolonged withdrawal from the vital money circulation would certainly have a negative impact on the economy.)

The examples given here just have to encourage us to totally trust God, don't you think? The Bible is so clear that there is no limit to what He can do to advance His Kingdom. But He never uses debt financing, for His people to accomplish His will.

> "It is really just as easy for God to give beforehand. He prefers to do so. He is too wise to allow His purpose to be frustrated for lack of a little money; but money wrongly placed or obtained in unscriptural ways is sure to hinder blessing. [...]

And what does going into debt really mean? It means that God has not supplied your need. You trusted Him, but He has not given you the money; so you supply yourself, and borrow. If we can only wait up right to the time, God cannot lie, God cannot forget: He is pledged to supply all your need." (Hudson Taylor, 1832-1905, missionary to China, founder of China Inland Mission)

The devil is happy when we borrow as it forces us to serve his evil system. But he is even more pleased when God's people borrow heavily to invest in tangible assets, particularly when it concerns the church.

Empirical studies show that the church worldwide spends $250-300 billion/year just to pay off, maintain and administer dead buildings and structures. The early church didn't bother with that at all. They focused on people.

So why do we do it when living people need resources to live? The more we are enslaved to paying off lifeless items the less we are able to invest into people, God's living temple *(1Pet 2:5; Heb 3:6; 1Cor 3:16-17)*. Yet it is the latter, not the first, that is God's way for us to store up treasures in heaven *(Matt 19:21; Mark 10:21; Luke 12:33)*.

No debt, no investment? That was the question for this section. Investments are part of God's Kingdom as much as they are of the world, although believers are warned not to use debt financing. We therefore are counselled to not employ the laws and logic of the world money system *(Rom 12:2)*, which play into Satan's hands, but to rely on the incredible abilities of God Almighty.

Borrowing And Lending – Unscriptural At All?

The Bible clearly warns against getting into debt for the consequences are heavy. Borrowing and lending is no sin, but the abuse associated with it is condemned. Lending to the needy is even encouraged. Yet, in God's Kingdom the conditions for borrowing and lending differ greatly to the world's financial system. Let's see.

1. Foundation

Disobedience to God forces people to borrow. They can't lend. The Bible calls this being the tail, being dragged along, being at the bottom, being enslaved:

They will lend to you, but you will not lend to them. They will be the head, but you will be the tail [...] because you did not obey the Lord your God and observe the commands and decrees he gave you. (Deut 28:44+45b)

Conversely, obedience to God puts His people in a position where they can lend freely, but do not have to borrow anymore. The Bible terms this as being the head, being at the top, i.e. being free and not enslaved:

You will lend to many nations but will borrow from none. The Lord will make you the head, not the tail. If you pay attention to the commands of the Lord your God that I give you this day and carefully follow them, you will always be at the top, never at the bottom. (Deut 28:12b+13; see also Deut 15:6, 8)

2. Lending Conditions

Jesus says that when you lend you should not expect to get it back *(Luke 6:34-35; see also Sirach 8:12)*, for your lending is considered an expression of your love for your neighbour. By implication you can regard it as unexpected 'gain', should you receive it back.

We may have less problems meeting this condition in the private environment, from person to person. However, when it comes to commercial loans (banks, businesses, organisations, institutions, governments, etc.), it's different, isn't it? But God makes no difference.

If anyone is poor among your fellow Israelites [...] do not be hardhearted or tightfisted toward them. Rather, be openhanded and freely lend them whatever they need. (Deut 15:7-8; see also Matt 5:42; 1 John 3:17)

The idea is to help those in need to get back on their feet. But helping those in need must never be exploited. Therefore, charging interest *(Ex 22:25; Lev 25:36-37; New 5:7-11)* or taking vital items as collateral *(Ex 22:26-27; Deut 24:6, 12-13)* is prohibited amongst believers. This throws a different light on the common practices of the worldly money lenders, doesn't it? We'll look in more details at the topics '41. Interest' and '42. Collateral' as we progress.

We know that the number seven is very prominent in Scriptures and stands for 'completion'. So it may not come as a surprise that the biblical lending period is restricted to a maximum of seven years. If the debtor does not manage to pay back his borrowing by the end of that time, his debts must be cancelled *(Deut 15:1-2, 31:10; Neh 10:31)*. The debt period ends.

Since we do not know the future *(James 4: 14-15)*, seven years seems to be a manageable time frame at the end of which things should be completed. Here are some examples from the Bible, both positive and negative:

- Jacob laboured seven years for Leah and seven years for Rachel *(Gen 29)*.

- Joseph oversaw the economic affairs of Egypt and the future nation of Israel for seven abundant and seven lean years *(Gen 41)*.
- Since Israel did evil in God's sight, He handed them over to the Midianites for seven years *(Judg 6:1)* to be chastised.
- In Elisha's time God decreed a famine of seven years *(2Kings 8:1-3)*.
- King Nebuchadnezzar was driven from the people and had to live amongst wild animals for seven years until he finally acknowledged God *(Dan 4)*.
- The time of tribulation is going to be seven years *(Matt 24:15-22)*.

3. Borrowing Conditions

Regardless of the borrowing context, the borrower must be committed to pay back what he borrowed. His obligation is to do that as as soon as he possibly can, but at least stick to the agreed terms and not let the lender suffer. Paying back has preference over financing own wants, etc. *(Sirach 18:33; 29:1-3, 6-7; Rom 13:7-8; Luke 6:31; 16:12)*. A half-hearted pay back as suggested in the secular book quoted under 'Obligation To Fulfil' earlier is out of question.

Debt-free financial transactions, regardless of context, are likely to be a massive challenge when we move from a world system modus operandi to a Kingdom approach. But there is no other way.

> *Don't copy the behaviour and customs of this world, but let God transform you into a new person by changing the way you think. Then you will learn to know God's will for you, which is good and pleasing and perfect. (Rom 12:2, NLT-SE)*

41. Interest

The burning question here is this: Does God allow or prohibit the use of interest? Most believers have no problem with the use of interest and cite the parable of the Ten Minas *(Luke 19:11-27)* as a justification. That needs to be challenged.

The parable is about a nobleman who is to be crowned king. For that he must travel to a distant country and then return. He gives ten of his servants a mina each (= three months wages) to put it to work until he is back. His subjects try to get rid of him, but he still returns as king. The servants give an account of how they handled the entrusted money. The first one returns his mina with a tenfold profit. For that the king puts him in charge of ten cities. The next one returns his mina with a five-fold profit, receiving charge over five cities as a result. The next servant, however, just returns the very mina he had received. The king, visibly annoyed about his disobedience, instructs the mina to be taken away from him and be given to the one with the ten. The bystanders protest about this injustice but are told that everyone who has will receive more, while those who don't have will lose even what they have. Last but not least, the subjects who reject the nobleman to be their king are ordered to be executed in the king's presence.

There is much debate about this parable's meaning. Some believe it talks about Jesus and the Kingdom of God. Others are convinced it's exactly the opposite. We will not solve this difference here. But we'll scrutinise the issue of interest in both views to check if there's grounds for Christians to charge it. *Luke 19:23* reads,

> *Why then didn't you put my money on deposit, so that when I came back, I could have collected it with interest?*

If the parable is about an unjust lord and an evil, corrupt kingdom, then we can dispel the above verse as an authorisation for taking interest straight away. Why? Because believers mustn't follow evil ways and worldly patterns *(Rom 12:2)*.

If, however, this parable is about Jesus and the Kingdom of God, then we need to have a bit more context. So let's read from *verse 20*,

> *Then another servant came and said, 'Sir, here is your mina; I have kept it laid away in a piece of cloth. I was afraid of you, because you are a hard man. You take out what you did not put in and reap what you did not sow.' His master replied, 'I will judge you by your own words, you wicked servant! You knew, did you, that I am a hard man, taking out what I did not put in, and reaping what I did not sow? Why then didn't you put my money on deposit, so that when I came back, I could have collected it with interest?' (Luke 19:20-23)*

The third servant finds an excuse for his unwillingness (or laziness?) to use the entrusted mina. He calls the newly crowned king a hard man, i.e., someone who takes out what he hasn't put in and reaps what he hasn't sown *(V21)*. But he is exposed as a liar *("I will judge you by your own words" – V22)*, for if he truly meant what he said, then he would have deposited the money with a bank to gain interest. That would have enabled the king to take out what he didn't put in, and reap what he never sowed, since this is what hard men do *(V23)*. In the final analysis this little discourse simply exposes a disobedient, lying servant. But it doesn't offer believers any justification for the use of interest.

So is there anything else God is saying about the use of interest? Yes, there is.

- God didn't permit Israelites to charge interest to each other *(Deut 23:19-20)*, especially not to the poor and needy *(Ex 22:25; Lev 25:35-37, Prov 28:8; Neh 5:7-11)*, as this is considered exploitation.
- Charging interest to foreigners was allowed, though *(Deut 23:20)*.
- *Ezek 18:8-17* lists dealings that deserve the death penalty. Charging interest (amongst Israelites) is one of them.

A valid principle from this for today would be this: No interest charge of any kind amongst believers, but charging interest to non-believers is permitted.

But how much interest may a believer charge to non-believers? What is legit and what excessive? Sadly many differentiate between 'interest' and 'usury' today, regarding the first to be acceptable, the latter to be excessive interest. But since the word 'usury' simply means 'interest', regardless of its rate, that's not helpful here. So to arrive at a satisfactory answer a couple of issues must be considered.

First, the effects of interest. Let's list them again:

- Interest creates money out of money and thus turns the economic process on its head. Now money creation dictates the productive economy.
- Interest means an income without work for the lender and is thus in violation of *2Th 3:10*. The borrower works to enrich the lender; Interest is, thus, an advantage for the lender and disadvantage for the borrower, unless he can pass this burden on to others. It is an arithmetical law that interest makes the rich richer and the poor poorer.
- Lending money for interest represents a risk-free investment for the lender. The complete risk of earning the loan plus interest has been passed on to the borrower. This constitutes unfair exploitation.
- Interest causes finances to be granted to the safest borrowers rather than the most productive ones.
- Interest is not only paid by those who borrow but by everyone. Since interest is included as a cost factor in the price of everything we buy, it makes products and services more expensive than they should be.
- Interest supports the concentration of wealth into increasingly fewer hands.
- The commonly used compound interest with its exponential growth pattern leads to an unhealthy, destructive exploitation of natural resources.

Second, Jesus' admonition to do to others what you would have them do to you *(Matt 7:12; Luke 6:31)*. So if you don't want to pay any interest yourself, then don't charge it to others. If you do not mind paying low interest rates then make sure that you only charge low interest rates yourself.

We can't prohibit others from using interest, but as believers we can check in our spirits whether it should be part of our financial arsenal. Would Jesus charge it? Based on the circumstances and situation, our decision may or may not open or close the door to God's Kingdom for unbelievers.

> "Besides the devil there is no bigger enemy on earth than the scrooge and usurer, because he desires to be over somebody." (Martin Luther)

> "Usury is the safest means to profit, albeit one of the worst since it means nothing else but to eat your bread at the sweat of the faces of the other." (Francis Bacon, 1561-1626, British writer and philosopher)

> "Taking interest means living at the expense of other people's work without providing any service in return. Interest means a heavy violation of the right to equality. Christianity and interest are incompatible." (Johannes Ude, 1874-1965, Dean of the Catholic Theological Faculty, Graz/Austria)

> "The root of the evil lies in our current monetary system and the uncritical faith in the flawlessness of interest. But interest makes the rich even richer and the poor poorer, because it is not just paid as direct credit interest, but included as a cost factor in all prices." (Catholic Family Association, archdiocese in Vienna, 1990)

42. Collateral

A collateral is 'something delivered as security for the keeping of a promise or the payment of a debt or as a guarantee of good faith', and 'property used as security against a loan'. Synonyms for collateral are 'backing, bond, guarantee, pledge, security, surety'. A 'pledge' is also 'a promise to donate money, for example, to a charity or political cause'.

Lets talk about the second meaning of 'pledge' first to get this out of the way. Pledges are fairly popular in Christian circles. Quite often congregation members are manipulated into making pledges to contribute to building funds and such like. This goes even so far that they are 'encouraged' to empty their whole bank account(s) or take out a loan to fulfil that pledge or vow. Hoodwinking fellow believers into doing this violates *2Cor 9:7*, which encourages us to never ever give under compulsion and manipulation. If you still feel you should pledge, the least you should ensure is to not pledge beyond your means *(Sirach 8:13)*.

However we are not talking about these kind of pledges here, but about things that are given to back up debts.

When we borrow a large amount (e.g. for a home or a business investment), the bank requires collateral (tangible asset) to back up the loan. The home or the tangible assets we acquire are normally used as collateral. So that's an easy hedging for the bank, but a massive burden for us, because if we cannot service our debts, we will lose our collateral. If we want to avoid the very real possibility of losing our collateral to the bank, we should not borrow. This is what the Bible advises us anyway, because the borrower is slave to the lender *(Prov 22:7)* (see also topic '40. Borrowing And Lending').

When we borrow smaller amounts from a money lender, we must, as a rule, provide a written guarantee from a creditworthy person who is willing to pay off our debts if we default. It's an easy backup for the lender. For the guarantor it is a big commitment. To avoid the very real possibility of someone having to bail us out, it is best not to borrow at all. Which is God's advice for us anyway (see topic '40. Borrowing And Lending').

Collaterals as described above, have negative impact on our relationships, both with God and others. By making debt I show my distrust into God's provision abilities and then trust stuff or others to bail me out if that decision turns sour. In my relationships with others the use of collateral can easily lead to irritation and resentment. This is a bad basis for loving neighbourly relations.

Again, by borrowing we enslave ourselves to the lender. But this also means that we are consuming now what should be at the disposal of the next generation. We are stealing from their future, thus become thieves, and leave them with a debt burden instead, thus become responsible for their enslavement. So by giving surety for debts we are acting no better than the borrower. We become part of the evil system.

By not borrowing, we would avoid collateral in any way, shape or form and many headaches. But people always have and always will borrow, which requires such backup. The Bible considers this a bad practice *(Job 22:6; Prov 20:16; 27:13; Ezek 18:7+16)*, and therefore offers some guidelines for a more considerate approach *(Ex 22:25-27; Deut 24:10-12)*.

There is no biblical law against or punishment for providing collateral, regardless of its form. But just like the warning about debt, the Bible warns against securing someone's debt, too. This makes sense, because if the borrower becomes a slave to the lender, then the one providing surety for that debt also does. But God does not want us ever to become slaves to other people again *(1Cor 7:23)*.

> *My son, if you have become security for your neighbour, if you have given your pledge for a stranger or another, You are snared with the words of your lips, you are caught by the speech of your mouth. Do this now [at once and earnestly], my son, and deliver yourself when you have put yourself into the power of your neighbour; go, bestir and humble yourself, and beg your neighbour [to pay his debt and thereby release you]. (Prov 6:1-3, AMP)*

> *Whoever puts up security for a stranger will surely suffer, but whoever refuses to shake hands in pledge is safe. (Prov 11:15)*

> *Don't agree to guarantee another person's debt or put up security for someone else. (Prov 22:26, NLT-SE)*

'Another' or 'someone else', as used here, does include a stranger, neighbour, friend, associate, companion or any other person, even a family member. It does not matter who we provide a guarantee for, the Bible always considers it a poor decision. The obvious reason is that it is out of our control whether the person we give surety for fulfils his obligations. We may end up having to pay the price for this person's default.

> *Being surety has ruined many who were prosperous, and has tossed them about like waves of the sea; it has driven the influential into exile, and they have wandered among foreign nations. […]. Assist your neighbour to the best of your ability, but be careful not to fall yourself. (Sirach 29:18-20, NRSV)*

43. Limited Liability

Limited liability provides legal protection for the shareholders of a bank, a private or listed company. It guarantees the shareholders to be only liable for debts and obligations to the maximum of their shareholding.

At first glance, limited liability looks like a great solution to bolster and stimulate business activity. But this legal framework, created by governments for just that reason, has two sides to it.

The one side concerns the liability of the shareholders, i.e., those responsible for the business. For them being released by law from full liability by stroke of a pen is like a jackpot. It is a legalised invitation to take excessive risks to achieve short-term profits without having to fear major consequences. A license for unlimited profits with limited losses, so to speak.

The other side concerns the liability for everything beyond what is covered by the shareholders' limited liability. As this liability does not simply dissipate, it remains with the bank or company as the legal entity. On paper this may appear correct and fair. But the reality is that the legal entity can't pay. Any shortfall is borne by those who are not responsible for the problems. It is a heavy price that is paid by the struggling company's employees, contractors, suppliers, and customers.

Limited liability undermines healthy business practices by effectively eliminating the natural restriction of risks. The result is the increase in impulsive, unqualified business decisions, and the ability for banks and corporations to operate on a large scale without fear of grave ramifications if things go wrong.

The use of limited liability puts strain on Christians' relationship with God as it shuns the full accountability God demands from everyone *(Rom 14:12)*. Avoiding full liability and passing it on to the innocent is corrupt and creates a destructive foundation for relationships with those concerned (see also '59. Accountability').

Without limited liability, large corporations would be rare since the risk in case of bankruptcy would be too big for those responsible. The possibility to shift the risk of wrong decisions, i.e. deficits, from the responsible to the innocent has, thus, contributed to the creation of large companies. As if the unfair distribution of risk were not enough injustice, these large companies are now able to dominate the markets and so deprive small and medium-sized enterprises of their existence.

There is no explicit law in the Bible prohibiting limited liabilities, ergo no penalty to enforce it. Yet, some biblical principles, as listed below, oppose the concept of 'limited liability'. This should persuade us to voluntarily reconsider the use of this type of enterprise.

- A limited liability or responsibility may well meet worldly standards, but not God's. Every human being must give an account of his entire life to His Creator *(Ezek 18:20; Rom 14:12; Gal 6:7-8; 1Pet 4:5)*. This includes the accountability in entrusted financial enterprises *(Luke 19:12-27)*.

- Taking the profits but passing liabilities on to the innocent is a form of theft, so violates the 8th commandment, *'You shall not steal' (Ex 20:15; Luke 18:20)*.

- Limited liability also represents a form of exploitation, resulting in unrighteous wealth for the shareholders. It violates *Ezekiel 22:29* and *James 2:6, 5:1-6*

- The fundamental biblical principle that all debts must be repaid *(Psa 37:21; Rom 13:8)* is treated with contempt, as limited liability allows shareholders to avoid full responsibility for their companies financial obligations.

- Jesus challenges us to count the cost before we commit ourselves financially so that we can complete what we started *(Luke 14:28-29)*. Limited liability clearly bypasses this principle of good, faithful and healthy stewardship.

- From a spiritual point of view, only those who are willing to assume other people's liability can also remove other people's liability. Jesus did that for us by dying on the cross for our sins. By reducing the full liability of some and shifting the difference to others, governments have violated this spiritual law because they themselves do not assume this liability.

Business owners and shareholders would be much more cautious in running their business if there were no limited liability laws. Board of directors would be forced to do a much better job in reviewing the dealings of the businesses management.

With the abolishment of limited liability laws, there would be an end to the practise of privatising profits (shareholders) and socialising losses (employees, contractors, customers, suppliers). Those benefitting in good times would now carry the loss in bad times. The result would be a much better and more faithful stewardship of entrusted resources.

44. Bankruptcy, Insolvency

A biblical contemplation of filing for bankruptcy must begin with the cause of the indebtedness. As mentioned under '40. Borrowing And Lending' the motivation and reasons for indebtedness can be very numerous and diverse. The Bible warns against debt, but also recognises that there are circumstances beyond a person's control that can lead to indebtedness. Therefore, we can divide debt into the two main categories of 'voluntary/deliberate' and 'involuntary/forced'.

Scriptures are clear that debts falling into the first category must be paid back, i.e., the relevant contracts must be honoured *(Prov 3:28; Eccl 5:4-5; Rom 13:8; James 5:12)*. Or else the borrower becomes a thief *(Psa 37:21; Sirach 29:2+6)*.

In Israel at the time, it was up to family members, relatives and the community to help those who got indebted through hardship *(Lev 25:35-37; Deut 15:7-10)*. However, at the end of seven years the remaining debt that the debtor wasn't able to repay had to be forgiven *(Deut 15:1-23)*. Debt forgiveness was to be an active act of the creditor, because it meant he had to give up part of his wealth.

Therefore, according to biblical guidelines, it seems wrong to give those who have deliberately and voluntarily become indebted an easy way out of their responsibilities by allowing them to file for bankruptcy. In the secular world this might look helpful, but from a spiritual point of view it turns the debtor into a thief, violating the 8th commandment *(Deut 5:19; Mark 10:19)*. The legal option to file for bankruptcy furthermore ignores the spiritual law of full accountability to God *(Rom 14:12)*.

For those, who are indebted through misfortune, debt forgiveness should be granted by their creditors, for they are affected by it as their wealth is reduced. Here we need to restate what we stated under topic '43. Limited Liability'. From a spiritual point of view, only those who are willing to assume other people's liability can also remove other people's liability. Jesus did that for us by dying on the cross for our sins. By passing a bankruptcy law that allows debtors to get rid of their liability and shifting it to the creditor, governments have violated this spiritual law because they themselves do not assume this liability.

In reality, not all bankruptcy cases are so clear-cut that you can put them in the one or the other category. Each single case has its individual influencing factors and dynamics and thus needs to be assessed and treated accordingly. However, taking into account the spiritual law of accountability, it is simply wrong for a government to grant all debtors carte blanche that allows them to avoid their responsibility for paying their debts.

The impact bankruptcy or insolvency has on our relationship with God and our neighbour is similar to what is noted under '43. Limited Liability'.

45. Partnerships

When we speak of partnership we speak of either marriage or business. The first is an intimate, close relationship with a single person, with whom we share all areas of our lives for the rest of our lives. The second is a confidential relationship with one or more people with whom we share a part of our lives for some time (we are not talking about employment here).

For either one, the biblical foundation is the same: Believers should not be yoked together with unbelievers as their driving force in life and their perspective on life are kind of opposite. The central point in the believer's life is his relationship to God and his faithful obedience to Him. The life of the unbeliever, however, is characterised by egoism, that is, the rebellion against God. The Bible calls this contrast light and darkness. They have nothing in common.

> *Do not be yoked together with unbelievers. For what do righteousness and wickedness have in common? Or what fellowship can light have with darkness? (2Cor 6:14)*

> *For you were once darkness, but now you are light in the Lord. Live as children of light. [...] Have nothing to do with the fruitless deeds of darkness, but rather expose them. (Eph 5:8, 11)*

> *If we claim to have fellowship with him and yet walk in the darkness, we lie and do not live out the truth. (1John 1:6)*

It is said that money ruins friendship. In reality, money has the ability to destroy any relationship, regardless of its context. That's why it is most important to find out if the potential partner is primarily driven by money or recognises God's authority in his/her life and serves Him above all else *(Matt 6:33)*. Not without reason does Jesus say that we cannot serve both God and money *(Matt 6:24, Luke 16:13)*. Also, how about the potential partner's character, integrity, values, vision, and goals? Is it a kind, loving, friendly, generous, reliable, trustworthy and fun-to-be-around person?

In business people often enter into a partnership because they desperately need money, possibly knowhow and assets, too. But every partner also brings some personality flaws, negative character traits and burdensome 'baggage' into the partnership. A careful consideration of all the above points is, therefore, very important as they have more impact on the success or failure of the partnership than knowhow, assets and money.

It is also said that opposites attract. If opposite characters balance each other out in a partnership, that is certainly positive. But if it means that partners are pulling in opposite directions, then that's a recipe for disaster.

Choosing the wrong partner (unbeliever) for the wrong reason (money) surely displeases God. It shows Him that we are driven more by money rather than our service for Him. Though the world might not have a problem partnering with others for money, biblically this is questionable. It amounts to taking advantage of the partner(s), which is not 'love your neighbour'-based, is it?

Do not plow with an ox and a donkey yoked together. (Deut 22:10)

Woe to those who call evil good and good evil, who put darkness for light and light for darkness, who put bitter for sweet and sweet for bitter. (Is 5:20)

For of this you can be sure: No immoral, impure or greedy person—such a person is an idolater—has any inheritance in the kingdom of Christ and of God. Let no one deceive you with empty words, for because of such things God's wrath comes on those who are disobedient. Therefore do not be partners with them. (Eph 5:5-7)

A rich person will exploit you if you can be of use to him, but if you are in need he will abandon you. If you own something, he will live with you; he will drain your resources without a qualm. When he needs you he will deceive you, and will smile at you and encourage you; he will speak to you kindly and say, "What do you need?" He will embarrass you with his delicacies, until he has drained you two or three times, and finally he will laugh at you. Should he see you afterwards, he will pass you by and shake his head at you. (Sirach 13:4-7, NRSV)

There is no biblical law that punishes partnerships between believers (those who walk in the light) and unbelievers (those who walk in darkness). But the Bible trusts in the understanding of its readers that light and darkness can never make a spiritually successful partnership *(John 8:12; 12:46; Acts 26:18; Rom 13:12; 1Cor 4:5; 1Pet 2:9).*

46. Planning

"God beckons storm clouds, and they come. He tells the wind to blow and the rain to fall, and they obey him immediately. He speaks to the mountains, "You go there," and He says to the seas, "You stop here," and they do it. Everything in all creation responds in obedience to the Creator ... **until we get to you and me. We have the audacity to look God in the face and say, "No."**" (David Platt, 'Radical', page 31, emphasis added)

The wild animals honour me, [...]. Yet you have not called upon me, [...]. (Is 43:20+22)

Plans are established by seeking advice; [...] (Prov 20:18)

The process of planning involves more than creating a budget. A budget is simply the financial expression of something more tangible. Yet when Christians advise

that you must plan and plan wisely as a good steward, meaning to use your God-given brain, they normally think of budgets.

The classical biblical accounts used to cement the argument to employ your brain are Joseph in Egypt *(Gen 41)*, the example of the ant *(Prov 6:6-8)* and the wise builder *(Luke 14:28-30)*. However, Joseph was tasked to use the abundance of seven years of plenty to provide food for seven lean years; an ant plans food storage for the imminent season, not for seasons ahead; and the builder shouldn't even think about starting to build if he can't afford to finish.

Sadly, if using our God-given brains is all we need, this tends to result in a secular planning process with a secular outcome. Our plans and budgets become an expression of human intelligence, logic, common sense, history, experience, available options, own potential, trends and market research, empirical values, probabilities, good expert advice, and so forth. Occasionally, these plans and budgets are then submitted to God for correction and approval.

Such a planning approach only makes our creator a rubber stamp and that is not conducive for our relationship with Him. The result of such planning may affect our relationships with our neighbours negatively, too.

Such an approach runs the risk of missing the real thing, because God declares,

> *"For my thoughts are not your thoughts, neither are your ways my ways," […] "As the heavens are higher than the earth, so are my ways higher than your ways and my thoughts than your thoughts. (Is 55:8-9)*
>
> *For our knowledge is fragmentary (incomplete and imperfect), […] (1Cor 13:9, AMP)*

A good biblical approach, therefore, is a reverse process in which God is involved right from the start, and not just roped in at the end. As a matter of fact He is the One providing vision and giving direction to His people based on His overarching plan anyway, thus laying the foundation for plans and budgets. He is the Alpha and Omega, the beginning and the end *(Rev 1:8; 21:6; 22:13)*. Please note that this here isn't about the ordinary things in life that you know to be God-pleasing anyway. It's about plans that line up with His plans and purposes for our life, privately and professionally.

A planning process driven by the Lord of all plans will result in less stress, greater efficiency, minimal risks, minimum wastage, better timing, and less frustrations for us, and greater success and benefit for His Kingdom. Remember, even Jesus could only be successful by doing what the Father told Him to do *(John 5:19)*?

So using our brains begins with listening to what He has to say and then following His plans and instructions in obedience.

> *[...] apart from Me [cut off from vital union with Me] you can do nothing. (John 15:5b, AMP)*

> *Why do you call me, 'Lord, Lord,' and do not do what I say? As for everyone who comes to me and hears my words and puts them into practice, I will show you what they are like. They are like a man building a house, who dug down deep and laid the foundation on rock. When a flood came, the torrent struck that house but could not shake it, because it was well built. But the one who hears my words and does not put them into practice is like a man who built a house on the ground without a foundation. The moment the torrent struck that house, it collapsed and its destruction was complete. (Luke 6:46-49)*

> *He who is not with Me [siding and believing with Me] is against Me, and he who does not gather with Me [engage in My interest], scatters. (Luke 11:23, AMP)*

The above Scriptures are clear and challenging, don't you think? Working without Jesus is like working against Him.

The Bible is filled with accounts that show how obedience to God brings success, while disobedience leads to failure. Other passages expose the challenges linked to breaking free from well-trodden paths to follow God. And yet other incidents encourage to turn back to God when our human plans find His disapproval. So let's list some of those accounts and elaborate further.

1. Success due to obedience

- Noah builds the ark *(Gen 6:8-22)*
- Moses leads Israel through the Red Sea *(Ex 14)*
- Moses builds the tabernacle with all its articles *(Ex 25-30)*
- Joshua conquers Jericho *(Josh 5:13-6:27)*
- Gideon conquers a vastly superior army with just 300 men *(Judg 7)*
- Elijah is fed by ravens in a brook during a famine *(1Kings 17:1-6)*
- Solomon builds the temple *(2Chr 2-4)*
- Jesus turns water into wine *(John 2:1-11)*
- Jesus feeds thousands twice with next to nothing *(Matt 14:13-21, 15:29-39)*
- Jesus organises temple tax from a fish's mouth *(Matt 17:24-27)*

And don't forget God's promise to meet our daily needs if His Kingdom agenda is driving our daily life and we act on His principles *(Matt 6:33; Luke 12:31)*.

2. **Failure due to disobedience**

   At times we may act presumptuously in executing God's plan. Two incidents, taken from *Num 20:8-12* and *2Sam 6:1-3*, illustrate this well.

   In the first account Moses ignores that he was instructed to speak to the rock for water to come out. Instead, he hits it just as he was instructed to do the first time *(Ex 17:6)*. Considering the tense situation with an angry, constantly complaining people, there were probably good reasons for this oversight. However, what sounds like a minor detail miss had grave consequences for Moses future. He was no longer allowed to enter the Promised Land. Unfair?

   In the second account David brings the Ark of the Covenant back to Jerusalem. Though God approves of it, David executes things wrongly. Instead of letting the priests carry the Ark on poles as per God's original dictate, he puts it on a cart. A well-intentioned change with tragic consequences. The oxen stumble, the cart threatens to tip over, so Uzzah secures the Ark with his hands. It's an irreverent act, which costs him his life and makes David angry.

   The Bible also offers numerous examples where people did not just miss fine details but flatly refused to follow God's plan and instructions. It too always ended in disaster. Remember, Israel's defeat at the first battle of Ai was a result of Achan's disobedience to God in the conquest of Jericho *(Josh 7:1-26)*. Or, how king Saul's refusal to fully execute God's judgment on the Amalekites *(1Sam 15)* turned his life upside down, ending in his suicide *(1Sam 16-31)*.

3. **Challenge to leave well-trodden path**

   At times the Lord's instructions may appear rather wacky. Think of Peter, when he came home with his crew, exhausted and empty-handed from a nocturnal fishing trip. Approaching the shoreline, someone he did not recognise at first, challenged him with the mind-boggling advice to,

   > *"Throw your net on the right side of the boat and you will find some." When they did, they were unable to haul the net in because of the large number of fish. (John 21:6)*

   Left side or right side of the boat, does it make any difference? If it does, why did these professional fishers, experts in their field, not think of it? And why go out now, when every experienced fisherman knows that fishing in the early morning hours does not work? We know that Peter's obedience to Jesus' instruction led to the biggest catch ever. But when he had to decide whether to follow this strange plan or not, he had to consider risking his reputation as a seasoned fisherman. So God's plans and their execution may require us to leave our well-trodden paths.

4. Turning back to God

What about when we are confronted with the fact that the plans we made and set into motion are against God's will? Well, the Bible offers advice on that, too. Here is an example.

When Israel and Judah were separate kingdoms, Amaziah king of Judah had planned to go to battle against Edom. So besides mustering his own Judaean troops, he hired a hundred thousand Israelite soldiers to fight for him. As he was ready to execute his plan and march out, a man of God approached him. He warned him of relying on Israel's help since God was not with them. Even if he went and fought bravely, God would still deliver him to his enemies on account of unfaithful Israel. We then read,

> *Amaziah asked the man of God, "But what about the hundred talents [of silver] I paid for these Israelite troops?" The man of God replied, "The LORD can give you much more than that." (2Chr 25:9)*

So Amaziah had to come to terms with losing a fortune (about $2.1 million in today's value) due to an ungodly alliance. But the man of God assured him that God would be able to easily make up for it if the king was to be obedient. Amaziah listened to God and dismissed the Israelite troops, who were furious.

Another, rather sad example, is found earlier in the same book.

> *But Jehoshaphat said to the king of Israel, "First, please ask what the LORD's will is." (2Chr 18:4, HCSBS)*

Ahab, Israel's evil king, wanted to win Jehoshaphat, Judah's king, as an ally for his attack on Ramoth Gilead. However, Jehoshaphat did not want to join in without first asking God for His will in this. Ahab reluctantly agreed to question Micaiah, the only true prophet of God around. But Micaiah did not provide a favourable answer from the Lord. So the kings ignored the warning and went ahead as planned, which ended tragically for everyone involved *(2Chr 18:1-19:3)*.

So you wonder, what good is it to ask for God's will if you continue with your own plans anyway? Totally wasted effort.

*They set up kings **without my consent**; they choose princes **without my approval**. With their silver and gold they make idols for themselves **to their own destruction**. (Hos 8:4, emphasis added)*

This is what the LORD says: Cursed is the one who trusts in man, who draws strength from mere flesh and whose heart turns away from the LORD (Jer 17:5)

By my observation, God has largely been banned from Christianity's planning and its resultant budgeting processes. On the whole, visions, missions and business plans resemble more of a worldly approach. His divine insight and understanding has been substituted by secular methods and common sense. In private life, in churches, businesses, organisations, public offices, government, you name it. Many believers organise resources and money in unbiblical ways for what they perceive as God's direction and Kingdom mandate. This is usually done through loans and mortgages, in short, with funds that God has not entrusted to them. No wonder paying off this heavy load is so frustrating, joyless, exhausting, tiring, restricting, disabling ... It's obvious, God is not in it.

The problem with basing our plans and the resulting budgets solely on our skills, ability to work, expertise, imagination, ingenuity, intelligence and wisdom is this: we just don't know what will happen to us and/or our businesses tomorrow. Our plans are based more on guesswork and potential opportunities than on facts, which can cost us and others dearly.

*Come now, you who say, "Today or tomorrow we will travel to such and such a city and spend a year there and do business and make a profit." You don't even know what tomorrow will bring—what your life will be! For you are like smoke that appears for a little while, then vanishes. Instead, you should say, **"If the Lord wills**, we will live and do this or that." (James 4:13-15, HCSBS, emphasis added)*

If I remember my fifteen years as a financial controller in different corporations, then reality turned out to be always different from business plans and budgets. It is commonplace to constantly explain why things are not going according to plan. Honestly, is it really wise to plan knowing that it will turn out different anyway?

"The only function of economic forecasting is to make astrology look respectable." (John Kenneth Galbraith, 1908-2006, famous Canadian-American economist and author)

The fear of the Lord is the beginning of true wisdom and knowledge *(Job 28:28; Psa 11:10; Prov 1:7, 9:10)*. Col 1:16-17 says everything was created by Him (not us), for Him (not us) and everything holds together in Him (not us). It is thus foolish not to make God's plans and intentions the basis of ours. Actually, as per *Job 5:12; Psa 33:10; 140:8; Is 29:15; 30:1; Jer 18:12; Rom 13:14;* and *2Cor 1:17* it's really dangerous to make any plans without involving Him. After all,

> Many are the plans in a man's heart, but it is the Lord's purpose that prevails. (Prov 19:21)

> [...] the Lord's plans stand firm forever; His intentions can never be shaken. (Psa 33:11, NLT-SE)

The secular world plans and budgets based on secular understanding. Believers should not. Again, God gives vision and plans for His children in accordance with His overarching plan, so He must be the source of our plans and budgets. Thus, it is of vital importance to be firmly 'grafted' in Jesus *(John 15:1-10)* and to make God's Kingdom our driving force *(Matt 6:33, Luke 12:31)* in life rather than our own plans. If that's the case then we know we ask Him with right motives *(James 4:3)* and then it doesn't really matter anymore what we are ask for – He will grant it *(Psa 34:10; John 14:4, 15:7, 16:24; Phil 4:6)*.

47. Investment

There are private, public and corporate investors. They may be secular or faith-based. Their investments may range from tiny to extremely large amounts, which may be owned or borrowed. The reasons for investing may be many: retirement; enrichment; real estate; diversification; expansion; maintenance, replacement or modernisation of equipment, machinery and buildings; efficiency; competitive pressure; you name it. Similarly the motivation may also be quite diverse: hubris, arrogance, fear, greed, gamble, speculation, strategic, pressure, manipulation, carelessness, survival, etc.

A biblical perspective of this rather complex subject must begin with ownership. Everything belongs to God *(Job 41:11; Psa 24:1, 50:12; 1Cor 10:26)*, which means it's His prerogative to decide over its use, including whether or not, where, when and how to invest. As His stewards it is our responsibility to act faithfully in His interest *(Matt 24:45; Luke 16:12; 1Cor 4:2)* and to do this really well *(Matt 25:14-30)*. We therefore can't follow the secular investment path as outlined in most of the above paragraph. The Bible warns in this regard.

There is a painful tragedy that I have seen under the sun: Riches lead to the downfall of those who hoard them. These hoarded riches were then lost in bad business deals. The owners had children, but now they have nothing to give them. (Eccl 5:13-14)

Do not wear yourself out to get rich; have the wisdom to show restraint. Cast but a glance at riches, and they are gone, for they will surely sprout wings and fly off to the sky like an eagle. (Prov 23:4-5)

Those who want to get rich fall into temptation and a trap and into many foolish and harmful desires that plunge people into ruin and destruction. (1Tim 6:9)

So, in terms of investment, what exactly does it mean to act faithfully in God's interest? In a nutshell it means emulating Jesus by doing exactly as God tells us to *(John 5:19+39)*, which, of course, requires that we hear and understand Him. Since God's instructions may not make sense to us, our obedience is even more of great import.

The prophet Jeremiah, e.g., provides us a case in point: While he was imprisoned in Jerusalem and the city was besieged by the Babylonians and about to be overrun, burned and destroyed, and the inhabitants to be taken into captivity to Babylon, God instructed Jeremiah to buy a certain piece of land. From a worldly point of view this is the most ridiculous investment advice you can get. Why should you buy land that will be taken away soon by your enemy anyway? Yet, It was a prophetic act that Jeremiah had to carry out to show that Israel will buy land again there once her imminent 70 years of captivity in Babylon are over.

The point is that, even if God's instructions don't make sense to our human mind, we must follow them. Investments done by believers should be in line with God's plans and purposes. If they are not, they are probably a waste of resources and may end up in disaster.

An example for this is an incident involving Amaziah, king of Judah *(2Chr 25)*. He had invested about $2.1 million today's value in conscripting the Israelite army for a military campaign. But God warned him that he should distance himself from this plan since it would not end well. So the king had to decide. Either follow God's instructions, give up his own plans and accept a significant financial loss as a learning effect. Or, as so often done in the world, ignore divine counsel and still try to get the most out of this doomed mission. Amaziah was obedient.

On closer examination, the Bible provides ample advice (warnings and approvals) on investment decisions. With a good deal of info also contained in other topics of this book the next table may provide a helpful overview regarding warnings.

Topic	Bible Reference	Other Related Topics
Questionable Investments – investments driven by, based on or resulting in:		
Fear	1John 4:18	54. Fear Factor
Worry	Matt 6:34; Luke 12:22	
Greed, Speculation	Luke 12:15; Eph 5:3; Col 3:5; 1Tim 6:9	53. Get-Rich-Quick Schemes
Deception, Lies	Lev 6:2, 19:11; Prov 10:2, 13:11, 21:6	
Theft, Exploitation	Ex 20:15; Prov 22:22; Luke 18:20; Rom 13:9; James 2:6	51. Marketing, Advertising 63. Honesty
Debt	Deut 28:12-13, 44; Prov 22:7	13. Growth Compulsion 40. Borrowing And Lending
Proliferation of Armament	Ex 20:13; Deut 5:17; Mark 10:19; Eph 6:12; 1John 3:12	13. Growth Compulsion 24. War And Capital Destruction
Ecological Destruction	Gene 2:15; Deut 20:19; Jer 2:7; Ezek 34:18; Rev 11:18	13. Growth Compulsion 23. Ecological Exploitation, Ruination

There is much talk today about ethical investments, although 'ethical' often does not seem to be clearly defined. The word 'ethical' means, 'consistent with agreed principles of correct moral conduct'. The believer's mode of conduct is defined as 'utilising and managing all resources for the glory of God and the betterment of His creation'.

Consequently, all projects in line with God's plans, purposes and principles are ethical and worthwhile investments that find God's approval. They show that we are serving God instead of money *(Matt 6:24; Luke 16:13)*.

> *Find out what pleases the Lord. Have nothing to do with the fruitless deeds of darkness, but rather expose them. (Eph 5:10-11)*

Summarised, investing into anything that contradicts God's plans, purposes and principles, can be ruled out as God-pleasing. Logically it will ultimately also effect our relationships with others negatively, because the reason for such investments is always selfishness instead of love for others.

Our focus should be on treasures in heaven *(Matt 6:20, 19:21; Luke 12:33, 16:9, 18:22; 1Tim 6:19)*, not on fading financial profits *(1Pet 1:18)*. Treasures in heaven aren't gold (that's paving material there) or other stuff. Treasures in heaven are people. They are the only ones passing into eternity. Everything else is temporal and will be replaced by something new and better anyway. Thus, proper biblical investments will help people for the right reasons.

Much can be done to slow down, possibly stop or even reverse the continuous destruction of creation and the relentless exploitation of its natural resources. Or to provide affordable and healthy living standards. Investments into,

- alternative, low cost energy;
- water production and purification;
- more natural, uncontaminated food production and supply;
- true medical care incl. natural remedies instead of dependency on chemical-based pharmaceuticals;
- provision of shelter and other basic needs;

are but some examples here.

Finally, provided there are sufficient investments funds available, a diversification of risks is surely wise advice:

> *Invest in seven ventures, yes, in eight; you do not know what disaster may come upon the land. (Eccl 11:2)*
>
> *Sow your seed in the morning, and at evening let your hands not be idle, for you do not know which will succeed, whether this or that, or whether both will do equally well. (Eccl 11:6)*

48. Land, Buildings

At creation, God entrusted all land into man's care *(Gen 1:26, 2:15)*. Because of the Fall, land was subjected to the curse and the resulting evil influence of Satan *(Gen 3:17-19, 23)*. It was only when God chose Israel to be His people that He decided to cleanse specific land for them from evil control for them to occupy and utilise *(Ex 3:8+17; 13:5, 34:11-16)*. In this setting, God gave Israel instructions that provide us today with a biblical base and advise on land and building issues:

- God owns the whole earth *(Ex 9:29; Job 41:11; Psa 24:1, 89:11; 1Cor 10:26)*.

- He distributed the land designated for Israel fairly amongst His people and they were mere tenants or stewards of God's property *(Lev 25:23)*.

- The entrusted land was to be well stewarded and treasured, not abused – no defilement or pollution through bloodshed, law transgression, unfaithfulness, hatred, denial of God, idolatry, etc. *(Lev 18:25+28; Num 35:33-34; Is 24:5; Jer 16:18; Hos 4:1+3)*.

- The entrusted land was to have a Sabbath rest *(Lev 25:2-5)*, that is, lie fallow every seventh year to allow restoration of its nutrients.

- God's land could never be sold permanently, neither to outsiders nor amongst His people *(Lev 25:23)*.

- Land sale amongst God's people was possible when people became poor, but the sale was only temporary. The price was based on the remaining harvests until the year of Jubilee arrived. However, the sold land could be redeemed (bought back) at any time, either by the nearest relative or by the seller himself if his economical fortune turned for good. The price for the buyback was the balance of the original selling price minus the value for the harvest years since it was sold. *(Lev 25:14-17, 24-27)*

- If the poor person could not redeem his land, he received it back in the year of Jubilee *(Lev 25:28; 27:24)*, i.e., every fiftieth year. This way God made sure all land was returned to its original possessor (steward) to avert impoverishment amongst His people. Therefore, every person had access to productive land at least once in his lifetime.

- The year of Jubilee was also to be a full years rest for the ground *(Lev 25:11)*.

- Unlike land, houses could be sold permanently as long as they were part of a walled-in city. The seller had one year to buy it back, after which the house became permanent property of the new owner and did not have to be returned in the year of Jubilee *(Lev 25:29-30)*.

- Houses in villages without walls around them, however, were classed as open country and treated like land, i.e., had to be returned to its original possessor in the year of Jubilee *(Lev 25:31)*.

The OT reveals that the state of the land is a reflection of man's relationship with God *(2Sam 21:1-14; 2Chr 7:13-14)*. There is a strong link between land quality and the morality and spiritual condition of those living in it. Spiritual pollution leads to environmental pollution. Disobedience to God damages the habitat.

> *I will bring on you sudden terror, wasting diseases and fever that will destroy your sight and sap your strength. You will plant seed in vain, because your enemies will eat it. […] I will break down your stubborn pride and make the sky above you like iron and the ground beneath you like bronze. Your strength will be spent in vain, […] your soil will not yield its crops, nor will the trees of your land yield their fruit. (Lev 26:16, 19-20)*

Conversely, obedience to God results in environmental quality.

> *If you follow my decrees and are careful to obey my commands, I will send you rain in its season, and the ground will yield its crops and the trees their fruit. Your threshing will continue until grape harvest and the grape harvest will continue until planting, and you will eat all the food you want and live in safety in your land. […] You will still be eating last year's harvest when you will have to move it out to make room for the new. (Lev 26:3-5, 10)*

What does all that mean for today's handling of land and buildings?

- God still owns it all *(Ex 19:5; 1Cor 10:26)*, irrespective of its current occupants (believers or non-believers) or spiritual influence (God or Satan).

- Believers can buy land and buildings from non-believers, therefore increase Kingdom influence. However, such property needs to be spiritually cleansed from sin, corruption, idolatry, and bloodshed attached to it.

- Believers can buy or sell land and buildings for the common good of the Body of Christ *(Acts 4:32-37)*. Sales should be done within the Body of Christ to ensure that Kingdom property remains under God's rule and influence.

- Other than the world, believers should not aim to become large building and landowners to enrich themselves. The Bible condemns the accumulation of wealth and land in the hands of a few, because it harms the poor and needy *(Is 5:8, Mic 2:2, Luke 6:24)*. Jesus expressly condemned the scribes (lawyers) strongly for devouring particularly widow's houses *(Mark 12:40)*. By implication they had devised ways within the law to expropriate the needy of their property.

- Land and buildings in the hands of believers should be managed in obedience to the owner, God. It is first and foremost to be used for His glory and the betterment of His creation, not for personal enrichment. For example, this can mean to provide affordable living space for those in need, or land for natural food production, etc.

- Agricultural land in any form should be used according to biblical standards, which includes a Sabbath year.

Just to be clear, there is no law in Scriptures that regulates the handling of land and buildings and punishes its violation. Following biblical patterns is, therefore, completely voluntary, the benefit of it a certainly stronger community.

The secular use of land and buildings almost always violates biblical guidelines. Assets are not used to truly help people but to maximise monetary profits. Such selfishness is an unhealthy foundation for our relationship with God (He abhors egotism) let alone our relationship with others (no-one likes to be exploited).

49. Payment Terms

One of the results of our debt-based financial system is that you can buy stuff now and pay for it later. As if the seller had only the good of the customer at heart, long payment periods or even whole payment plans are often offered as an aid to the buyer. In truth, businesses are under growing pressure to increase revenue to cover the exponential growing compound interest burden. Therefore they need to find ways to lure customers to buy, even if they can't afford it right now. Long payment terms and payment plans play a part in this.

If we had the choice to be paid immediately on delivery of our products and services or, alternatively, in 30, 60, 90 or more days, what would we choose? Surely, everyone appreciates immediate payment, right? It reduces the time for pre-financing relevant material input and allows us to use revenue right away. So if we appreciate being paid immediately then, from a spiritual point of view, we should start paying promptly ourselves.

> *So in everything, do to others what you would have them do to you, for this sums up the Law and the Prophets. (Matt 7:12; also Luke 6:31)*

The benefit of paying bills right away is that we no longer have to worry about them and the risk of penalties for late payment is eliminated.

> *Do not withhold good from those who deserve it, when it is in your power to act. Do not say to your neighbour, "Come back later; I'll give it tomorrow" – when you now*

have it with you. (Prov 3:27-28)

That's a precise instruction, right? Upon delivery of goods or services in accepted condition, the supplier has the right to immediate payment. If this is not possible then the product or service should not be ordered to begin with. Such conduct is part of good stewardship.

If you do not pay for ordered goods or services on delivery, then you are from a biblical point of view in debt, no matter how the world defines that condition.

Let no debt remain outstanding, except the continuing debt to love one another, […]. (Rom 3:8)

By letting the debt remain outstanding, you deprive the other side of your love, because love treats the other person the way you want to be treated yourself.

Good stewardship means working faithfully with entrusted goods. If you order what you can't afford, that is not good stewardship. The key here is to avoid the subtle, unnoticed enslavement that comes by not paying your debt *(Prov 22:7)*.

The Bible offers no penalty to force immediate payment. It is a voluntary act that demonstrates the payer's reliability and care to the supplier. It thus strengthens relationships.

50. Pricing

How should believers as self-employed, freelancers, entrepreneurs or managers set prices for their goods and services? Should they be based on production costs plus a reasonable profit? And how much profit is justifiable? Are market prices a good and fair gauge or not?

Many Christians believe in the market price approach and fight vehemently for it. But how do market prices come about?

According to economic textbooks market prices in free market economies, which most countries boast to have, are created by supply and demand:

- If demand exceeds supply, prices rise as products and services are scarce.
- If supply exceeds demand, prices fall as there are more products and services on offer than can be purchased.

Market prices seem to be an indicator of what consumers can pay for goods and services, or are at least willing to pay. It is said that the greater the competition and the more price wars there are, the more the consumers benefit from lower prices. Sometimes this is true but not always. The flip side is that companies may struggle for survival, which brings workplaces in jeopardy. Also, monopolists and large corporations are known to use their power to manipulate prices to rake in massive profits.

Unlike a proper production cost analysis, market prices do not show if businesses break even, let alone earn decent profits. In reality, the market price approach allows some businesses and service providers to make enormous profits. Others cope relatively well while still others struggle to survive.

By employing the world's finance system in our economies, we essentially defeat ourselves. Most businesses finance parts of their operation through debt today. Thus they must increase production and sales to cover the exponentially growing compound interest. The output increase often leads to oversupply. That in turn leads to lower market prices, commonly precipitating insufficient cost coverage. This is chiefly counteracted with laying off employees to reduce cost, leading to lack of income for the dismissed, which reduces the customer base even more.

In light of this, is market price the correct pricing approach for believers? From a biblical point of view, this method raises questions. Here are a couple of reasons:

- The potential use of price manipulation and overpricing defies God's demand for using honest measures, scales and weights, i.e., prices *(Lev 19:36; Deut 25:15; Prov 11:1, 16:11; Ezek 454:10; Mic 6:11)*.

- Market prices tend to fuel extortion, exploitation and at times constitute theft from the most vulnerable. Yet God hates when people take advantage of each other, especially of the poor *(Ex 22:22; Lev 25:14, 17; Deut 24:17; Prov 22:22; Is 58:3; 2Cor 12:17-18; 2Pet 2:3)*.

The worker deserves his wages. (1Tim 5:18b, also Luke 10:7)

As producers and service providers we should think about what constitutes a fair and justified price to charge based on our production cost and reasonable profit. Maybe we find out that our production costs are too high or our profit margins are too big and hence need to be adjusted. But if we can say in good conscience that it is not, then we can trust God to bless our business with enough customers willing to pay those fair prices if that business is what He calls us to do *(Deut 28:1-14; Matt 6:33; Luke 12:31; John 14:12-14, 15:5-8, 16:23)*.

As a consumer, we need to think about what is a reasonable, fair and justifiable price for the product or service offered to us. This doesn't mean that we expect things to cost next to nothing, which, in most cases, would also result in a form of theft and exploitation. As a result we might no longer buy products or services that don't pass our value-for-money assessment. It doesn't automatically mean that things are too expensive, but simply that we cannot or will not afford it.

> *So then, whatever you desire that others would do to and for you, even so do also to and for them, for this is (sums up) the Law and the Prophets. (Matt 7:12, AMP — see also Luke 6:31)*

Pricing our products and services as self-employed, freelancers, entrepreneurs or managers isn't always easy and straight forward in Kingdom context as we follow God's instructions. But if, as His stewards, we provide, with a clear conscience, products and services that benefit people at a price they can afford and that sustains us, then we are surely on the right path. Remember, it is God,

> *[…] who gives you the ability to produce wealth, and so confirms his covenant, which he swore to your forefathers, as it is today. (Deut 8:18)*

51. Marketing, Advertising

> *A merchant can hardly keep from wrongdoing, nor is a tradesman innocent of sin. Many have committed sin for gain, and those who seek to get rich will avert their eyes. As a stake is driven firmly into a fissure between stones, so sin is wedged in between selling and buying. If a person is not steadfast in the fear of the Lord, his house will be quickly overthrown. (Sirach 26:29-27:3, NRSV)*

It is one thing if you make consumers aware of your products and/or services and inform them about quality, benefits, specifics, and so forth. It is another thing if you entice people to buy what they don't need, with money they don't have, to impress people they don't like. Both paths use marketing and advertising to get the message out there. The first is based on verifiable facts, offering a solution to a potential and perceived need. The second appeals chiefly to people's emotions and feelings, hopes and desires, selling an unreal sense of life.

As enterprises today are typically in debt, they must persistently increase their revenues to service the exponentially growing debt interest. It is for this reason that marketing and advertising almost solely follow the second path. Without having any qualms, an entire industry uses deceptive and often intentionally false or limited information to make people do something they wouldn't otherwise do.

> "The truly important things in life aren't those you own, but those that own you!" (from a Seat commercial on German TV, 2008)

In the commercial, the above statement was heard in the background, after all the strong points and the luxury of the advertised vehicle were touted in a feel-good setup and a paradisiac scenery with only happy people. It is easy to see how consumers are beguiled by these dreamy, deceptive presentations. In the hope to buy the shown, appealing lifestyle, they get tempted to buy the advertised car, although another, cheaper, perhaps even used one would be quite sufficient. That is exactly what the sales pitch must accomplish: instil hunger and desire by use of non-factual, emotion-based means with the goal of increasing sales. We are inundated with thousands of such commercials year in year out.

The above cited punchline of the Seat commercial clearly opposes biblical truth,

> *[...] you are slaves to whatever controls you. (2Pet 2:19, NLT-SE)*

Christians are not supposed to be controlled and owned by anything or anyone, not even a Seat car. We are God's children and belong to Him 100%. That's it. So we can dismiss the stated commercial punchline as utter nonsense.

However, it is not always as obvious when marketing and advertising campaigns oppose the Word of God. We may think that all this doesn't influence us, but in reality it works like the constant dripping that wears the stone.

When tobacco advertising was banned almost all over the world because of its misleading information and the obfuscation of its harmfulness to health, there was hope that this would change the way the industry works. It didn't. Regardless which products and services are offered, marketing campaigns and advertising still tend to be driven by misinformation, including a deliberate omission of the whole truth. This is called deception and lying. The Bible warns us,

> *Do not lie. (Lev 19:11; the 9th commandment)*

> *Therefore each of you must put off falsehood and speak truthfully to your neighbour, for we are all members of one body. (Eph 4:25)*

> *Do not lie to each other, since you have taken off your old self with its practices. (Col 3:9)*

> *Let no one deceive you with empty words, for because of such things God's wrath comes on those who are disobedient. Therefore do not be partners with them. (Eph 5:6-7)*

Believers must operate in truth and hence cannot truly be part of this practise. If God calls a believer to work in this industry, then surely to make a difference, to be salt and light there. There can be no other reason. God does not tolerate lies and deception, which are devices of the devil. If we don't like to be deceived, we can't be part of deliberate deception of others. We must treat others the way we want to be treated ourselves *(Matt 7:12; Luke 6:31)*. **Period.**

When it comes to marketing or promoting products or services, be it our own or those of others, be it for us or on behalf of others, transparency and truth must be essential to us. It fosters reliable relationships. Woe to us if we ignore it.

> *Woe to those who call evil good and good evil, who put darkness for light and light for darkness, who put bitter for sweet and sweet for bitter. (Is 5:20)*

52. Competition

> *No one can say, "This is not as good as that," for everything proves good in its appointed time. (Sirach 39:33, NRSV)*

In the world there is an unrelenting competition for available resources, market shares, income, jobs, positions, provision, and so on. In fact, it's the world money system with its compound interest-driven growth compulsion that forces people into constant competition.

Competition is often seen as the engine of progress. But it seems unfair to reduce the innovation and ingenuity of all inventors and developers to a mere contest with others. It also casts a false light on God, the genius Creator par excellence, who gifted people to be inventive. Being created in His image, we are generally endowed with many gifts, talents, and amazing ingenuity. Personally, I know a number of inventors, developers and engineers who 'simply' translate into the physical, visible, what God shows them in spirit. They are not driven to make money and get rich, but to help people, especially the poor and needy.

Christians that are part of a secular approach to competition must know that this ruthless and indeed harmful way of securing a lifeline or supremacy isn't biblical. Trying to limit and harm others ignores the law to love God and neighbour.

From a spiritual point of view, competition is a driving force in Satan's realm of influence. Being the prototype deceiver and destroyer, he loves it when mankind deceives and destroys itself in hard contested economic fields. The world's picture of competition is not God's idea and there is no biblical justification for it.

> *For as in one physical body we have many parts (organs, members) and all of these parts do not have the same function or use, so we, numerous as we are, are one body in Christ (the Messiah) and individually we are parts one of another [mutually dependent on one another]. (Rom 12:4-5, AMP)*

When the parts of a body fight and outsmart each other, the body is completely ineffective, at best impeded. Scripture leaves no doubt that believers are part of one and the same spiritual body *(1Cor 10:17; 12:12-13, 20; Eph 3:6; 4:4, 25; Col 3:15)*. They therefore need to learn to work together practically and spiritually. This means that they complement each other instead of competing with each other. That also applies in the financial and economical sector.

Jesus didn't come to earth to compete with people. He came to serve them with all He had and embodied *(Matt 20:28, Mark 10:45)*. Seeing that Jesus focused solely on what the Father told him *(John 5:19)*, even the kingdom of darkness was no competitor to Him. Having grown up in a godless world that competes and compares, we must learn to emulate our Servant King. He refused to be implicated in any political power games and never made potential financial gain the basis for His ministry and decisions.

The media portray the economy and the financial world as war zones. It's about battles for currencies, profits or market shares, hostile takeovers, dominance through innovation, market leadership, etc.. Blackmail, exploitation, betrayal, nepotism, influence peddling, breach of secrecy, bribery, theft, fraud, lies, falsification of documents, discrediting others, etc. are only some of the weapons used. Fully aware of the warlike environment we are living in, Jesus says,

> *But I tell you, love your enemies and pray for those who persecute you (Matt 5:44)*

> *But to you who are willing to listen, I say, love your enemies! Do good to those who hate you. Bless those who curse you. Pray for those who hurt you. (Luke 6:27-28, NLT-SE)*

> *Bless those who persecute you; bless and do not curse. On the contrary: If your enemy is hungry, feed him; if he is thirsty, give him something to drink In doing this, you will heap burning coals on his head. Do not be overcome by evil, but overcome evil with good. (Rom 12:14,20-21)*

All that doesn't exactly sound like a call to compete, does it? Jesus' admonition to love, pray, do good and bless, is diametrically opposed to a competitive attitude. Should we not take this to heart and put an end to fighting about everything? If we truly seek God's Kingdom and His righteousness first *(Matt 6:33; Luke 12:31)*, then we must stop acting in the typical competitive mode of the world.

> *Do nothing from factional motives [through contentiousness, strife, selfishness, or for unworthy ends] or prompted by conceit and empty arrogance. Instead, in the true spirit of humility (lowliness of mind) let each regard the others as better than and superior to himself [thinking more highly of one another than you do of yourselves]. Let each of you esteem and look upon and be concerned for not [merely] his own interests, but also each for the interests of others. (Phil 2:3-4, AMP)*

This instruction is also quite obviously directed against the slightest semblance of rivalry or competition, don't you think? In addition, Jesus gave us clear orders to treat others the way we want to be treated *(Matt 7:12, Luke 6:3)*. So if we do not want to be treated like an enemy or a threat, we have to stop treating others that way. The initiative lies with us, not with the others.

The big question then is, can God provide sufficiently even if we do not engage in active competition? Well, He clearly promised to take care of our needs when His Kingdom and His righteousness are our driving force *(Matt 6:33, Luke 12:31)*. That holds for both private and professional life. Bear in mind that reckless competition, as practiced in the world, leads to the destruction of the economic supply of other people. Does this fit with *Rom 12:14, 20-21*, which we have just read?

We can't prevent others from competing with us. But instead of focusing on what they do, we should concentrate on obeying what the Lord tells us. I have seen companies consciously supporting and recommending their competitors. What a tremendous testimony that must be for their competitors as well as for their mutual customers.

> *Do not let yourself be overcome by evil, but overcome (master) evil with good. (Rom 12:21, AMP)*

It is possible to be loving, considerate and caring in a typically hostile economic environment, in which only money and profits have the say. In that we do not need to worry not being cared for. *Deut 28:1-14* and *Matt 6:19-34* promise God's full care for those who obediently follow His instructions.

> *Do not conform to the pattern [framework, system, order, method, structure, plan, format] of this world, but be transformed by the renewing of your mind. Then you*

will be able to test and approve what God's will is – his good, pleasing and perfect will. (Rom 12:2)*

53. Get-Rich-Quick Schemes

"Wall Street is doing nothing evil; it is merely doing its job - separating fools from their money. […] the whole edifice of Wall Street is built on a hollow wish: that you can get something for nothing." (Bonner & Wiggin, 'Empire Of Debt', page 309)

"The stock market isn't God, The Wall Street Journal isn't the Bible, your asset manager isn't your priest, and financial experts aren't prophets. (Prophets were put to death when their prophecies didn't come true!)" (Randy Alcorn, 'Money, Possessions, And Eternity', page 350)

Earlier in this book we read the global financial transactions to be 70 times bigger than the productive economy. With the global GDP currently standing at $75.4 trillion (2017) it puts the annual financial dealings at a staggering $5,278 trillion. Most of these transactions relate to speculative financial products with no tangible backup. Although it is an extremely risky business, making money with money is very attractive to many because it promises quick wealth. The stock exchanges have become hubs of a booming financial industry, which in turn has become a monetary slave-master of the manufacturing and services sectors.

"The lottery is a tax on people who are bad in math." (Bumper sticker)

Those who lack the means to play in this casino of the rich, play in the casinos of the poor, which are called lotto, lucky draws, pyramid schemes and the like. Lotto is the most used and most popular of them all. People spend their last pennies there, even if the odds of winning the jackpot are just 0.00000001% at best. It's like the modern day gold rush.

Since time immemorial, the devil has been trying to seduce mankind into getting rich quick. He knows that this will likely separate man from God and eventually destroy him *(Matt 6:24; Luke 16:13; 1Tim 6:10)*, which is his goal. So he paints this appealing picture of becoming an instant millionaire without doing anything for it. And many fall for it. To the believers, he even suggests that they could use this money for a good cause in God's Kingdom. And many fall for this, too. But whether casino of the rich or the poor, only a very small number of players win, and always at the expense of the vast majority. All get-rich-quick schemes are evil devices that produce nothing tangible and useful to mankind, yet skim enormous resources, exploit most of it's participants and ruin a good deal of individuals. God does not work that way.

The Bible contains accounts of people whom God bestowed with great wealth. However, get-rich-quick schemes are not scriptural. And for good reasons.

First, God expects us to work for a living and not "let the money work for us".

Money does not work. People work. So money can only pay people for work. The phrase "money works for us" is a clinical term for living from the work of others, which the Bible calls exploitation and robbery. This certainly doesn't foster loving and trustworthy relationships with God and neighbour.

> *By the sweat of your brow, you will eat your food [...]. (Gen 3:19)*

> *[...] The one who is unwilling to work shall not eat. (2Th 3:10; also 4:11)*

Second, God's standard is a steady, step by step accumulation of wealth.

> *[...] whoever gathers money little by little makes it grow. (Prov 13:11)*

Third, we need to prove to be trustworthy in handling the little we have to qualify for handling more.

> *Whoever can be trusted with very little can also be trusted with much, and whoever is dishonest with very little will also be dishonest with much. (Luke 16:10)*

> *[...] Well done, good and faithful servant. You have been faithful over a little; I will set you over much. [...] (Matt 25:21; also Luke 19:17)*

Fourth, money, especially lots of it, carries a great deal of negative, destructive potential, if it is not handled in a godly manner.

> *Of what use is money in the hand of a fool, since he has no desire to get wisdom? (Prov 17:16, NIV 1984)*

> *For the love of money is at the root of all kinds of evil. And some people, craving money, have wandered from the true faith and pierced themselves with many sorrows. (1Tim 6:10, NLT-SE)*

> *Wealth from get-rich-quick schemes quickly disappears; (Prov 13:11a, NLT-SE)*

The trustworthy person will get a rich reward, but a person who wants quick riches will get into trouble. (Prov 28:20, NLT-SE)

There is a painful tragedy that I have seen under the sun: Riches lead to the downfall of those who hoard them. These hoarded riches were then lost in bad business deals. The owners had children, but now they have nothing to give them. (Eccl 5:13-14, GWORD)

Better a little with the fear of the LORD than great wealth with turmoil. (Prov 15:16)

Fifth, a believer's wealth should be a result of his relationship and walk with God, because then it can be safely enjoyed.

But remember the Lord your God is the one who makes you wealthy. He's confirming the promise, which he swore to your ancestors. It's still in effect today. (Deut 8:18, GWORD)

And it is a good thing to receive wealth from God and the good health to enjoy it. […] (Eccl 5:19, NLT-SE)

The blessing of the LORD makes a person rich, and he adds no sorrow with it. (Prov 10:22, NLT-SE)

Satan offered all the riches of the world to Jesus in a quick-fix, when he tempted Him in the desert. Jesus declined. The devil is also offering quick riches to us. What is our response?

54. Fear Factor

General

"Reserves are crutches and props which become a substitute for trust in the Lord." (William McDonald, 1917-2007, American preacher and bestselling author)

'Fear' is defined as 'an unpleasant emotion caused by the belief that someone or something is dangerous, likely to cause pain, or a threat', and 'a feeling of anxiety concerning the outcome of something or the safety and wellbeing of someone'. Fear is horrid for we do not know what's coming and expect the worst. Therefore, people are trying to do everything possible to make arrangements and control events to kill or at least alleviate these hideous feelings.

A Zimbabwean friend believes 'fear' is an acronym for 'false evidence appearing real'. There is a lot of truth in this. God's Word tells us that,

> There is no fear in love. But perfect love drives out fear, because fear has to do with punishment. The one who fears is not made perfect in love. (1John 4:18)

Principally, every believer should live a life without fear as the above and many others Scriptures make clear *(Num 21:34; Deut 3:2; Judg 6:10; 2Kings 17:35-38; Psa 94:19; Eccl 1:10; Is 8:12; 35:4; 41:10, 13; 43:1; 51:7; 54:4; Jer 10:5; 30:10; 46:27-28; Lam 3:57; Zeph 3:16; Hag 2:5; 1Peter 3:14; 5:7)*.

According to the Bible we should only fear, i.e., revere, honour, respect, be in awe of God *(Job 1:9; Psa 55:19; 66:16; Eccl 5:7; 8:12-13; 12:13; Luke 23:40; Acts 13:16, 26; 1Pet 2:17)*.

Many people's lives are controlled by questions starting with 'What if?'. These are questions that cause insecurity, fear, anxiety and worry. They generally query God's goodness, promises, abilities, power, love, care, etc., and, as a result, His instructions. Such questions are reminiscent of the doubt that the devil had implanted in Eve's spirit in Eden, *'Did God really say?' (Gen 3:1)*.

As a consequence, man has begun to make his own arrangements for the 'what if's', which are more often than not contrary to the Word of God. The results are social systems and structures that look divine but are a death sentence for the God-ordained personal duty of care in families and communities.

Insurances (= Warranty Against Loss)

> "With insurance to compensate us for losses due to death of loved ones, earthquakes, floods, winds, fires, hospitalisation, unemployment, law suits, burglary, car wrecks and other calamities – who needs God?" (Harry Bethel, Bethel Ministries, USA)

> "Would Jesus have bought an insurance policy if one had been available? How about the apostles? If not, why not?" (Randy Alcon, 'Money, Possessions, And Eternity', page 348)

Insurances are not a modern day invention. E.g., OT Babylon and ancient Greece had already maritime insurances. But financial protection plans aren't God's way of shielding His people from calamities. Regrettably we don't appreciate His ways and offers. We rather rely on our own ingenuity to deal with those 'what if's'.

As a result we do have untold insurance varieties and options today. In Germany, for instance, you are offered protection against almost all eventualities with an assortment of at least 24 different insurance types. There are even bad debt and contingency insurances as well as an insurance against insurance default. Hmmm

So frankly, even if we say we do trust God, we don't really need Him since we are covered. We rely on secular institutions to shield us from all sorts of troubles, and then give God the glory for it? In reality, an insurance is man's attempt to protect himself from the curses that fall to those who disobey God *(Deut 28:15-68)*. Anyone who trusts in insurance, doesn't really trust God. Insurances can damage relationships with others, because the idea of hedging can lead to carelessness.

Ever thought about what insurance companies do with our premiums and into what schemes they invest to keep their promise to pay out when needed? If we did, we would be amazed how evil and exploitative some of their investment plans are. This ranges from speculation on exchanges to investments in the war industry. This isn't biblical, and so, as believers, we simply cannot be part of this machinery. We are well advised to reconsider our entire approach in this regard.

Sure, depending on a nation's laws, some insurances are obligatory. Statutory health insurance for employees or car insurance is compulsory in most countries. But many insurance policies are voluntary and so we can decide.

> *What the wicked dread will overtake them […] The fear of the Lord adds length to life, but the years of the wicked are cut short. (Prov 10:24a+27)*

Buying a protection (insurance) for a guarantee of being compensated for the loss of possessions or loved ones is totally foreign to Scriptures.

> *Follow my decrees and be careful to obey my laws, and you will live safely in the land. Then the land will yield its fruit, and you will eat your fill and live there in safety. (Lev 25:18-19)*

> *Command those who are rich in this present world not to be arrogant nor to put their hope in wealth, which is so uncertain, but to put their hope in God, who richly provides us with everything for our enjoyment. Command them to do good, to be rich in good deeds, and to be generous and willing to share. In this way they will lay up treasure for themselves as a firm foundation for the coming age, so that they may take hold of the life that is truly life. (1 Tim 6:17-19)*

Actually, *Deut 28* is a case in point. In *V1-14* God describes the good that will happen to those who obey Him, which includes comprehensive protection and insurance. Read for yourself. In *V15-68* God describes all the bad His people have to face if they are disobedient to Him. Much of it is exactly what we have insurance policies for today. In other words, we are trying to cancel the effects of the curses we brought on ourselves. Again, take the time and read it for yourself. Our only insurance should really be our obedience towards God. Or, as somebody said, prayer is a Christian's insurance.

These statements are certainly not well received by many, especially those who work professionally in this field. But that doesn't help. Job's life offers us amazing insights into a godly dealing with serious disasters. Let's take a good look at it:

CASE 1 – Job loses all his property and children *(Job 1:13-19)*. Some people can identify with those traumatic and devastating experiences. Yet, it's still difficult to understand what Job has gone through. – But here is his amazing response to it,

> *He said, "Naked I came from my mother's womb, and naked I will depart. The Lord gave and the Lord has taken away; may the name of the Lord be praised." (Job 1:21)*

CASE 2 – Satan attacks Job's health most violently *(Job 2:7-8)*, so that even his wife (!) turns against him and advises him to, *'Curse God and die' (Job 2:9)*. Try to put yourself in this cruel situation where your health condition is unbearable and your spouse is feeling depressed and giving up on you. How would you react? – Here is Job's response,

> *He replied, "You are talking like a foolish woman. Shall we accept good from God, and not trouble?" In all this, Job did not sin in what he said. (Job 2:10)*

We know today that God allowed Satan to test Job for his righteousness. But Job did not know that. He also did not know that God would bless him afterwards in the way the Bible describes. The lesson is that we don't need to be afraid, hence don't need insurance for what we fear, because God is in complete control of all and everything *(Heb 1:3; Acts 17:28; Col 1:16-17)*.

Retirement, Pensions

> *"If you young fellows were wise, the devil couldn't do anything to you, but since you aren't wise, you need us who are old" (Martin Luther)*

Whatever the context for Martin Luther's statement a few hundred years ago, it almost prophetically points to a biblical view of the modern idea of retirement. To arrive at a biblical position on today's retirement concept, we have to ask a few questions to begin with:

- Is it biblical for us to work until a certain age and then withdraw, enjoying life to its fullest without obligation, commitment or worry?

- Who can preset a proper age at which people in general are to retire?

- Is retirement, a stress free time where we can enjoy leisure, a biblically legit reward for a lifetime of hard work?

- Does God want us to save and bunker as much money as we can to live on when we don't work anymore, so that He no longer needs to provide for us?

- Is it biblically justified for the working world to treat people from a prescribed age as rejects and for the most part discard their gained experience, expertise, wisdom and maturity as no longer needed, valuable and beneficial?

- Is God pleased with us as a progressive, modern society for outsourcing our God-given, personal, social responsibility (caring for the aged, the sick, the poor, needy and disadvantaged) to distant, impersonal, secular organisations, institutions and governments, who only assume that responsibility on a profit and loss basis?

- If the western world's idea of retirement is truly biblical, are then all nations that don't have such systems doomed?

- Who provides for those who have no access to retirement/pension funds?

- Since nobody knows what will happen tomorrow, can anyone really guarantee that we can enjoy the pension benefits we pay for our entire working life? And if not, is it really wise then and good stewardship to pay into pension funds?

- Are we aware that most of these funds operate unbiblical with the money entrusted into the whole world of financial chicanery and requiring maximum returns?

- If the secular idea of retirement does not agree with the word of God, then what does? What is God's view here?

- Who is more reliable, powerful, capable, trustworthy, caring, committed to us, etc. – our compassionate God or a ruthless world serving money?

- Whose wisdom is greater? The infinite wisdom of the One who thought it all up and created everything in His infinite power? Or the finite wisdom of His creation?

Examining these questions makes it clear that the secular idea of retirement has little biblical foundation.

Paid Work For A Limited Time – Then Retire?

Astonishingly, only two out of a massive 31,170 Bible verses provide us with a direct reference to retirement. Those two verses are found in *Numb 8:25-26* where God instructs Moses to ensure that the Levites (God's chosen spiritual leaders of the Israelites) officiate in the service at the Tabernacle only from age 25 to 50. After that they were to retire from this specific active duty. That didn't mean, though, that they switched to a life without obligation, commitment or worry for the remainder of their time on earth. Rather, their job scope changed, as they were now to assist the younger Levites by serving as guards at the Tabernacle.

And that's about the closest we can find in the Bible regarding our modern day's retirement concept. No other passage anywhere in Scriptures hints at a limited work time or an age at which to leave our productive work and enjoy the rest of our lives in idle comfort and pursuit of pleasure. Exactly the opposite is the case. Right after the Fall, God decreed for man to work hard for a living until the end of his days *(Gen 3:17-19)*. To say it bluntly, a biblical retirement age is individual and always evoked by death. We won't find a universal preset retirement age by human authorities in the Word of God.

Almost all biblical characters worked until their death in their official duty, in their learned profession and in their vocation. Jesus' work didn't nullify the *Gen 3* decree for Christians. In the Bible there is simply no law prescribing retirement, no regulation setting a stop to productive work at a pre-specified age.

Undoubtedly, our physical and mental fitness play a major role to what extend we can continue in the daily grind of our profession and tasks. That's why it makes sense that we do find frequent hints in the Bible that the role of people or the scope of their job changed as they got older. For instance, we read at least seven times about the 'elders at the gate' who now use their knowledge and wisdom for the benefit of society. Or in *Titus 2* Paul charges that older men and women are to teach, by example, younger men and women how to live. These are clear indications that the older generation could and should serve as consultants, teachers, trainers, guides, or any other assisting capacity to the younger people. The fact that today the old are often treated with contempt and parked at old-age homes where they can't interfere with the energetic lives of the young doesn't render this biblical approach invalid.

In *1Kings 12* we read about the sad consequences when the young flatly refuse to consider mature advice of the more experienced and seasoned old. When Solomon's son Rehoboam assumed kingship over Israel, he immediately had to deal with a rebellion in his own camp. Its instigator, Jeroboam, approached him to lift the heavy burden (slave work) of Solomon from the people. If he would do that, Israel would serve Rehoboam. After listening to their petition, the king told Jeroboam and Israel to come back in three days for an answer.

Then Rehoboam did two things. First he consulted the old people who had served his dad during his lifetime. They advised him to give the people a positive answer, which would make them serve Rehoboam for the rest of their lives. But he rejected their counsel and then consulted, as a second measure, the young men who had grown up with him. They, because of their young age completely oblivious to the intricate realities of what was at stake, advised the king in their naivety and youthful stupidity to make the heavy yoke of his dad even heavier for the people. They wanted him to show who the boss was. Rehoboam followed his peer's advice. It backfired mightily and split a united kingdom into two, heralding the start of some bloody, mostly evil and painful centuries in the nation's history.

Things haven't changed. The young still discard the old too swiftly as out of touch with a fast changing world and unable to adapt to the new realities. As a result, the often over decades painfully acquired experience, expertise and wisdom, which actually was foundational for what the young inherited, is substituted by the dynamic, roughshod approaches of the young. We are doomed to repeat 'history'.

In summary, being productive for a certain time and then retire into leisure to make room for the next generation is not a biblical concept. It is more a necessity of the world's interest-driven money system. So, if we are going to retire just because people have set an age limit when to end our working life, what does it say about our relationship with God? And what does it say about our relationship to each other when we are forcefully withdrawn from active service?

Saving Up To Finance Retirement?

Since *Num 8:25-26* is the only Scripture alluding to retirement or pension, the Bible lacks references to support the building of respective funds. But we get good clues on God's view.

> *Then Jesus said to his disciples: "Therefore I tell you, do not worry about your life,*

what you will eat; or about your body, what you will wear. For life is more than food, and the body more than clothes. Consider the ravens: They do not sow or reap, they have no storeroom or barn; yet God feeds them. And how much more valuable you are than birds! Who of you by worrying can add a single hour to your life? Since you cannot do this very little thing, why do you worry about the rest? (Luke 12:22-26)

Both in *Matt 6:24-33* and *Luke 12:22-31* Jesus describes extensively how the unbelievers worry about their daily provision (food, drink, clothing). He then states firmly that believers mustn't worry. Instead, He concludes, by seeking the Kingdom of God and His righteousness first, we'll receive everything the Gentiles need to worry about. It's a passage often used in sermons, but rarely as a radical challenge to rethink our provision plans.

The Bible offers no time limit to this amazing provision-promise. Nowhere do we read about God instructing us that we must make provision for our retirement age so He can stop providing for us.

Granted, these passages are only talking about food, drinks and clothing. So what about all the other needs? Well, *Deut 28:1-14, Mark 11:22-25* and *John 14:12-14* substantiate that our complete provision depends on our connection to the Lord and our obedience to Him. But read *John 15*, where Jesus says,

> *I am the Vine; you are the branches. Whoever lives in Me and I in him bears much (abundant) fruit. However, apart from Me [cut off from vital union with Me] you can do nothing. If a person does not dwell in Me, he is thrown out like a [broken-off] branch, and withers; such branches are gathered up and thrown into the fire, and they are burned.* **If you live in me [abide vitally united to me] and my words remain in you and continue to live in your hearts, ask whatever you will, and it shall be done for you.** *When you bear (produce) much fruit, My Father is honoured and glorified, and you show and prove yourselves to be true followers of Mine. (John 15:5-8, AMP, emphasis added)*

Sure, many are forced by law to pay into pension schemes. But many also give in to the fear ('what if?') that all this will not be enough and must be supplemented with additional funds. Or they don't know what the Bible says on this subject.

> *And he [Jesus] told them this parable: "The ground of a certain rich man yielded an abundant harvest. He thought to himself, 'What shall I do? I have no place to store my crops.' " Then he said, 'This is what I'll do. I will tear down my barns and build bigger ones, and there I will store my surplus grain. And I'll say to myself, "You have plenty of grain laid up for many years. Take life easy; eat, drink and be merry."' "But God said to him, 'You fool! This very night your life will be demanded from you. Then who*

will get what you have prepared for yourself?' "This is how it will be with whoever stores up things for themselves but is not rich toward God." (Luke 12:16-21)

Most people would probably consider the rich man's plans wise. Christians would see this as clever stewardship. But Jesus calls this guy simply a fool, because his reasoning is through and through selfish, worldly and totally discards God.

As Christians, we have to grapple with this issue from God's perspective rather than simply accepting the worldly, i.e., secular take. What does that say about our relationship with and our trust in God when we spend our whole work life to pay into a scheme that is not of His design? Are we good and faithful stewards of His entrusted resources? If God's blueprint for taking care of the old is by way of family and close-knit community involvement, what does choosing a distant, impersonal scheme reveal about our relationship with others and current lifestyles?

This passage from *Luke 12* is a good description of our pension schemes where you store up treasures to be able to enjoy times of inactivity. But will we be still alive when those funds become available to us? Or are our pensions really safe and available when we need them? No one, except God, knows what tomorrow brings. Who would have ever predicted that negative interest is now destroying pension funds? The world financial system is very fragile and unpredictable. So who can assure us that we can eventually reap the fruit of our work when we retire?

Then I saw all that God has done. No one can comprehend what goes on under the sun. Despite all his efforts to search it out, no one can discover its meaning. Even if the wise claim they know, they cannot really comprehend it. (Eccl 8:17)

Friends in Zimbabwe have lost their whole pension to hyperinflation. Decades of faithful laying aside were wiped out by first unforeseeable and later unstoppable events. They were left with nothing. Others who wanted to be smart by shifting their savings to Europe lost everything when the recommended bank surprisingly collapsed in the financial crisis. So who can give unshakeable guarantees?

My people have committed two sins: They have forsaken me, the spring of living water, and have dug their own cisterns, broken cisterns that cannot hold water. (Jer 2:13)

Some nations employ a so-called generational contract. The compulsory pension contributions of the current workforce pay the pensions of those already retired. Such a system depends on enough children being born to later pay as employees the pension of the parents. But many couples opt to pursue their careers rather than starting a family, which means that the children of others must pay their pension. So when, as in many Western countries, the age pyramid turns upside down, problems ensue. More and more retirees mean a growing pension burden that has to be borne by fewer and fewer employees. To avoid the collapse of the system, pension rights are continually adjusted downward. Although this is theft by a government institution, it goes unpunished. Instead, people are pushed to supplement their dwindling statutory pension with a private one. The entire system is unrighteous and in violation of Paul's statement anyway,

> *After all, children should not have to save up for their parents, but parents for their children. (2Cor 12:14)*

God alone can really guarantee something. Scriptures tell us that His Word stands firm and forever *(Psa 119:89; Is 40:8)*. So why don't we begin to trust in His provision and protection promises again? This could free a fortune from the claws of the evil one to be used for God's Kingdom purposes. After all,

> *For in him [God] we live and move and have our being. (Acts 17:28)*

> *He is before all things, and in him all things hold together. (Col 1:17)*

> *In their hearts humans plan their course, but the LORD establishes their steps (Prov 16:9)*

> *And my God will meet all your needs according to the riches of his glory in Christ Jesus. (Phil 4:19)*

> *Trust in the LORD with all your heart and lean not on your own understanding; in all your ways submit to him, and he will make your paths straight. (Prov 3:5-6)*

Defence And Security Systems

Is 30:1-5 makes us witness the devastating criticism of God's people by the Prophet. Why? Because the kings of Israel asked the kings of Syria and Egypt for protection. They relied on the extremely limited powers of man instead of God Almighty. This is not part of God's plan for His people.

If you've ever been burgled, you know the terrible sense of your privacy being invaded and violated by strangers, especially when you have a family. The natural response seems to be an upgrade in protective measures and safety systems. Boundary walls, barbed wire, electric fences, CCTV cameras, security locks, alarm systems, burglar bars, security guards, the options are endless. But it is debatable whether these solutions ward off or attract criminals, according to the motto 'With so much protection, they must hide something valuable'.

Anyway, today entire industries (production, services) exist and thrive on man's fear of being burgled, mugged, attacked, kidnapped, and killed. They provide a vast array of defence and security solutions and services to minimise risks of falling prey to such events. No matter what you choose, it is always costly and never provides total protection. The question is, is it worth it, or is it pure waste of valuable resources that could be better utilised?

God offers much better and more comprehensive protection for free. Only, do we believe His promise and accept this offer?

> *If you listen carefully to what he says and do all that I say, I will be an enemy to your enemies and will oppose those who oppose you. (Ex 23:22)*

> *Follow my decrees and be careful to obey my laws, and you will live safely in the land. (Lev 25:18)*

> *The Lord will rescue me from every evil attack and will bring me safely to his heavenly kingdom. To him be glory for ever and ever. (2Tim 4:18)*

Notably since the 9/11 events, laws, regulations, security measures, systems, controls and much more become persistently more complex and rigorous. As a result many people are increasingly restricted in their daily lives and their privacy violated. Technological advance turns man progressively into transparent beings whose lives can be fully monitored. Most people accept restrictions and surveillance as a price for perceived safety. It is all fear-driven. John tells us,

> *There is no fear in love. But perfect love drives out fear, because fear has to do with punishment. The one who fears is not made perfect in love. (1John 4:18)*

Computer hackers show us that every system can be hacked into, every security can be breached, and every protection mechanism can be removed or corrupted. A simple power failure can render the safest and most expensive electronic system useless. History shows that neither walls, gates, fences, and trenches, nor all the weapons in the world can ultimately keep us from harm. No car, as safe as they might be, can shield us from the reckless driver causing a crash. No shelter can truly protect us when natural forces like torrential floods, tsunamis, hurricanes, heavy earthquakes, scorching heat, freezing blizzards and iciness, etc. hit with immeasurable force. We witness that year in year out, don't we? This list is not exhaustive, but the message is clear, isn't it?

> *For whoever wants to save their life will lose it, but whoever loses their life for me will find it. (Matt 16:25)*

There is, in the end, only One who truly has the power and ability to protect us from any kind of harm – God. He promised to be an enemy to our enemies if we carefully follow His instructions. For us as fallible humans in a fallen world, there will always be inadequacies causing problems, neglect and pain. Or, with God's permission, we are simply tested by Satan and his cohorts like Job was. In other words, there is always a chance where our safety and security is compromised. But it is up to us who we trust to intervene effectively, powerless man or God Almighty? Why don't we choose our omnipotent Creator in whom everything holds together *(Col 1:17)*?

Maybe we should think about radical changes in this area, too? It's not about being reckless and careless. But about trust in the abilities and faithfulness of our heavenly Father instead in man-made security systems and measures. It would free immense resources from a fear-driven world system for the Kingdom of God. It will reveal our confidence in God and show that we are not driven by fear. It would also be a sign of trust in our neighbour rather than mistrust.

55. Giving

Giving money is a very sensitive issue in Christian circles. While tithing is deemed almost a legal duty, offerings are generally considered voluntary. Many a time churches push for tithes and offerings in a manipulative manner to make people feel guilty if they don't give. This leads either to an angry and stubborn refusal or to a helpless and frustrated yielding. Both reactions are not in line with Scriptures and aren't exactly expressing the freedom for which Jesus Christ has set us free *(Gal 5:1)*. So lets have a look at what Scriptures have to say on giving.

Tithe

Amongst believers tithing is more contested than giving an offering. This may be down to its regular, continuous payment nature. Very few pastors seem to be relaxed about it, while many church leaders fight for tithes as if their lives depend on it. Perhaps this is because church resources would otherwise dry up?

Tithes (together with offerings) finance pastors, apostles, prophets, evangelists, teachers, deacons, buildings, equipment, utilities, publications, recordings, programs, and perhaps even outreaches, mission works, the soup kitchen for the poor, a bible school, and what have you. However, it is hypocrisy when leaders encourage their flock to trust God wholly for daily provision, but they themselves rather trust in the tithes (and offerings) of people. Giving, but especially tithing, has become an emotional issue in the church. So lets try to free this topic from this emotional baggage and have a balanced view.

1. What is a tithe and what not?

The tithe is not 'firstfruits'. Firstfruits depict the first part of a harvest but don't relate to a specific quantity. They were given as a recognition that God is in control of provision. The tithe on the other hand refers always to one-tenth of a whole, or ten percent out of a hundred. It is taken from the wealth increase (income, profit), thus from the newly added part that wasn't there before.

2. Old Testament

The tithe is first mentioned in *Gen 14:20*. Abram was returning home from a successful rescue operation in which he had recovered his nephew Lot, Lot's possessions, the women and all the other people from the hands of marauders. It was there that Melchizedek, the king of Salem, who served God as a priest, met and blessed him in the Name of the Lord. At that Abram gave 10% of everything he had seized from the enemy kings to Melchizedek. As the story about Abram-turned-Abraham progresses we never ever read anything about a tithe anymore.

- CONCLUSION – Here the tithe was given only once from war booty.

The tithe is mentioned next in *Gen 28:22*. On his flight from his brother Esau, Jacob had to spent a night outdoors, in the course of which he had an amazing encounter with God. At that Jacob promised to give God 10% of everything He would bless him with, provided God would be with him and take care of all his needs on his journey.

- CONCLUSION – Jacob's vow to give the tithe was conditional. God had to fulfil Jacob's demands, otherwise he didn't have to tithe.

The next occurrence of the tithe is some 430 years after Abraham, in the context of the Mosaic Law. Here it becomes a regular payment for the first time *(Lev 27; Num 18; Deut 12, 14, 26)*. However, the Mosaic Law talks about three different tithes. The first is given continuously for the Levites and priests. The second is reserved for one's own family and is due once a year. And the third is set aside for the poor, widows, orphans, and foreigners, and is due every third year.

- CONCLUSION – Broken down into a monthly tithe, the Israelites had to pay 23.3% of their increase.

The entire passage on tithing in *Mal 3:8-12*, the last book of what we know as the Old Testament, is particularly drastic and challenging for any reader. God's people are warned that they are thieves and live under a curse (the power to fail) when they are not tithing. On the other hand, faithful tithing brings food into God's house, leading to blessings and protection for the giver.

3. New Testament

The NT begins with the four Gospels, i.e., records of Jesus' life and ministry on earth. Till Jesus' death, resurrection and ascension at the end of the Gospels, even the Gospels are set in an OT context. This is because a testament (or will; here the one of Jesus Christ) becomes effective only after death (see also *Heb 9:16-17*). Thus the NT only really starts with the book of *Acts*.

Of the few references to tithing, all but one are found in the Gospels, thus still in OT context. They are used in conjunction with a severe admonition of the Pharisees, the teachers of the OT Law that includes tithing. In *Matt 23:23* and *Luke 11:42* Jesus rebukes them severely that tithing is irrelevant if the more important matters of justice, mercy, faithfulness and the love of God are neglected. *Luke 18:10-13* accounts the self-righteous prayer of a Pharisee that includes a reference to tithing.

The only passage relating to the tithe outside the Gospels is found in *Heb 7:1-10* where Melchizedek's priesthood is explained. It is here that Abraham is mentioned as the first giver of a tithe, but his offspring (the Levites) also as the recipients. *Heb 7:11-8:7* though goes on to explain, why the old covenant (which included the Levitical priesthood and the law) needed to be replaced by a better and superior one through Jesus Christ. This also suggests that tithing, as part of the law, needed to be replaced by something better.

Bottom-line, it is difficult to deduct any clear instruction from this.

4. And Today?

The question of whether tithing is still applicable to us today occupies many and often leads to heated discussions and disputes. If we assume that tithing is valid for us today, then we have only OT references to define its application. But this creates a dilemma as the following questions highlight:

- Do we give, like Abraham, only once a tithe from a war booty? And then, what would a war booty in our modern day context be?
- Do we give, like Jacob, the tithe only if God fulfils our demands? And what should these demands be?
- Do we give, like the Israelites, a regular tithe on our financial gain? And if so, do we also give an average of 23.3% for the three different tithes, as laid down in the Mosaic Law?

Today we no longer follow the written law like Israel of old, but the Spirit of Truth, who leads us to live in a godly way. That includes financial giving.

Since everything belongs to God *(Psa 24:1; 1Cor 10:2; Col 1:15-19)* He has the right to decide on its use. Thus, the question, 'Do we have to tithe?' is the wrong question to ask. Why should we give God 10% when 100% belongs to Him anyway? From a stewardship position it's not about how much or little we must give to God to stay obedient. Rather how much of what He entrusted to us is for us, and what we must do with the rest. Only personal communication with Him will reveal this information. A statutory tithe does not do it justice.

5. Summary

In OT times, tithing was enshrined in the Mosaic Law as a reminder that God is the Provider of His people. Nothing has changed, the Lord still is Jehovah Jireh, our Provider today. However, with the Holy Spirit dwelling in us, the dynamics of acknowledging this have changed. We work on the law written on our hearts. From within the Holy Spirit is leading us into a God-pleasing lifestyle as faithful stewards of everything He has entrusted to us. That's not limited to a fixed percentage on our wealth increase.

Offering

Offerings, the other form of giving taught in churches, are much less questioned than tithing. That may be because it is a voluntary, irregular contribution and not a regular payment of a fixed percentage.

1. What is an offering and what not?

An offering is neither a tithe nor the 'firstfruits'. Depending on its context, an offering can be something that is always very clearly defined for a specific purpose (OT), or it can be completely undefined and given in response to God's prompting (OT and NT).

2. **Old Testament**

   References to offerings abound in the OT (675x), but they have very little to do with the giving-concept taught in most churches today. The Torah (first five books of the Bible) has the by far largest contingent (83.5%) of passages on offerings. We can derive a list of voluntary or mandatory sacrifices as part of the Mosaic Law from it. Even in all other OT books almost all references to offerings allude to those sacrificial laws (burnt offering, meal or grain offering, peace or fellowship offering, sin and guilt offering, etc.). They define precisely what has to be given when, by whom, and for what purpose. These sacrificial laws were fulfilled through Jesus and are therefore obsolete today.

   But there are OT passages that come close to the current church definition of offerings (to give for specific purposes). They always include elements of gratefulness towards the Lord *(Ex 36:3-7; 1Chr 21:24; Ezra 8:28)*, **generosity** *(Deut 15:14; 2Chr 7:5)*, **and voluntariness** *(Ex 35:5, Psa 37:21; Ezra 8:28)*.

3. **New Testament**

   The law of Moses was unable to save us because of the weakness of our sinful nature. So God did what the law could not do. He sent his own Son in a body like the bodies we sinners have. And in that body God declared an end to sin's control over us by giving his Son as a sacrifice for our sins. He did this so that the just requirement of the law would be fully satisfied for us, who no longer follow our sinful nature but instead follow the Spirit. (Rom 8:3-4, NLT-SE)

   Since the sacrificial OT offerings have become obsolete, we find almost no such requests and references in the NT, except

   - in direct allusion to Jesus *(Eph 5:2; Heb 10:5-7)*,
   - in connection with Jews, who, of course, were still living based on the Mosaic Law *(Matt 5:23; Acts 21:26; Heb 13:11)*,
   - or from the mouth of Paul about himself, who understood that his own life as a follower of Christ has to be sacrificial *(Phil 2:17; 2Tim 4:6)*.

   All other mention of offerings are either a direct hint that our lives will have to be sacrificial, too *(John 16:2; Rom 15:16; 1Pet 2:5)*, or they refer to financial/material support for others *(Acts 10:4; 2Cor 8:19; Phil 4:18)*.

4. Summary

All we have belongs to God *(1Cor 10:26)*, not us, which gives Him the right to decide on the use. So is today's teaching on offerings, as we hear it taught in churches up and down the country, biblical?

Despite *Acts 10:4; 2Cor 8:19;* and *Phil 4:18* talking about financial offerings, a biblical teaching on offering would never be a mere appeal to give money. It would be an appeal to a sacrificial life in every way, poured out for the purposes of God's Kingdom, just as Jesus did and asked us to do as well *(Matt 10:38; 16:24; Mark 8:34; Luke 9:23; John 11:26)*.

It would be liberating if the churches would teach the subject on giving from a true Kingdom perspective rather than monetary self-interest. There would be no reason anymore to force and manipulate believers to give. There is no biblical grounds for that practice anyway *(2Cor 9:7)*.

A Generous (Giving) Lifestyle

Somewhere during the last 1900+ years, the church has lost its financial compass. She started with a dynamic, voluntary, relationship-based support system that propelled God's Kingdom. Today, however, in their efforts to transform the world, most churches are run financially just like secular businesses using world system methods. It does not work. At least not as expected.

> *Give, and it will be given to you. A good measure, pressed down, shaken together and running over, will be poured into your lap. For with the measure you use, it will be measured to you. (Luke 6:38)*

A pastor had the ushers collect the tithes and offerings as usual. All baskets were emptied in a drum at the back of the church, which was then brought to the front and placed next to the pulpit. As the pastor began to preach on giving, he set the tithes and offerings in the drum alight. Shocked, some people jumped from their seats and angrily asked to know why he was doing this with their money. And that's exactly the point this pastor wanted to bring across: believers give from their entrusted finances, but with strings attached. They don't really release it, as they still want to have a say in what is happening with it (this is not to be mixed up with giving for a specific purpose). It must have been quite an embarrassing experience for those people, especially after the pastor revealed that the drum with the real money was secretly swapped with a similar drum prepared for this demonstration beforehand.

But remember the LORD your God, for it is he who gives you the ability to produce wealth, and so confirms his covenant, which he swore to your forefathers, as it is today. (Deut 8:18)

Once, the devil was approaching Jesus about the price for a person's life (perhaps mine or yours). He reasoned with himself, 'If I ask too much then Jesus will decline and I will have missed a great chance to become richer. Conversely, if I ask too little I might loose out on a good deal.' So he proposed a price of $150,000 to the Lord. But Jesus declined. Afraid that, indeed, he had gone too high Satan quickly lowered his offer to $100,000. But the Lord declined again. Perturbed and somewhat desperate, the devil asked Jesus how much He then was willing to pay, to which the Lord replied, 'Everything!'

This fictional story conveys biblical truth. For the devil we are neither important nor valuable. On the contrary, we will be quickly 'disposed of' if it is beneficial for him. But for Jesus we are everything. We are so important and valuable to Him that He rather 'disposed of' Himself to save and protect us than vice versa.

You can't be more generous than giving your life as the ultimate price for those who don't deserve it, can you? Considering such generosity on the side of our Lord and Saviour we may have to reconsider our own attitude. Are not we acting in exactly the opposite spirit as believers, when we, in our stinginess, try to find out how little we can give to still be considered obedient? Of course, a generous lifestyle expresses itself not only in financial giving, but our money dealings speak volumes about our heart attitude and true allegiance *(Matt 6:21, 24; Luke 12:34; 16:31)*. God desires us to give generously according to our ability to give, and to give cheerfully from the depth of our hearts. This may well be less or significantly more than a tenth or any other predefined percentage.

Remember this: Whoever sows sparingly will also reap sparingly, and whoever sows generously will also reap generously. Each of you should give what you haves decided in your heart to give, not reluctantly or under compulsion, for God loves a cheerful giver. (2Cor 9:6-7)

The above reminder reveals some interesting aspects relevant to us, too:

- Giving is not limited to a specific, legally prescribed percentage; we should be generous *(V6)*.
- We decide (guided by the Holy Spirits' soft, gentle voice in our hearts) what and how much we give, not the law or anyone else *(V7)*.

- We should never give reluctantly, but freely; giving ought to be an enjoyable experience *(V7)*.
- We should not give under compulsion; nobody should force us to give *(V7)*.

If our lifestyles are to be by generous, then we need to know what generosity actually means. Generosity is defined as 'having or showing a willingness to give money, help, or time freely (without strings attached) in great measure'.

Hence our challenge here in this book's context is to give money freely (without strings attached) and in great measure. It is the exact opposite of the world's approach of sharing as little as possible to avoid running out of funds. Not surprisingly, in contrast to this human logic, the Bible teaches that generous giving will even bring us success:

Good will come to those who are generous and lend freely, who conduct their affairs with justice. (Psa 112:5)

A generous man will prosper; he who refreshes others will himself be refreshed. (Prov 11:25, NIV 1984)

The generous will themselves be blessed, for they share their food with the poor. (Prov 22:9)

Don't I have the right to do what I want with my own money? Or are you envious because I am generous? (Matt 20:15 — from the parable of the workers in the vineyard*)*

Money has no lasting value, if it even has value at all. We can't take it with us into eternity, but what we do with it can have eternal effects.

Teach those who are rich in this world not to be proud and not to trust in their money, which is so unreliable. Their trust should be in God, who richly gives us all we need for our enjoyment. Tell them to use their money to do good. They should be rich in good works and generous to those in need, always being ready to share with others. By doing this they will be storing up their treasure as a good foundation for the future so that they may experience true life. (1Tim 6:17-19, NLT-SE — from Paul's charge to his spiritual son Timothy*)*

Money should be used to build the eternal Kingdom of God instead of building our own 'little private kingdom' here on this fallen planet. First, private kingdoms don't tend to last long. Second, we simply don't know who will ultimately inherit and perhaps even spoil and corrupt what we have gathered and built *(Psa 39:6, 127:2; Luke 12:20)*.

The following Scriptures should be a wake-up call for us, as they underscore the common practice of today, where generosity just goes as far as our own front door. The bigger picture that includes others is hardly considered. Consequently, they are in stark contrast to God's instructions to His people.

When you ask, you do not receive, because you ask with wrong motives, that you may spend what you get on your pleasures. (James 4:3)

Now listen, you rich people, weep and wail because of the misery that is coming upon you. Your wealth has rotted, and moths have eaten your clothes. Your gold and silver are corroded. Their corrosion will testify against you and eat your flesh like fire. You have hoarded wealth in the last days. Look! The wages you failed to pay the workers who mowed your fields are crying out against you. The cries of the harvesters have reached the ears of the Lord Almighty. You have lived on earth in luxury and self-indulgence. You have fattened yourselves in the day of slaughter. You have condemned and murdered innocent one, who was not opposing you. (James 5:1-6)

If we as stewards are determined to use God's entrusted resources according to His instructions, a generous lifestyle should become natural and easy. If we can slowly but surely adopt an open-handed lifestyle, discussions about tithing or donations will become superfluous. If we really allow God to tell us what to do with His property, stinginess, greed, etc. will no longer be an issue.

It's Not About Stuff

Looking for example at the extremely generous contributions for the tabernacle, the ark of the covenant, and all the other artefacts, or the temple in Jerusalem with all its magnificent interior, could lead to this assumption: The contribution of huge sums of money to build churches and to buy furniture and equipment is still biblically justified today. But that's wrong as we no longer need designated places and means to meeting together with God. Since God now lives in us through the Holy Spirit, each believer is God's temple *(1Cor 3:16)*.

Therefore, the emphasis for our generosity cannot lie in financing dead buildings, structures, furniture, equipment, cars, planes, and stuff. Sadly, Christian leaders around the world are tirelessly harassing believers to generously give for just that. This is in stark contrast to the way the early church lived and operated. The believers then were indifferent to buildings and items but very concerned about helping people in need and bringing them the Gospel.

It's About People

The underprivileged, deprived, disadvantaged, the poor and needy tend to suffer immensely because the resources that would help them to get even the bare necessities are rather spent on dead buildings and structures. Giving towards physical stuff isn't wrong per se, but it should never be our main emphasis. Buildings and material goods are not really that important to God, yet people are and what truly benefits them. Jesus didn't come to build a worldly kingdom with lifeless materials but God's Kingdom with living stones *(1Pet 2:5)*. Thus our focus must be people, people, people.

> *The Spirit of the Lord [is] upon Me, because He has anointed Me [the Anointed One, the Messiah] to preach the good news (the Gospel) to the poor; He has sent Me to announce release to the captives and recovery of sight to the blind, to send forth as delivered those who are oppressed [who are downtrodden, bruised, crushed, and broken down by calamity]. (Luke 4:18, AMP)*

The destruction of Sodom is credited to the arrogance and sexual perversion of its inhabitants. However, few people know that the root of their sexual sin was their refusal to help the poor and needy in spite of their material wealth, abundance and ease of life *(Ezek 16:49-50)*. That should make us think.

Jesus left no doubt that helping the poor and needy is more valuable than keeping all possessions for ourselves, its reward means storing up treasures in heaven *(Matt 19:21; Mark 10:21; Luke 12:33)*. Indeed, He sees our concern for the hungry, strangers, sick and imprisoned a service to Himself *(Matt 25:31-46)*.

God puts a strong emphasis on helping the most destitute *(Lev 19:9-10; Deut 15:1-11; 24:14, 19-21; Acts 10:4; Rom 15:26-27; 1Tim 6:17-19; James 2:6)*. He wants us to be personally involved in helping those in need *(Prov 31:9; Matt 6:2-3; Luke 14:13)*, probably because that keeps our hearts soft and humble. It's difficult to show 'agape', the selfless, active love, compassion and mercy without a face-to-face involvement, don't you think? Personal involvement does cost us something, whereas our handouts to readily available impersonal and corporate aid and support schemes are quite often just a means to ease our conscience.

> *If anyone has material possessions and sees a brother or sister in need but has no pity on them, how can the love of God be in that person? (1John 3:17)*

The Greek *theoreo*, translated here with 'see', means 'to see, look at, watch closely; perceive, experience', clearly indicating a personal involvement. But that doesn't mean we shout from the rooftops what we do and are involved in.

Be careful not to do your good works in public in order to attract attention. If you do, your Father in heaven will not reward you. So when you give to the poor, don't announce it with trumpet fanfare. This is what hypocrites do in the synagogues and on the streets in order to be praised by people. I can guarantee this truth: That will be their only reward. When you give to the poor, don't let your left hand know what your right hand is doing. Give your contributions privately. Your Father sees what you do in private. He will reward you. (Matt 6:1-4, GWORD)

Taking care of the poor and needy includes family members *(1Tim 5:4-21)* and results in the following:

(1) It honours God *(Prov 14:31)*,

(2) makes us complete and perfect *(Matt 19:21)*,

(3) leads to rewards or blessings *(Prov 19:17; Luke 14:13-14)*, and

(4) makes sure we won't lack anything *(Prov 28:27)*.

Summary

God doesn't want us to give routinely based on laws like in OT-times. Our loving and personal relationship with Him should make us good and faithful stewards, who use His entrusted resources for His glory and the betterment of His creation. He wants us to become generous, open-handed as much as He is. God's heart is for people, not for stuff. If we help those who can't help themselves or pay us back, we demonstrate that we live on His two foundational laws *(Matt 22:37-40)*.

> **Good will come to those who are generous** *and lend freely, who conduct their affairs with justice. (Psa 112:5, emphasis added)*

> *In everything I did, I showed you that by this kind of hard work we must help the weak, remembering the words the Lord Jesus himself said:* **'It is more blessed to give than to receive.'** *(Acts 20:35, emphasis added)*

56. Refund, Restitution

Refund

Whether we are responsible for large or small sums of money in the world, God seems to test our integrity in handling trifles to see if He can trust us to handle funds for His Kingdom. For example, if we get too much change at the till, what do we do with it, especially if it's only a few cent? Remember?

> *Whoever can be trusted with very little can also be trusted with much, and whoever is dishonest with very little will also be dishonest with much. So if you have not been trustworthy in handling worldly wealth, who will trust you with true riches? And if you have not been trustworthy with someone else's property, who will give you property of your own? (Luke 16:10-12, emphasis added)*

The few cents that we consider negligible may be not as unimportant to God as we believe, because principle is principle. It has no respect for persons and also no regard for sums. The way we handle trivial amounts that others may not even notice provides God with valuable details about our character and obedience, and the resulting qualification to deal with larger things.

Perhaps you know the movie 'The Family Man'? It's a really nice story that shows how empty and pointless the hunt for money is compared to a life with family. In one of the scenes, a man (an angel sent to show the main character what he really misses in life) stands behind the cash register of a small grocery store. A girl approaches to pay something small with a $1-note. Intentionally, the angel gives her change on a $10-note to see her response. First, the girl is baffled and deep in thought about what to do with the too much change. But then she takes it all and leaves the shop without comment. This prompts the angel to note to the main character, 'Did you see that? It all boils down to character.'

Yes, it all boils down to character. How often have we returned or kept too much change? How many times have we overcharged others without refunding it? How often have we been involved in injustice and not rectified it? What's the state of our character? Do we belong to those who take advantage of the innocence, kindheartedness or credulousness of people and punish them this way for their trust in us? Would we like to be treated this way? Or would we prefer people to treat us with honesty and integrity?

> *Do to others as you would have them do to you. (Luke 6:31)*

To refund means 'to repay', and 'to return in payment or compensation what has been taken', and 'to restore the remainder', and 'to return money to somebody, because he or she paid too much or did not receive what was paid for'.

God's financial standards are quite different from the secular ones. The world might say that on a larger scale things will balance out. But God expects us to do financial transactions with a serious commitment to righteousness and honesty (see topics '62. Integrity, Transparency' and '63. Honesty'). He requires us to live up to His principle of refunding what was overcharged or wrongly taken *(Prov 3:27-28, Lev 25:27, 51-52)*. In fact, if we know we have received too much change or have overcharged and don't make this right, we are stealing, thus violating the 8th commandment *(Ex 20:15; Deut 5:15; Matt 19:18; Rom 13:9)*.

Restitution

Restitution means 'to return something to its rightful owner', and 'compensation for a loss, damage, or injury'.

Restitution goes beyond mere refunding as it not only refunds the original loss but also compensates for the negative consequences of it. *Luke 19:1-10* is a good biblical reference here. It's the narrative of tax collector Zacchaeus meeting Jesus. Being visited by the righteous Son of God must have had a massive impact on this unrighteous customs officer. Because he immediately pledged to give half of his possessions to the poor and repay anyone he had cheated on anything fourfold.

In those days, tax collectors had to secure a certain area in which and for which they could collect taxes. For that they had to agree to pay a certain amount of all the tax collections to the Roman occupying powers. It was common for those toll-keepers to shamelessly exploit and heavily fleece the traders that either had to pass through or needed to enter their collection area for their trading activities. So when Zacchaeus announced his restitution, we can safely assume that it must have cost him everything he had justly and unjustly accumulated until then.

> *And Samuel said to all Israel, I have listened to you in all that you have said to me and have made a king over you. And now, behold, the king walks before you. And I am old and grey, and behold, my sons are with you. And I have walked before you from my childhood to this day. Here I am; testify against me before the Lord and Saul His anointed. Whose ox or donkey have I taken? Or whom have I defrauded or oppressed? Or from whose hand have I received any bribe to blind my eyes?* **Tell me and I will restore it to you** *[make restitution; GH]. (1Sam 12:1-3, AMP, emphasis added)*

The principle of restitution is part of God's training program for us as described in *Luke 16:12*, so we do well developing an attitude like Samuel was displaying here.

And again, the 8th commandment, *'you shall not steal' (Ex 20:15; Deut 5:15; Luke 18:20; Rom 13:9)*, is as relevant in this context as is *Exodus 22*, which speaks of restitution. Scriptures like *Luke 3:14* (John's exhortation not to get money by dishonest means) and *Rom 13:7-9* (Paul's invocation to give others what is due to them) must also find consideration in this regard.

We can state that if we refuse to provide any necessary refund or restitution, we treat our relationship with neighbour and God with contempt.

57. Inheritance

In OT times most people were poor and lived at a subsistence level. Thus leaving an inheritance (normally land) was vital to enable the following generation(s) to continue farming and raise livestock, without getting enslaved. The distribution of the inheritance was executed like this: usually daughters did not receive land, for they commonly lived with their parents until they married, after which they benefitted from their husband's land; but all sons received an equal portion of land except the firstborn son who got double *(Deut 21:17)*; only if there were no sons, daughters would inherit; with no daughters the brothers of the deceased would be in line; with no brothers the nearest relative would inherit *(Num 27:1-11)*. Ultimately, even if land was sold at some stage, it remained in the family line as it reverted to them in the year of Jubilee, when all debts were cancelled. All this is background to the following Scriptures:

> *Good people leave an inheritance to their grandchildren [...] (Prov 13:22, NLT-SE)*

> *Houses and wealth are inherited from parents, [...]. (Prov 19:14)*

If we wanted to derive a law from the above to be adhered to today, we'd also need to follow the biblical distribution pattern, i.e., giving only to sons and to the oldest one a double portion, etc.. However, whilst especially in the subsistence/small scale farming sector land is still passed on to the next generation, it's fair to say that biblical inheritance patterns are generally not followed at all.

The reason may be that, especially in industrial countries, the entire economical landscape has changed leading to a different inheritance approach. Most people have no land and those who still have, rarely own productive grounds. Children tend to leave their parents early and seldom carry on with the family business, if there is one. They move to economic hubs where they build their own careers and mostly become financially independent. When they inherit real estate, these are typically sold. It provides a windfall for them that is not necessarily needed but welcomed to improve the living standard. The family property, however, is gone.

So what's a biblical approach to inheritance then today?

I have seen a grievous evil under the sun: wealth hoarded to the harm of its owners, or wealth lost through some misfortune, so that when they have children there is nothing left for them to inherit. (Eccl 5:13-14)

Someone in the crowd said to him, "Teacher, tell my brother to divide the inheritance with me." Jesus replied, "Man, who appointed me a judge or an arbiter between you?" Then he said to them, "Watch out! Be on your guard against all kinds of greed; life does not consist in an abundance of possessions." (Luke 12:13-15)

Both Scriptures hint at the importance to handle wealth correctly, which applies to both parents and children.

To be clear, there is nothing wrong with leaving a material or financial inheritance to our children, if we are able to. Likewise, we also decide on the time of transfer. However, the parable of the Prodigal Son *(Luke 15:11-31)* shows that there are no guarantees as to how the children will see their inheritance (older son) or use it (younger son).

The question is, have we prepared our children for handling it well? Teaching and demonstrating the biblical approach to money is a vital part of the heritage that parents should give to their children. It is even more important than material wealth itself as it may prevent the child's destruction by money *(1Tim 6:10, 2Tim 3:2, Heb 13:5)*.

For Christians, every inheritance remains the property of God and must therefore continue to be administered in His interest. Only the trustee has changed. Thus, parents need to teach their children what good stewardship means, and be an example what it means that you can't serve God and money at the same time *(Matt 6:24)*. Teaching God's principles and ways, imparting spiritual truth and wisdom, is an inheritance of eternal value in itself, and must never be underrated *(see Prov 1-7)*.

> "If you wish to leave much wealth to your children, leave them in God's care. Do not leave them riches, but virtue and skills. For if they have the confidence of riches, they will not mind anything besides, for they shall have the means of screening [hiding; GH] the wickedness of their ways in their abundant riches." (John Chrysostom, 347-407, Archbishop of Constantinople)

> "The easiest way for your children to learn about money is for you not to have any." (Katharine Whitehorn, British journalist, writer, and columnist)

Any financial inheritance is worthless, and usually wasted quickly, if the spiritual foundation for dealing with it properly isn't laid *(Prov 20:21)*. After all, a material inheritance cannot be taken to eternity, but a spiritual inheritance helps to determine how the heir will spend eternity. The most important and powerful inheritance parents can pass on to their children is to show by their own lives that God is an omnipresent reality; that He is trustworthy in every way including provision; that He is full of love, care, compassion and eagerly interested in His children's success and fulfilment. If parents fail to do this, they rob their kids of an inheritance of everlasting value.

58. Taxes

Taxes and levies are paid to finance the government and the public sector. They provide in return services to all people of the nation, such as education, welfare, health care, retirement, defence, infrastructure, programs to overcome poverty and inequality, etc. This constitutes an unbiblical outsourcing of mostly personal obligations to impersonal entities and institutions and comes at a heavy price tag.

Recently, media reported that on average Germans are now officially working the first half of the year for those taxes and levies before starting to create wealth for themselves. Fact is that in most countries such tributes have become so high that people feel deprived by the government and public sector. Though a typically complex tax distribution system tries to provide justice to everyone, there is still a permanent dissatisfaction with the use of these levies. So it's easy to see why people think it's their 'God-given' right to avoid as many of them as possible.

As a result, and probably also due to greed, tax evasion has shot up, especially among the big-earners and capital owners, but also in the financial, service and productive industry. Tax evasion is defined as 'an illegal activity in which a taxpayer seeks to hide taxable income or claims unauthorised tax deductions'. So based on the law of the land it's a criminal act and liable to prosecution.

There is nothing wrong with using laws that allow tax deduction, of course only if that does not violate the Word of God. In that case, we ought to obey God's commandment rather than the law of man *(Acts 5:29)*. For the fact that man legalises wrongs as right (e.g. abortion, simple and compound interest, different kinds of bribery, etc.), doesn't make them right to God *(Is 5:20; Eph 5:11)*.

While fabricating scenarios that allow legal tax deductions is a criminal offence in the world, it is unrighteous in God's eyes for it constitutes a lie, violating His 9th commandment *(Lev 19:11;* see also *Col 3:9)*.

The Pharisees tried to trap Jesus on the question of paying taxes. They thought if He confirmed that they were to pay taxes, the common people and the Zealots would turn against Him. And if Jesus said they shouldn't, it would be a sign of His open rebellion against the Roman occupying power. His answer, *'give to Caesar what belongs to Caesar' (Matt 25:21)*, was rather sidestepping the trap than giving a clear directive on paying taxes.

Elsewhere, just to avoid offending the authorities, Jesus paid temple tax to enter His Father's house *(Matt 17:24-27)*. Sounds absurd, but He did it. However, it was a 'religious', not a secular state tax. So it's hard to build a case pro or contra state taxes on this.

The apostles Paul and Peter gave the clearest indication that we must submit to our worldly authorities and therefore pay taxes, even if we disagree with them.

> *This is also why you pay taxes, for the authorities are God's servants, who give their full time to governing. Give to everyone what you owe them: If you owe taxes, pay taxes; if revenue, then revenue; if respect, then respect; if honour, then honour. (Paul in Rom 13:6-7)*

> *Submit yourselves for the Lord's sake to every human authority: whether to the emperor, as the supreme authority, or to governors, who are sent by him to punish those who do wrong and to commend those who do right. For it is God's will that by doing good you should silence the ignorant talk of foolish people. (Peter in 1Pet 2:13-15)*

In a God-pleasing set up like He laid out for His people at the time, we would not have to pay taxes, or very little at best, as most of today's tax-funded tasks would have been covered by extended families and the close-knit communities. Central government wouldn't be needed. However, since we are not living in such a setup (yet), we Christians should follow Paul's and Peter's advise.

Character

It is said that the way we behave when no one is looking shows our character.

"The best index to a person's character is how he treats people who can't do him any good, and how he treats people who can't fight back." (American advice columnist and radio show host Pauline Phillips aka Abigail Van Buren, 1918-2013)

The Character of a person is defined as 'the mental and moral qualities distinctive to that individual'. In the secular world, a person's character or moral qualities are practically always secondary. All that counts are professional qualification, competence and experience, for it's about getting a job done, no matter how. Large parts of this book show the negative effects of this.

Good character, i.e., good morals are considered a hinderance to the materialistic vision of the capitalistic world system. The burgeoning suspicion that things are wrong and harmful to many rather than beneficial is not always appreciated.

In a Kingdom economy it is exactly the opposite. Because it is relationship-based, character is of the essence. No one with a bad character can live based on the two basic laws of the kingdom, i.e., to love God and neighbour *(Matt 22:37-40)*.

So let's look at some character traits and their impact on a Kingdom economy.

59. Accountability

When Israel left Egypt, the Amalekites perfidiously attacked and destroyed their tired and exhausted rearguard, which consisted mainly of women, children and the old. Because of this God condemned the Amalekites to complete annihilation *(Deut 25:17-19)*. Round about 400 years later king Saul was ordered to enforce this sentence *(1Sam 15:2-3)*. Nothing belonging to them was to be left intact and no-one was to be left alive, not even their animals.

So Saul mustered his army to get this job done, but was not consequential in the execution. As happened before, his disobedience to the Lord showed.

> *When Samuel reached him, Saul said, "The LORD bless you! I have carried out the LORD's instructions." But Samuel said, "What then is this bleating of sheep in my ears? What is this lowing of cattle that I hear?" (1Sam 15:13-14)*

Saul and his army had not killed all the animals of the Amalekites. Slaughtering the healthy and strong sheep, goats, donkeys and cattle was, from an economical point of view, a total waste of resources and thus unreasonable. Yet it was part of what God ordered Saul to do and made him responsible for. When Samuel pointed to this blunder, Saul was quick to make excuses, saying

The soldiers brought them from the Amalekites; [...]. (1Sam 15:15)

Now that's remarkable. King Saul shifted the blame onto his soldiers, the very ones who were under his authority and had to follow his command. No wonder God regretted making him king *(1Sam 15:11)*. Blame shifting is a sign of weakness, a lack of backbone, and a refusal to act on the spiritual law of responsibility and accountability *(Matt 12:36; Luke 16:2; Rom 14:12; Heb 4:13; 1Pet 4:5)*.

But Saul wasn't finished, as he continued,

[...] they [the soldiers] spared the best of sheep and cattle to sacrifice to the Lord your God, but we totally destroyed the rest. (1Sam 15:15)

Again, that is truly amazing. Saul maintains that the soldiers are still to blame *("they spared the best of sheep and cattle")*. He excludes himself here, but then he includes himself in the totally-destroying-part *("but we totally destroyed the rest")*. And on top of it, he tries to sell Samuel the story that the only reason for taking the good and unblemished cattle and livestock was because they wanted to sacrifice them to the Lord.

This is schizophrenic argumentation as Saul literally said, 'the soldiers wanted to bless God by being disobedient'. No wonder God got angry.

But Samuel replied, "What is more pleasing to the LORD: your burnt offerings and sacrifices or your obedience to his voice? Listen! Obedience is better than sacrifice, and submission is better than offering the fat of rams. Rebellion is as sinful as witchcraft, and stubbornness as bad as worshiping idols. So because you have rejected the command of the LORD, he has rejected you as king." (1Sam 15:22-23, NLT-SE)

And that was the end of Saul's career. God removed His hand from him and the years that followed remain a very sad account of a once promising servant of God. Saul lost everything, his kingship, and his family, and in the end he took his own life prematurely.

For God will bring every deed into judgment, including every hidden thing, whether it is good or evil. (Eccl 12:14)

How can God work with somebody who refuses to be accountable or answerable for his own decisions and actions? It is easier for Him to work with somebody who is humble enough to admit his disobedience, like king David, than with somebody who is too proud for that and tries to find excuses, like king Saul. In a way, blame shifting-behaviour appears to resemble the lukewarmness of the Laodicean church that God finds disgusting *(Rev 3:14-22)*.

Sadly, lack of accountability is widespread theses days and permeates all spheres and levels of society. We are confronted with it on a daily basis in politics. We witnessed the devastating results in the world of finance when most perpetrators of the financial crisis refused to take responsibility for the financial mayhem they caused. At the moment it's visible in the car industry, where against all evidence especially German car makers deny a deliberate data manipulation resulting in the deception of their customers and national authorities. But that's just a very small part of the daily occurrences on that front.

It is very difficult to trust people that refuse to be accountable for their actions and decisions. How can we be sure that they do what they say and say what they do? Our 'yes' should remain a 'yes', our 'no' a 'no', and shouldn't change with the wind *(Matt 5:37; James 5:12)*.

Luke 16:10-12 points out that someone who can't be trusted with little, can't be trusted with much. Untrustworthy people can't handle money, spiritual wisdom, or other people's properties. The lack of or complete denial of accountability is a clear sign that you cannot trust a person. Those who refuse their accountability, don't value their relationship with God and destroy the foundation for a healthy relationship with others.

60. Corruption

The dictionary defines corruption as 'dishonest exploitation of power for personal gain', and 'loss of integrity, which means loss of the quality of being honest, incorrupt and morally upright, and loss of the condition of being whole and undivided', and 'immorality', and 'wickedness'.

Alas, this fairly clear definition is rarely interpreted the same in different cultures and societies. For example, the Western world considers nepotism to be corrupt, thus punishable by law. Yet in most African societies it is an accepted component of great import. No wonder that it is difficult to find a common basis for fighting corruption across cultures and societies. Moreover, corruption is today usually reduced to the first definition, i.e., in connection with power or money.

Only fools say in their hearts, "There is no God." They are corrupt, and their actions are evil; not one of them does good! **God** *looks down from heaven on the entire human race; he looks to see if anyone is truly wise, if anyone seeks God. But no, all have turned away; all have become corrupt. No one does good, not a single one! (Psa 53:1-3, NLT-SE, emphasis added)*

[…] as Scripture says, "Not one person has God's approval. No one understands. No one searches for God. Everyone has turned away. Together they have become rotten to the core. No one does anything good, not even one person. (Rom 3:10-12, GWORD)

From a biblical point of view the definition of corruption does not change with society or context. It is measured against God's absolutes that are valid all over the world, all the time, without respect for anyone. Hence, the biblical definition of corruption is wider and more comprehensive than the worldly one. Here is a (probably incomplete) listing of what the Word of God defines as corruption:

- **Idolatry** *(Deut 4:16, 25)*
- **Denying God's existence** *(Psa 14:1; 53:1)*
- **Doing bad** *(Psa 14:3; 53:3)*
- **Disobedience towards God** *(Deut 9:12; Is 1:4; Jer 2:21)*
- **Pollution of the land** *(Ezra 9:11)*
- **Destructive talk** *(Prov 4:24; 6:12; James 3:6; 2Pet 2:10)*
- **Destruction of wisdom** *(Ezek 28:17)*
- **Using Godliness for financial gain** *(1Tim 6:5)*
- **Promoting injustice** *(Prov 19:28; Judg 2:19)*
- **Destruction of good character** *(1Cor 15:33)*
- **Denying absolutes** *(Titus 1:15)*

As a matter of fact, everyone who lifts himself up against God, who denies God's existence and refuses to act on God's laws, decrees and principles, is corrupt. Everyone who is living and acting other than the way God created him for is corrupt. We are only whole and complete in connection with our Creator *(John 15:1-10)*. That's how we have been made. If we deny Him as our Maker and Lord, an integral part of our being is missing. We are not whole and complete anymore. We are divided and incomplete. We are corrupt.

Economic corruption finds its expression in a multitude of different ways: bribery, fraud, favouritism, self-enrichment at the cost of public funds, conflict of interest, influence peddling, misuse or abuse of government property, breach of secrecy, leaking of unauthorised or confidential information, gossiping, creating false claims or budgets, tax evasion, falsification of documents, obtaining goods or money under false pretence, extortion or blackmail, lying, stealing, cheating, blame shifting, cover up, nepotism, overworking, laziness, greed, debt, idolatry, and many more. In the further course of the book we will take a closer look at some of those.

Please note that most of these expressions have to do with personal financial gain. That makes sense as living without God forces us to take care of ourselves. We can't rely on our Creator's provision.

> *These people are springs without water and mists driven by a storm. Blackest darkness is reserved for them. For they mouth empty, boastful words and, by appealing to the lustful desires of the flesh, they entice people who are just escaping from those who live in error. They promise them freedom, while they themselves are slaves of depravity—for **"people are slaves to whatever has mastered them." If they have escaped the corruption of the world by knowing our Lord and Saviour Jesus Christ and are again entangled in it and are overcome, they are worse off at the end than they were at the beginning**. It would have been better for them not to have known the way of righteousness, than to have known it and then to turn their backs on the sacred command that was passed on to them. (2Pet 2:17-21, emphasis added)*

If, in a financial context, we can see corruption as an unjust means of personal enrichment, then we are already sensitised. As God's stewards we are to use everything entrusted to us for the glory of God and the betterment His creation. Corruption clearly violates this mandate and destroys the relationship base with God and neighbour.

61. Bribery

Bribery means 'giving money or some other incentive to persuade somebody to do something, especially something illegal or dishonest, that the individual would otherwise not do'. In reality, bribery happens both for legal and illegal activities. And it works in two directions, too. There are those who offer bribes and those who demand bribes. Both ways pervert justice, hence are corrupt.

A Price To Pay

Several days later Felix came with his wife Drusilla, who was Jewish. He sent for Paul and listened to him as he spoke about faith in Christ Jesus. As Paul talked about righteousness, self-control and the judgment to come, Felix was afraid and said, "That's enough for now! You may leave. When I find it convenient, I will send for you." **At the same time he was hoping that Paul would offer him a bribe, so he sent for him frequently and talked with him.** *When two years had passed, Felix was succeeded by Porcius Festus, but because Felix wanted to grant a favour to the Jews, he left Paul in prison. (Acts 24:24-27, emphasis added)*

A fascinating biblical account that is. Though Paul was unjustly imprisoned, the ruler kept him in jail hoping to be paid a bribe for releasing him. This went on for two whole years (!), yet Paul never succumbed to the bribe demand and, as a result, remained innocently imprisoned. He chose to suffer for righteousness sake rather than bribing his way from corrupt plots into freedom.

This account also depicts today's reality as those who refuse to pay bribes face disadvantages and suffer. Sadly, for many such a prospect is too high a price to pay. And so they capitulate to bribe demands, even if they hate it. Perhaps they don't realise that in this way they are accomplices in an ungodly, corrupt act.

[…] Do not accept a bribe, for a bribe blinds the eyes of the wise and twists the words of the innocent. (Deut 16:19)

The Bible leaves no doubt that Christians must make the same decision as Paul did when facing bribe demands. Otherwise they support an ungodly system of exploitation and perverting justice *(Ex 23:8; Deut 16:19-20, 27:25; Job 15:34-35; Prov 15:27, 17:23; Sirach 20:29)*.

Some Christians argue that without bribing they won't get access into a country, won't receive a passport, or this or that. Essentially they state that anything is justified to promote the Kingdom, even corruption. But this is a contradiction in terms and as stated by the above Scriptures believers must not act like that. Unrighteousness can't advance righteousness and injustice can't advance justice. Jesus refused to compromise righteousness for personal benefit. That's why we must follow this example.

Bribing God

We are warned not to try bribing God. Mmmhhhhh, how on earth can a person bribe God? Most likely by trying to buy His favour and approval when investing into churches and Kingdom projects.

Drug lords have tried to buy their way into the Kingdom by generously donating money to the church. Freemasons have financed whole church buildings. Corrupt business people, shamelessly exploiting their customers, have paid tithes and offerings to ease their conscience.

> *If one sacrifices ill-gotten goods, the offering is blemished; the gifts of the lawless are not acceptable. The Most High is not pleased with the offerings of the ungodly, nor for a multitude of sacrifices does he forgive sins. (Sirach 34:21-23, NRSV)*

Corrupt people and organisation may be able to buy their say and influence in governments and the economy with illegal money, but money can't buy God.

> *For the LORD your God is God of gods and Lord of lords, the great God, mighty and awesome, who shows no partiality and **accepts no bribes**. (Deut 10:17, emphasis added)*

> *Give to the Most High as he has given to you, and as generously as you can afford. For the Lord is the one who repays, and he will repay you sevenfold. **Do not offer him a bribe, for he will not accept it**; and do not rely on a dishonest sacrifice; for the Lord is the judge, and with him there is no partiality. (Sirach 35:12-15, NRSV, emphasis added)*

The issue isn't that God could be tempted to look away and accept corruption, because *James 1:13* tells us that God cannot be tempted. So this has more to do with the wrong heart attitude or motivation of the one who tries to blind God's eyes with a bribe (see also topic '64. Motivation').

Bribe Or Not?

National laws and regulations make it easy to conceal bribes as marketing or representation cost and such like. In some countries kickbacks can even be declared as tax deductibles. But that doesn't make illegal payments legal in God's eyes. Only in a world that is driven by financial gains, the end justifies the means.

There is no such approach in God's Kingdom. He looks at man's heart. Thus taking a customer out for lunch or an entertaining evening, becomes a bribe if there are strings attached or a hidden agenda. A relationship-based economy suffers from corrupted relationships, which is exactly what bribery results in.

As an aside, have you ever wondered how God pictured the large sums of money and gifts that ancient rulers from Israel and Judah paid to pagan rulers to buy their allegiance? The world may rate that as an ingenious, wise political move. But God? Can one buy true friendship and allegiance? What if the enemy tops the original gift and offer, as frequently reported in the annals of God's people? Isn't that exactly what defines bribery – buying favour?

Bad Results

No matter why bribes are paid or demanded, they always promote injustice, selfishness, inequality and unrighteousness. In his farewell speech to Israel *(1Sam 12)*, Samuel expressed the godly desire to make right, if they thought he had been involved in bribery. That's a good example to emulate if we have been involved such acts ourselves.

Conclusion

We shouldn't bribe at all for at least six good reasons:

1. We would lose our protection *(Psa 15:5; Is 33:15; Sirach 40:12)*
2. It's a matter of life and death *(Ezek 22:12; 2Macc 10:20)*
3. We would twist the truth *(Ex 23:8; Deut 16:19)*
4. Our hearts would be corrupted *(Job 36:18; Prov 17:8; Eccl 7:7)*
5. It perverts justice and brings injustice *(2Chr 19:7; Prov 29:4; Is 1:23; 5:23; Amos 5:12; Mic 3:11; 7:3; 3Macc 4:19; 4Macc 4:45f)*
6. It blinds the eyes of the wise *(Deut 16:19)*

62. Integrity, Transparency

"The United States brags about its political system, but the President says one thing during the election, something else when he takes office, something else at midterm and something else when he leaves." (Deng Xiaoping, 1904-1997, Chinese leader)

In our world today discerning truth from lies becomes increasingly difficult. Sure, discerning light (truth) from darkness (lies) has always been a problem since the Fall. But a flip side of technological advance today allows people to present and sell themselves much faster, more comprehensively and globally through media as someone they really are not. There is much more 'fake news' out there than we can perceive. This is called operating in darkness. Knowing the real face, true character and honest attitude of a person has become an enormous challenge. That should not be so, certainly not in God's Kingdom. God is very clear that His children should walk in integrity and transparency.

Integrity is 'the quality of being honest, incorrupt, and morally upright', and 'the condition of being whole or undivided'. God expects Christians to be people of integrity *(1Chr 29:17; Psa 51:6)*, i.e., living their life without pretence.

Transparency is 'the condition of being transparent', whereas 'being transparent' means 'allowing light to pass through so that objects behind can be distinctly seen'. God expects believers to live in the Light, so that Jesus can be seen in their life *(1Cor 11:1; Gal 3:27; Eph 5:1-2; 1Pet 2:12+21; 1John 2:6)*.

From a biblical viewpoint, integrity and transparency go hand in hand. Being real, without pretence, means being transparent and vice versa.

God Himself operates in the light, the devil in darkness. Transparency rules where light is. But in darkness the occult and obscurity rule, i.e., things are covered up, hidden. Jesus came as the Light into this world to expose the darkness and acted completely transparent. People may not always have understood Him, but He has never obscured His true intentions. Christians are light carriers *(Is 5:20; 1Th 5:5; 1John 1:6)* hence should expose darkness, too.

> *For you were once darkness, but now you are light in the Lord. Live as children of light. Have nothing to do with the fruitless deeds of darkness, but rather expose them. (Eph 5:8+11)*

> *You are the light of the world. A town built on a hill cannot be hidden. Neither do people light a lamp and put it under a bowl. Instead they put it on its stand, and it gives light to everyone in the house. In the same way, let your light shine before others, that they may see your good deeds and glorify your Father in heaven. (Matt 5:14-16)*

Jesus did not hold back when he exposed evil, wickedness, dishonesty and deceit in those who should know better.

> *Woe to you, teachers of the law and Pharisees, you hypocrites! You are like white-*

washed tombs, which look beautiful on the outside but on the inside are full of the bones of the dead and everything unclean. (Matt 23:27)

Now you Pharisees cleanse the outside of the cup and of the plate, but inside you yourselves are full of greed and robbery and extortion and malice and wickedness. You senseless (foolish, stupid) ones [acting without reflection or intelligence]! [...]. (Luke 11:39-40, AMP)

More than anyone, the Pharisees, the teachers of the Law of Moses, should have recognised Jesus as the Messiah they were waiting for. But first they failed to do so, and when they did after some time, they tried to cover up their blunder. They tried to maintain their good and holy appearance before the people, but inside they were as rotten and sinful as anyone. The outside didn't reflect the inside. That's the backdrop for Jesus' scathing attack on their hypocrisy *(esp. Matt 23)*.

A hypocrite is 'somebody who gives a false appearance of having admirable principles, beliefs or feelings'. So a hypocrite has no integrity. He deceives people, i.e., spreads fake news about himself. And this is exactly for which Jesus kept on rebuking them. As He threatened their false appearance they plotted to kill him.

King David was a man after God's own heart *(Acts 13:22)*, there was no pretence in him. Far from his predecessor king Saul, David was as he was, *'shepherding Israel with integrity of heart' (Psa 78:72)*. He was fully aware of his flaws and dependency on God's grace. He knew it was useless to pretend otherwise. Integrity doesn't mean that we are perfect, but we don't pretend we are.

Blessed are those whose lives have integrity, those who follow the teachings of the Lord. (Psa 119:1, GWORD)

The implication of the above Scripture is that those whose life has no integrity are cursed. Integrity therefore is a protection.

Let integrity and uprightness protect me, because my hope, Lord, is in you. (Psa 25:21)

God wants us to 'practice what we preach' *(Rom 2:17-24)*, unlike the Pharisees. Jesus Christ never changed his mind, reduced the weight of what He said, diluted the truth, wavered, swayed or retreated from his convictions. Hence He is called the Rock on which we can build and face all storms. We need to become like Him, reliable, sturdy, steadfast, immovable, solid, and indestructible.

Showing integrity may not be popular or easy, but it is crucial for keeping a right relationship with God. As people of integrity we can't associate with those who call themselves brothers and sisters in the Lord, but are knowingly doing wrong.

> *I wrote to you in my letter not to associate with sexually immoral people—not at all meaning the people of this world who are immoral, or the greedy and swindlers, or idolaters. In that case you would have to leave this world. But now I am writing to you that you must not associate with anyone who claims to be a brother or sister but is sexually immoral or greedy, an idolater or slanderer, a drunkard or swindler. Do not even eat with such people. What business is it of mine to judge those outside the church? Are you not to judge those inside? God will judge those outside. "Expel the wicked person from among you." (1Cor 5:9-13)*

An enemy to integrity is spiritual dishonesty. It's when sin is renamed to make it more acceptable or relieve the pain of violation. Here are a few examples:

- Adultery is called 'affair';
- Fornication is called 'living together';
- Homosexuals and lesbians live 'an alternative lifestyle';
- Stealing is called 'misappropriation of funds' or 'deferral of ownership';
- Hatred is regarded as 'inherited temper';
- Lying is called 'exaggeration';
- Pride is being 'his own man' or 'her own woman';
- Lust is labeled 'adult entertainment';
- Murder of unborn children is called 'removal of foetal tissue';
- Civil victims of war are called 'collateral damage'.

Though we are not born with integrity, we can become such people. Jacob didn't start off known for his integrity. He used an obvious weakness of his twin brother Esau to steal his birthright and then, helped by his mother, also stole the blessing of the firstborn. So he was forced to flee, hide and live with the ramifications of this for twenty years until he could be reconciled with Esau. But it took even much longer before we see him acting in integrity, at least based on what was recorded for us to read. During a famine Jacob sent his sons to Egypt to buy food. On their return the sons discovered that their money had been put back in their provision bags. So the next time Jacob sent them to Egypt to buy food, he gave them twice that amount to rectify the issue. That's proof of integrity *(Gen 43:12)*.

Psa 41:9-12 tells us that God upholds us in our integrity and sets us in His presence. What a promise. Here is a selection from a host of Scriptures that show how highly God regards integrity, but also reveal the antagonism it can cause.

> *Whoever walks in integrity walks securely, but whoever takes crooked paths will be found out. (Prov 10:9)*
>
> *The way of the LORD is a stronghold to those with integrity, but it destroys the wicked. (Prov 10:29, NLT-SE)*
>
> *Better a poor man who lives with integrity than a rich man who distorts right and wrong. (Prov 28:6, HCSBS)*
>
> *Bloodthirsty men hate a man of integrity and seek to kill the upright. (Prov 29:10)*
>
> *They hate the one who convicts the guilty at the city gate and despise the one who speaks with integrity. (Amos 5:10, HCSBS)*
>
> *Simply let your 'Yes' be 'Yes', and your 'No', 'No'; anything beyond this comes from the evil one. (Matt 5:37)*

Are we realising how much our fake appearance, our little so-called emergency lies and half-truths, our lack of commitment and reliability, our rebellion against God's morals, standards and principles, in short our masquerade to the outside world, really disqualifies us for handling God's resources?

> "A single lie destroys a whole reputation of integrity." (Balthasar Grecian, 1601-1658, Spanish Jesuit and baroque pose writer)

Integrity does not come cheap. In fact, it can cost us our life. The apocryphal book of *4 Maccabees 5-18* **gives us a horrid account of the potential cost for an uncompromising integrity. It's about the priest Eleazar and his martyrdom and a mother and her seven sons who are being tortured to death, all of them defying evil pressure to deny God. Only very few might have to pay that price but it is key for us to get our head around this question, 'Am I prepared to suffer rather than losing my integrity?'. Integrity does not just mean talking about trusting the Lord, but living it fully. If we want to become candidates for God's abundant provision, we should become people of integrity.**

> *The godly walk with integrity; blessed are their children who follow them. (Prov 20:7, NLT-SE)*
>
> *Moreover, it is required of stewards that they be found faithful. (1Cor 4:2, ESV)*

When we believe that we can get by without integrity in life, we effectively deny God's yardsticks for a divine character and risk our relationship with others. Because honestly, who likes the fake appearance in others?

63. Honesty

Honesty is 'truthfulness', i.e., 'adhering to the facts and reality of things'. So it's the exact opposite of various behaviours that are commonplace today and are often accepted as a valid means to economic, financial progress. Because God warns us not to behave that way *(Rom 12:2)*, we'll have a closer look at this.

Please note that all of the following ways of acting are very destructive to our relationships with our neighbours, therefore an expression of contempt, not love. They all represent an improper attempt for self-enrichment at the expense of others and are hence tools of darkness. Ergo they violate God's law to love our neighbours *(Lev 19:18; Mark 12:31+33)* and consequently are detrimental to our relationship with our Creator Himself.

Lying

Lying means 'to make an untrue statement with the intent to deceive', and 'to create a false and misleading impression'.

Some forms of lying have become fairly accepted in our societies. They are called 'white lies' or 'small lies' or 'emergency lies'. But they are still lies, even if they don't cover up serious wrongdoing. Fake news, a major topic these days, are lies, too, because anything that's not truth and fact-based falls into that category. Unlike man, God doesn't distinguish between lies to say what's acceptable and what not. His 9th commandment simply states, *'Do not lie' (Lev 19:11)*. So using any form of lies to deceive others to gain advantage, be it in private or professional context, violates God's directive.

God, being truth, cannot lie *(Num 23:19; Titus 1:2; Heb 6:18)*, but the devil does. In fact Jesus calls him the father of lies,

> *You belong to your father, the devil, and you want to carry out your father's desires. He was a murderer from the beginning, not holding to the truth, for there is no truth in him. When he lies, he speaks his native language, for he is a liar and the father of lies. (John 8:44)*

Thus, everyone who lies, regardless of the extent, reason and context, acts like a child of the devil, and must know that God hates lies *(Prov 6:16-17; 12:22)* and won't tolerate it *(Rom 1:18)*. To tell the truth isn't a suggestion but a command *(Psa 15:2; Zech 8:16; Eph 4:25)*. Truth is the bedrock of a Christian's relationship with God and others. Lies destroy that foundation.

Fraud, Cheating, Swindling

Fraud is 'a wrongful or criminal deception aiming to result in financial or personal gain'.

Cheating is 'to act dishonestly in order to win an advantage or profit', and 'to trick or deceive', and 'in a dishonest way prevent somebody from having something', but also 'to be unfaithful, especially in the context of marriage.

Swindling means 'to enrich yourself by fraud or deceit'.

So, save the specific definition of cheating concerning marital unfaithfulness, all three words are meaning more or less the same and thus are interchangeable.

> *Listen! The wages of the labourers who mowed your fields, which you kept back by fraud, cry out, and the cries of the harvesters have reached the ears of the Lord of hosts. (James 5:4, NRSV)*

Scriptures warnings against fraud, cheating and swindling are truly abundant *(Lev 6:2+4, 19:13, 35-36; 25:17+37; Num 26:52-54; Psa 55:11; Prov 10:2; 11:1; 13:11; 20:7+14+17; Ezek 18:18; Hos 7:1; Zeph 1:9; Amos 8:5; Mal 3:5; Acts 13:10; James 5:4; …)*. **But we want to focus on just three specific ones here:**

> *"Cursed is the cheat who promises to give a fine ram from his flock but then sacrifices a defective one to the Lord. For I am a great king," says the LORD of Heaven's Armies, "and my name is feared among the nations!" (Mal 1:14, NLT-SE)*

> *Should people cheat God? Yet you have cheated me! "But you ask, 'What do you mean? When did we ever cheat you?' "You have cheated me of the tithes and offerings due to me. You are under a curse, for your whole nation has been cheating me. (Mal 3:8-9, NLT-SE)*

> *The very fact that you have lawsuits among you means you have been completely defeated already. Why not rather be wronged? Why not rather be cheated? Instead you yourselves cheat and do wrong, and you do this to your brothers. Do you not know that the wicked will not inherit the Kingdom of God? (1Cor 6:7-9a)*

The first Scripture starts off quite threateningly with, *'cursed is the cheat'*. To curse means to empower to fail. Hence cheating God and others sets us up for failure.

The second passage tells how quickly we can cheat God. According to *Matt 25:40*, all that we do to God's children we do to Him. So cheating believers is cheating God.

The third passage talks about disputes between Christians who have cheated, defrauded and wronged each other. Cheating, defrauding and wronging each other is a bad testimony for Christians in itself. But taking each other to court for this is even worse. The Bible tells us to rather bear injustice and disadvantages *(1Cor 6:7-9)* instead of insisting on our rights. Because if we are driven by love and faithfulness *(Prov 3:3)* rather than by selfishness and disobedience then, *'[…] we will gain favour and a good name in the sight of God and man.' (Prov 3:4)* That is remarkable, isn't it?

Cheating/defrauding is commonplace today, but Christians mustn't take it lightly and brush it aside as too unimportant to deal with. Again, God hates it and thus doesn't tolerate it. It destroys our relationships with others, especially those we defraud our cheat. So if the Holy Spirit convicts us of cheating/defrauding, then we must make amends (see '56. Refund, Restitution'). A powerful case for that is the account of tax collector Zacchaeus *(Luke 19:1-10)*.

> *‹Later, at dinner,› Zacchaeus stood up and said to the Lord, "Lord, I'll give half of my property to the poor. I'll pay four times as much as I owe to those I have cheated in any way." Then Jesus said to Zacchaeus, "You and your family have been saved today. You've shown that you, too, are one of Abraham's descendants." (Luke 19:8-9, GWORD)*

God loves this kind of attitude and will wholeheartedly bless such a move.

Theft

The 8th commandment is unambiguous, *'You shall not steal' (Ex 20:15; Lev 19:11; Deut 5:15; Matt 19:18; Mark 10:19; Luke 18:20; Rom 13:9)*. The Hebrew word for stealing as used in *Ex 20:15* is *ganab* and both literally and figuratively means, 'to thieve; to deceive and carry away; to secretly bring away'.

Stealing means 'to take secretly without permission or legal right', or simply 'to take dishonestly'.

By definition you cannot borrow something from someone without this person's knowledge and permission. To borrow means asking the owner for permission to use something that is entrusted to that individual. If you don't ask, you steal. Even if you assume you would get permission but don't ask, you're still stealing. And we can't steal, thus violate one of God's commands and expect to be blessed by Him at the same time.

Theft can be very subtle and might not be recognised as such. Just listen to this:

> "Many go to work and steal from their bosses. They come to work late, take extra long lunch hours and go home early. They take home the pencils, paper, pens and paper clips that belong to the company, they make private copies on the boss's copy machine, private phone calls on the company's telephones and conduct personal business on company time. They steal time and materials, which should have been used productively for the company. These actions are no better than those of a thief who enters your home and takes your possessions because both result in the loss of goods that someone else has worked for to provide.

> "In an even broader sense, a thief is anyone who relies on the productiveness of another to provide for his needs because he is too lazy to meet them himself. If you are able to work and you're not working, you are stealing from those who are working. You're requiring them to provide what you could get for yourself if you worked. If you are eating but not working, or you are living in a house but not working, you are a thief. Taking the benefits of work without participating in the effort is theft.

> "Thus, a son who plays baseball all day then comes in and messes up the house his mother has spent all day cleaning is a thief. He has stolen her energy. Likewise, an adult child who is out of school, but lives at home, steals from his parents if he goes into the kitchen and eats from the pot that is on the stove without helping to provide what's in the pot." (Dr. Myles Munroe, 1954-2014, 'Releasing Your Potential', pg 138)

> "The Greek word for poor, as used by Jesus, is 'poucos', which means 'non-productivity'. That's what poverty is. To be poor doesn't mean you don't have anything. It means you aren't doing anything. Poverty is cured by hard work, not by stealing." (Dr. Myles Munroe, 1954-2014, ibid)

It's not unusual to justify such actions, possibly to silence the conscience. We can fool ourselves by doing this, but not God. Ultimately He will take us to account *(Rom 14:12; Heb 4:13; 1Pet 4:5)*. **So He instructs,**

Let the thief steal no more, but rather let him be industrious, making and honest living with his own hands, *so that he may be able to give to those in need. (Eph 4:28, AMP, emphasis added)*

Unjust overpricing of products and services, as well as artificial money creation (fiat money, fractional reserve banking, interest) results in unrighteous wealth transfer. This is as much theft as the physical robbery of other people's property. The apocryphal wisdom book *Sirach* even equates theft with murder:

Whoever builds a house with other people's money is like one who gathers stones for his burial mound. (Sirach 21:8, NRSV)

Like one who kills a son before his father's eyes is the person who offers a sacrifice from the property of the poor. The bread of the needy is the life of the poor; whoever deprives them of it is a murderer. To take away a neighbour's living is to commit murder; to deprive an employee of wages is to shed blood. (Sirach 34:24-27, NRSV)

Theft is an expression of God's apparent inability to provide for us and shows that we don't trust Him. Theft also ruins the trust base of our relationship with our neighbours, as no-one likes to keep a relationship with a person that robbed him.

Extortion (Blackmail)

Extortion or blackmail then goes a little further than plain stealing.

Extortion describes 'the crime of obtaining something such as money from somebody using illegal methods of persuasion', and 'the charging of an excessive amount of money for something', and 'the practice of obtaining something, especially money, through force or threats'.

Blackmail means 'demanding money from a person in return for not revealing compromising or injurious information about that person', and 'the use of threats or the manipulation of someone's feelings to force them to do something'.

The Bible condemns this practice, which is commonly used in the secular world system, albeit often cleverly disguised:

Do not take pride in extortion or take pride in stolen goods. (Psa 62:10)

Extortion turns a wise man into a fool, and a bribe corrupts the heart. (Eccl 7:7)

Will not all of them taunt him [the proud, arrogant, wicked person; GH] with ridicule and scorn, saying, 'Woe to him who piles up stolen goods and makes himself wealthy by extortion! How long must this go on?' (Hab 2:6)

Some other Scriptures to study on extortion are found in *Prov 1:10-19; Is 33:15-16; Jer 22:17; Ezek 18:18; 22:12, 29.*

> *Then some soldiers asked him, "And what should we do?" He replied, "Don't extort money and don't accuse people falsely—be content with your pay." (Luke 3:14)*

It is quite interesting that John the Baptist told the people, who came to him to be baptised, to restore economic justice and abstain from unrighteous ways of self-enrichment to express a godly way of living.

Exploitation

Exploitation is essentially in line with stealing and extortion as it means, 'the use of a situation or person in an unfair or selfish way', and 'the unfair benefit from the work of others, typically by overworking or underpaying them or not paying them at all'.

This predictably results in unrighteous gain for the one who exploits. At the end of the day, God speaks strongly out against exploitation *(Ex 22:21; Psa 146:7; Jer 22:3; Ezek 22:7, 29; James 2:6; 2Pet 2:3)* and even rates it equal to murder! Just listen to the following two accounts:

> *A rich person will exploit you if you can be of use to him, but if you are in need he will abandon you. If you own something, he will live with you; he will drain your resources without a qualm. When he needs you he will deceive you, and will smile at you and encourage you; he will speak to you kindly and say, "What do you need?" He will embarrass you with his delicacies, until he has drained you two or three times, and finally he will laugh at you. Should he see you afterwards, he will pass you by and shake his head at you. (Sirach 13:4-7, NRSV)*

> *Now listen, you rich people, weep and wail because of the misery that is coming on you. Your wealth has rotted, and moths have eaten your clothes. Your gold and silver are corroded. Their corrosion will testify against you and eat your flesh like fire. You have hoarded wealth in the last days. Look! The wages you failed to pay the workers who mowed your fields are crying out against you. The cries of the harvesters have reached the ears of the Lord Almighty. You have lived on earth in luxury and self-indulgence. You have fattened yourselves in the day of slaughter. You have condemned and murdered the innocent one, who was not opposing you. (James 5:1-6)*

As much as we would avoid entrusting thieves and those who exploit us with our financial affairs, God will certainly refrain from doing so. So, if we want to be candidates for God's blessing, we must stop blessing ourselves by illegally taking what we (not necessarily God) consider to be legitimately ours. If we want to bring about change to today's practices then the onus is on us to start walking the righteous road instead of waiting for others to do so first. This will certainly have positive implications for our relationship with other people and our Creator.

64. Motivation

The LORD's light penetrates the human spirit, exposing every hidden motive. (Prov 20:27, NLT-SE)

If I gave everything I have to the poor and even sacrificed my body, I could boast about it; but if I didn't love others, I would have gained nothing. (1Cor 13:3, NLT-SE)

A wide range of biblical accounts reveal people's heart, their inner driving force, motivation, ambition, or zeal. We read about the Pharisees trying to trap Jesus to justify their own legalistic and harsh treatment of others. And about the rich having such difficulty in letting their riches go. We meet sick people longing for healing and sinners looking for forgiveness and meaning in life. Sometimes motives are obvious, at other times they are concealed. We want to look at two examples here.

Freaky And Scary

When he arrived at the other side in the region of the Gadarenes, two demon-possessed men coming from the tombs met him. They were so violent that no one could pass that way. "What do you want with us, Son of God?" they shouted. "Have you come here to torture us before the appointed time?" Some distance from them a large herd of pigs was feeding. The demons begged Jesus, "If you drive us out, send us into the herd of pigs." He said to them, "Go!" So they came out and went into the pigs, and the whole herd rushed down the steep bank into the lake and died in the water. Those tending the pigs ran off, went into the town and reported all this, including what had happened to the demon-possessed men. Then the whole town went out to meet Jesus. And when they saw him, they pleaded with him to leave their region. (Matt 8:28-34)

This report, similarly narrated in *Mark 5* and *Luke 8*, reveals the heart attitude of those involved at that time, but also reflects the hearts of many people today. Undoubtedly, the people back then were terrified by what happened *(Luke)*. And undeniably, there was a heavy financial loss involved when the herd of about 2,000 pigs *(Mark)* drowned. Yet it wasn't Jesus who made the pigs jump down the cliff and drown. He only allowed the demons, which had tormented men (God's image) for too long already, to enter these ceremonially unclean animals.

Strange that people were not happy to have gotten rid of the aggressive and destructive force that harassed everyone. The loss of assets knocked out any celebration mood about the deliverance from demons. Financial loss killed the enthusiasm that people could now enter the cemetery without being harried. The culmination was peoples' rejection of Jesus – they beseeched Him to leave! God could have easily made up for that deficit had the people only welcomed His Son and embraced the Kingdom wholeheartedly. Sadly, He didn't get a chance.

Today it seems obvious that those people then were serving money rather than God. As somebody not being involved it's easy to come to that conclusion. But what would our reaction be in a similar situation, what would be more important to us? Seeing people free from eternal damnation or avoiding a great personal financial loss? The status of our society today shows that we are not any better.

The other account is from *Acts* and is about Ananias and Sapphira (see also '65. Greed'). It, too, narrates glaringly the destructive power of wrong motives.

First we read about Joseph, also called Barnabas (= son of encouragement), who sold one of his fields and brought the proceeds to the apostles' feet for them to use for the needy *(Acts 4:36-37)*. The beginning of the next chapter *(Acts 5:1-11)* describes that Ananias and Sapphira also sold some of their property to help the needy. But unlike Barnabas they kept part of the sales revenue for themselves and brought the rest to the apostles.

There's nothing wrong in keeping some of the money. Peter said, they could have even kept all of it. But they lied when they insisted it was the full sales proceeds they bought to the apostles. That cost them their lives. Instantly. We can assume that this event had enormous chastening effect on the motives of those who witnessed this in person and the church that heard about it. The couple wanted to look good and be highly regarded just like Barnabas, only without giving it all. Helping others wasn't their motivation, but their own ambition was.

What Is Driving Us?

God is looking for those sold out to His course. Radically. He is looking for those fired up and motivated to building His kingdom. Eternally. He is looking for those driven by His concern and love for people rather than any selfish ambitions.

If we want to find out whom we truly serve we must check our motivation. It's as simple as that. What's driving us, concern about ourselves, personal ambition? What comes first to our mind when we wake up in the morning and start getting ready for the day? What motivates us and keeps us going? Why we do what we are doing? Why are we involved in the business we are involved in? Why are we employed where we are employed? Why are we headed toward this or that?

Christians keep stressing that they want to make money to support the Kingdom of God. Sounds noble, unselfish, even kind of holy. But ask yourself,

- Does God really depend on us making money? – Creation happened without it, so why would He need it now?
- Are Christians staying true to their promise to invest the money they make into God's Kingdom? – History shows that this normally doesn't happen.
- Are moneymaking believers committed to keep on investing into the Kingdom if the money flow stops for some reason? – History testifies to the opposite.

So whom do Christians really serve then, above all? What is their true motivation for focussing on moneymaking businesses? Surely not the Kingdom? Our Lord is zealous and asks for our whole, undivided and full attention and dedication, and a radical shift from selfish (usually money-driven) ambitions to unselfish Kingdom affairs.

Love the Lord your God with all your heart and with all your soul and with all your mind and with all your strength. (Mark 12:30)

He [the Lord; GH] must increase in importance, while I must decrease in importance. (John 3:30, GWORD)

Both *Matt 6:24* and *Luke 16:13* clearly warn us that we cannot serve both God and money. Therefore, being motivated to make money for the Kingdom is a contradiction. In fact, an unrighteous dealing with money has the power to easily pull people away from God and destroy them. That's the exact opposite of what people profess they want to accomplish.

"If you make money your god, it will plague you like the devil." (Henry Fielding, 1707-1754, English novelist and dramatist)

For that reason a believer's highest priority, i.e., motivation in life must become the Kingdom of God. And the Kingdom is not about money but about God's eternal plans, which are always about people.

But seek first his Kingdom and his righteousness, and all these things will be given to you as well. (Matt 6:33, see also Luke 12:31)

God promises to take care of our every need, every day, when we seek His Kingdom (not ours) and His righteousness (not ours) before anything else in life. Hence, provision is secured if all we do is propelled by God's agenda (establishing His rule here) instead of our own moneymaking one.

We shouldn't be looking for jobs to make money to help the Lord out in financing His Kingdom. Instead we have to find out why God created us, what He purposed us for and how we can accomplish and fulfil our calling. In other words, it is not that we have to find a good job to build the Kingdom; we rather have to find our place in the Kingdom to do a good job. Put yet another way, we have to ask God what He wants us to be doing. And then we need to go about it in constant and close communication with Him.

Making money is a bad motivation for believers for if the driving force is money instead of God's affairs it's hard to enter His Kingdom *(Matt 19:23-24)*.

> "The man whose only pleasure in life is making money weighs less on the moral scale than an angleworm." (Josh Billings, 1818-1885, famous US writer)

Dependence on our destructive monetary system and its laws often forces us to act against God's laws and principles in order to make ends meet. Thus applying Kingdom principles and so trusting God to provide is a huge challenge to anyone. At the end of the day we must choose whom we trust, either God or the world.

But remember the LORD your God, for it is he who gives you the ability to produce wealth, and so confirms his covenant, which he swore to your forefathers, as it is today. (Deut 8:18)

When we ask God about our role in His Kingdom, we may end up doing the same work we did before and potentially enjoyed doing. However, now we have an entirely different motivation. We do it for God told us to. We've found purpose. Whatever it is we are called to do, it is about putting into practice the two basic laws of the Kingdom economy.

To love him with all your heart, with all your understanding and with all your strength, and to love your neighbour as yourself is more important than all burnt offerings and sacrifices." (Mark 12:33)

Do to others as you would have them do to you. (Luke 6:31)

From the outside, jobs can look all the same, but when it comes to decisions and actions, our motives make all the difference. It will quickly become clear why we are doing something, for ourselves and for money or for God and others.

Let's use a car dealer as an example. An unbeliever sells cars to make money. He doesn't care if people buy on credit. To sell, he is likely to tell anything that makes the customer buy. At times car dealers receive kickbacks from banks for securing credit deals. The prospect of additional income will motivate the trader to make customers to buy on credit instead of paying cash. The customer is only a means for the dealer's income.

If a Christian sells cars seeing that it's God's calling for him, then he can do it the Kingdom way. He can focus on what is good for his customers, not himself. He can be completely honest about the car and everything relating to it; no need for stories. Since debt enslaves *(Prov 22:7)*, thus breaches *Gal 5:1*, he can dissuade his customers to buy what they can't afford. He may lose out on a deal, but doesn't lure into evil, enslaving schemes (see '40. Borrowing And Lending').

To the secular mind such approach may be absurd, but from a Kingdom point of view the dealer may as well turn out to be a 'blessing in disguise'. Maybe he even becomes a long longed-for testimony for a caring salesman instead of the usually encountered rip-off and I-don't-really-care dealer.

Matt 6:33 and *Luke 12:31* motivate us to seek God's Kingdom first and act on His righteous precepts. Whether we do or not will reveal the level of trust we have in God's ability to provide.

Beneficial For The Kingdom?

As a general rule God gives, when it furthers His Kingdom, but withholds when our motives are wrong.

> *When you ask, you do not receive, because you ask with wrong motives, that you may spend what you get on your pleasures. (James 4:3, see also James 5:1-6a; 1Th 2:3-6)*

2 Maccabees gives vivid accounts of people who paid their way to become High Priest. They weren't religious leaders by calling but by bribing the authorities of the day. The sole purpose for this? Self-enrichment, but no real concern for God's people. Corrupt as they were they didn't carry any spiritual authority anyway.

> *[…] They have an unhealthy interest in controversies and quarrels about words that*

*result in envy, strife, malicious talk, evil suspicions constant friction between people of corrupt mind, who have been robbed of the truth and **who think that godliness is a means to financial gain**. (1Tim 6:4-5, emphasis added)*

When Simon saw that the Spirit was given at the laying on of the apostles' hands, he offered them money and said, "Give me also this ability so that everyone on whom I lay my hands may receive the Holy Spirit." Peter answered: "May your money perish with you, because you thought you could buy the gift of God with money! (Acts 8:18-20)

Conclusion

In a way it's fairly easy to fool other people about our true motives, at least for a while. But we won't be able to hoodwink the Lord about what is driving us. Not even for a single second. So why don't we allow the Lord to ignite and establish in us this driving force that is first and foremost concerned about the things of God. About issues of true and eternal value. About people and His eternal Kingdom. It would make us a great partner for God and we would be so much more fulfilled than we would ever be by running after worldly stuff.

65.   Greed

"You say, 'If I had a little more, I should be very satisfied.' You make a mistake. If you are not content with what you have, you would not be satisfied if it were doubled." (Charles H. Spurgeon, 1834-1892, famous British Baptist preacher)

The eye of the greedy person is not satisfied with his share; greedy injustice withers the soul. (Sirach 14:9, NRSV)

When we think of greed, we tend to think of the rich and famous, singers, sport and movie stars, bankers, corporate executives, corrupt politicians, and so forth. But greed is everywhere, permeates all areas of life, social classes, cultures, genders, beliefs and is independent of age.

Greed is the 'overwhelming desire to have more of something such as money than is actually needed'. Perhaps we all should ask ourselves every now and then, 'When last did we experience such desire and for what?'. The Bible warns a lot against greed. Here is a small selection of clear-cut statements from Scriptures:

A greedy man brings trouble to his family, [...]. (Prov 15:27)

From the least to the greatest, all are greedy for gain; prophets and priests alike, all practice deceit. (Jer 6:13)

Then he said to them, "Watch out! Be on your guard against all kinds of greed; a man's life does not consist in the abundance of his possessions." (Luke 12:15)

[...] the people of this world [...] are immoral, or the greedy and swindlers, or idolaters. [...] you must not associate with anyone who calls himself a brother but is sexually immoral or greedy, an idolater or a slanderer, a drunkard or a swindler. With such a man do not even eat. (1Cor 5:10-11)

But among you there must not be even a hint of sexual immorality, or of any kind of impurity, or of greed, because these are improper for God's holy people. [...] For of this you can be sure: No immoral, impure or greedy person — such a man is an idolater — has any inheritance in the kingdom of Christ and of God. (Eph 5:3+5)

Put to death, therefore, whatever belongs to your earthly nature: sexual immorality, impurity, lust, evil desires and greed, which is idolatry. (Col 3:5)

Sex, power and money, that's what is widely perceived to be the strongest driving forces in a person's life. People might have different opinions on the rank order, but money is certainly extremely commanding.

A rich man's wealth is his fortified city; (Prov 10:15a, HCSB)

No one can serve two masters; [...] . **You cannot serve God and mammon** *(deceitful riches, money, possessions, or whatever is trusted in). (Matt 6:24, AMP, emphasis added — see also Luke 16:13)*

The devil knows exactly about the power of money for He commands the spirit (mammon) behind it. Money is one of his strongest weapons to entice people to serve him rather than God. He literally controls people through their insatiable lust for money. It's called greed. Which is exactly why the Bible warns,

For the love of money is a root of all kinds of evil*. Some people, eager for money, have wandered from the faith and pierced themselves with many griefs. (1Tim 6:10, emphasis added)*

Keep your lives free from the love of money and be content with what you have*, because God has said, "Never will I leave you; never will I forsake you." (Heb 13:5, emphasis added)*

Believers are prone to greed as anyone. How does God perceive TV preachers, teachers, evangelists, apostles and whatever 'title' they carry, with all their wealth dangling on their arms and necks, etc? Why do they need to spend fortunes on big mansions, a fleet of cars, several airplanes, etc., when there are millions of people starving? Why do they fleece their audience for even more money to get more stuff? Isn't that a clear sign of greed, of being driven by the love of money?

> *Be shepherds of God's flock that is under your care, serving as overseers - not because you must, but because you are willing, as* **God wants you to be; not greedy for money but eager to serve**; *not lording it over those entrusted to you, but being examples to the flock. And when the Chief Shepherd appears, you will receive the crown of glory that will never fade away. (1Pet 5:2-4, emphasis added)*

The love of money promotes corrupt morals and perverted values. People start worshipping created things more than the Creator himself *(Rom 1:25)*. It is for this very reason that the devil tries to entice as many as possible in his schemes. He knows very well how useless and blinded we will be for the Kingdom once we fall for the overwhelming desire to have more of the stuff than we really need.

> *Do not store up for yourselves treasures on earth, where moth and rust destroy, and where thieves break in and steal. But store up for yourselves treasures in heaven, where moth and rust do not destroy, and where thieves do not break in and steal. For where your treasure is, there your heart will be as well. (Matt 6:19-21)*

In *Acts 5:1-10* we read the inglorious story of Ananias and Sapphira who wanted two things. They wanted to look good in the eyes of the church, and to double-cross the apostles with their greed. So like others before them they sold a piece of property to contribute to the wellbeing of the church. However, unlike those before them they didn't have the heart to lay the whole sales revenue at the apostles' feet. Yet they declared their reduced contribution as the full one. Greed made them lie to the Holy Spirit and that cost them their lives right then and there! It's hard to imagine the shock this incident caused in the church.

In his letter to Timothy Paul explains the destructive forces of greed quite plainly:

> *But godliness with contentment is great gain. For we brought nothing into the world, and we can take nothing out of it. But if we have food and clothing, we will be content with that. Those who want to get rich fall into temptation and a trap and into many foolish and harmful desires that plunge people into ruin and destruction.* **For the love of money is a root of all kinds of evil. Some people, eager for money, have wandered from the faith and pierced themselves with many griefs**. *(1Tim 6:6-10, emphasis added)*

Please note, it's not money that is bad or wrong or sinful as such or in itself (unless we talk about artificially created money, of course; see '7. Artificial Money Creation'). But Paul points out that the love of money is the real problem here, because it bears the danger of doing anything (evil) to get it. Which is precisely why the Bible considers it the root to all kinds of evil. The best way to break this love of money, this overwhelming desire of having more than needed, this spirit of greed, is by responding in the opposite spirit – through acts of generosity:

> Command those who are rich in this present world not to be arrogant nor to put their hope in wealth, which is so uncertain, but to put their hope in God, who richly provides us with everything for our enjoyment. Command them to do good, to be rich in good deeds, and to **be generous and willing to share. In this way they will lay up treasures for themselves as a firm foundation for the coming age (treasures in heaven)**, so that they may take hold of the life that is truly life. (1Tim 6:17-19, emphasis added)

The danger is to see greed solely as a problem of the greedy individual. But we cannot truly isolate its destructive nature and force from fellow men as the following vivid account proves. Innocent people suffer at the hands of corrupt individuals right unto death, simply because their leaders are so greedy that they rather let corruption prevail over justice. The following narrative is outrageous:

> Charges were brought against Menelaus about this incident. When the king came to Tyre, three men sent by the senate presented the case [about corrupt Menelaus; GH] before him [the king; GH]. But <u>Menelaus</u>, already as good as beaten, **promised a substantial bribe to Ptolemy** son of Dorymenes to win over the king. **Therefore Ptolemy**, taking the king aside into a colonnade as if for refreshment, **induced the king to change his mind. Menelaus, the cause of all the trouble, he** [the king; GH] **acquitted of the charges against him, while he** [the king; GH] **sentenced to death those unfortunate men**, who would have been freed uncondemned if they had pleaded even before Scythians. **And so those who had spoken for the city and villages and the holy vessels quickly suffered the unjust penalty**. Therefore even the Tyrians, showing their hatred of the crime, provided magnificently for their funeral. But **Menelaus, because of the greed of those in power, remained in office, growing in wickedness, having become the chief plotter against his compatriots**. (2Macc 4:43-50, NRSV, emphasis added)

The verdict is clear: greed is devastating, not only for the one who is greedy but also those (usually) innocent bystanders who suffer because of it. Logically, greed has no place in God's Kingdom.

66. Work Attitude

Avoiding Work (Laziness)

Naturally the working speed in hot climates is slower than in colder climates due to higher temperatures. Moreover, in contrast to cold climate people, hot climate people (e.g. South Europeans, South Americans, Africans, etc.) generally put greater value on relationships than on tasks and time. 'Time is money' does not have as high a priority as in colder climates because time is rather invested into relationships. Therefore seeing things working differently and slower in hot climate countries doesn't necessarily mean people are lazy.

Laziness is defined as 'being unwilling to do any work or make an effort', and 'contributing to an unwillingness to work or make an effort', and 'moving slowly'. So first of all, laziness is a question of attitude, regardless of where in the world we live. The Bible says,

> Lazy hands make a man poor, but diligent hands bring wealth. He who gathers crops in summer is a wise son, but he who sleeps during harvest is a disgraceful son. (Prov 10:4-5)

> As vinegar to the teeth and as smoke to the eyes, so is the sluggard to those who employ and send him. (Prov 10:26, AMP)

In his excellent booklet 'A Letter to Africa About Africa', **the late** Kasongo Munza (DR Congo) strikingly describes the context of African cultures and the resulting obstacles to development. He points out that one major obstruction to people is the perception that this world is only a temporary place. Consequently,

> "[…] it makes no sense to build good houses and roads in a place you will be occupying only temporarily. The concept of development is almost absent." (pg 13)

The Bible, also, makes clear that this planet in its current state is temporary and that we are only sojourners. However, there is concurrently a strong emphasis on maintaining this entrusted planet in pristine condition for our children to inherit. This requires active work and involvement.

Kasongo **then goes on to explain that many African proverbs agree in stating,**

"'This is how we received it; as we received it is how we have to leave it'. This includes style of life, housing, food, power, land or boundaries, and traditions. It is a taboo to try and change things."

Such mindset is indeed counterproductive and an open invitation to laziness. In many cultures the way family life is set up encourages the unwillingness to work. If one person in the extended family has paid work, the others see no need for it. Only if the breadwinner loses the job, someone else has to step in. After all, since everything in the house can be used by anyone who lives there, why work for things that you can have for free?

> *My child, do not lead the life of a beggar; it is better to die than to beg. When one looks to the table of another, one's way of life cannot be considered a life. One loses self-respect with another person's food, but one who is intelligent and well instructed guards against that. (Sirach 40:28-29, NRSV)*

Although the Bible undoubtedly calls for help for the needy, it does not tolerate laziness for healthy people who are able to work. On the contrary, Scriptures inform us about a host of penalties resulting from laziness, namely:

- **Hunger** *(Prov 13:4;19:3; 2Th 3:10)*
- **Isolation and shame** *(Prov 19:7; 2Th 3:6)*
- **Not be taken seriously because of all the excuses not to work** *(Prov 22:13)*
- **The inability to see the own need to get up and work** *(Prov 26:13)*
- **Increasing loss of ambition** *(Prov 6:6-11; 26:16)*
- **Desire to sleep** *(Prov 26:15)*
- **Inability to take pride in accomplishments since there are none** *(Prov 12:27)*
- **Slavery** *(Prov 12:24)*
- **Disqualification for handling money** *(Matt 25:26-28)*
- **Poverty, which is the cumulative result of the other penalties** *(Prov 6:10-11; 10:4; 14:23; 19:15; 20:13)*

Here is another great passage from the Bible that drives the principles home nicely. Yes, it's a long one, but it's very very worthwhile reading it in this context:

> *"Now we charge you, brethren, in the name and on the authority of our Lord Jesus Christ (the Messiah) that you **withdraw and keep away from every brother (fellow believer) who is slack in the performance of duty and is disorderly, living as a shirker** [idler, good-for-nothing; GH] and not walking in accord with the traditions*

*and instructions that you have received from us. For you yourselves know how it is necessary to **imitate our example, for** we were not disorderly or shirking of duty when we were with you [**we were not idle**]. **Nor did we eat anyone's bread without paying for it, but with toil and struggle we worked night and day, that we might not be a burden or impose on any of you** [for our support]. [It was] not because we do not have a right [to such support], but [**we wished**] **to make ourselves an example to follow**. For while we were yet with you, we gave you this rule and charge: **If anyone will not work, neither let him eat**. Indeed, we hear that **some among you are disorderly** [that they are passing their lives in idleness, neglectful of duty], **being busy with other people's affairs instead of their own and doing no work. Now we charge and exhort such person**s [as ministers in Him exhorting those] in the Lord Jesus Christ (the Messiah) **that they work in quietness and earn their own food and other necessities**. And as for you, brethren, do not become weary or lose heart in doing right [but continue in well-doing without weakening]. But if anyone [in the church] refuses to obey what we say in this letter, **take note of that person and do not associate with him, so that he may be ashamed**. Do not regard him as an enemy, but simply admonish and warn him as [being still] a brother." (2Th 3:6-15, AMP, emphasis added)*

Work is not God's punishment, rather,

It is a gift from God to be able to eat and drink and experience the good that comes from every kind of hard work. (Eccl 3:13, GWORD)

Wealth is produced by work and not by idleness, even if the secular world wants us to believe it ('let your money work for you'). To the extent people don't (want to) work, although they are capable, they don't create wealth. And those who don't create wealth become dependent on others for survival. They become a burden to others instead of being a blessing.

If you love sleep, you will end in poverty. Keep your eyes open, and there will be plenty to eat! (Prov 20:13, NLT-SE)

The late Dr. Myles Munroe **gave permission to use the following recording, which gives a good portrayal of people's attitude towards work. Where appropriate, I have added some Scriptures and two emphases:**

"Most people want a job but don't want to work. Nothing is as depressing and frustrating as having someone on a job that is not interested in working. God is more interested in your attitude towards work than in the status of your chequebook *(Matt 6:14)*. We make the mistake that we equate sin and work. Work does not exist because of sin but sin changed the conditions of work *(Gen*

3:17b-19). Work has to be seen as a blessing that reveals what you can do. When creating the world, God worked for six days and rested one *(Gen 2:2)*. He also instructed us to work six days and rest one *(Ex 23:12)*. Work always produces more personal growth and satisfaction than rest does. You can't run from work and expect to be happy. Work is the energy that keeps you alive. It's the stuff that gives life meaning. If you are unfulfilled you are probably resting too much.

"Just as a car runs on gasoline you run on work. God designed you to find satisfaction in looking at the fruit of your labor. That's why inactivity often brings depression and discouragement. You believe a lie if you think you can get something for nothing. You cannot fulfil your purpose without work. Through work God opens the door into your inner storehouse and teaches you how to use your talents and abilities to meet the many responsibilities of life.

"Have you ever noticed whom God uses? **God uses busy people**. When Jesus chose the first disciples he didn't go to the unemployed but fishermen who were busy working. God designed us to work. But we don't appreciate God's ways. We want results without the process. We seek promotion without responsibility. We desire pay without work. Even if no one ever pays you, your work profits you because you discover what you can do. **It is better to deserve an honour and not receive it than to receive an honour and not deserve it**. Work keeps you healthy, physically and emotionally. Poverty is cured by hard work. If you don't work you will end up begging. Look at the birds: God provides food for them, but they have to go and look for it. They have to dig and pull it out of the ground. So it is with you."

A 2015 study revealed that US workers squander more that two hours/day of their paid work for private stuff. It means $759 billion are paid in annual salary with no apparent productivity. The price of this non-productivity or laziness is passed on to consumers of the products and services through higher prices. Receiving pay for non-productivity is the same as receiving interest.

The secular world might accept much unrighteousness as a given necessity or an unavoidable evil, but God doesn't. The parable of the ten virgins in *Matt 25* makes it clear that access to the Kingdom is blocked for us if we want to profit from the diligence and readiness of others. We have to be ready and diligent ourselves. Jesus' statement in *Luke 12:47* sums it all up,

That servant who knows his master's will and does not get ready or does not do what his master wants will be beaten with many blows.

Whatever 'beaten with many blow' means, it sure doesn't sound appealing. The unwillingness to work (laziness) shows God that He can't count on us. That puts a strain on our relationship with Him. It also brings tension into our relationships with our neighbours because we expect them to take care of us, even though we could take care of ourselves.

Enslaved By Work (Workaholic)

Laziness marks the one side of the pendulum swing, working too much the other. If we look at the so-called developed nations (usually colder climates) there is an enormous pressure on people to perform. For many employees this results more often than not in long stressful workdays. The fear of losing their job makes them surrender to such enslaving demands.

Working too much is destructive to our body and since our body is the temple of the Holy Spirit *(1Cor 3:16-17)* we have no right to destroy a legal home for Christ. Working too much is also unhealthy for the relationships within the family and violates our role as stewards of our time, since work only falls into third place of priorities, after God and family. Working too much and too long normally keeps us from doing the really important things for God's Kingdom.

So hot climate people sacrifice a fair amount of Kingdom economy opportunities for relationships, while the colder climate people sacrifice relationships for tasks and work obligations. Both lack a healthy balance.

> *We are merely moving shadows, and all our busy rushing ends in nothing. We heap up wealth, not knowing who will spend it. (Psa 39:6, NLT-SE)*

> *If the Lord does not build the house, it is useless for the builders to work on it. If the Lord does not protect a city, it is useless for the guard to stay alert. It is useless to work hard for the food you eat by getting up early and going to bed late. The Lord gives food to those he loves while they sleep. (Psa 127:1-2, GWORD)*

People addicted to alcohol are called alcoholics. People addicted to work are called workaholics. Besides being forced to work long hours to avoid getting sacked, many workaholics work long hours for recognition or out of greed. Either way, the Bible tells us that we are slave to whatever controls us and we should check our motive as the price for that slavery might be too high.

> *A person is a slave to whatever he gives in to. (2Pet 2:19b, GWORD)*

> *And how do you benefit if you gain the whole world but lose your own soul in the*

process? (Mark 8:36, NLT)

Lets not forget the story of the prodigal son *(Luke 15:11-32)*. For most it is just a picture of how our benevolent heavenly Father welcomes us back into His arms and the sonship once we repent. But there is also the reaction of the older brother, who complained to his dad about how his younger brother squandered his inheritance. Why did he complain? Because he himself worked tirelessly (like workaholics do) but never received a welcome party like his brother did. His father's explanation that he really didn't have any grounds to be mad, because everything the father had belonged to him, his son, anyway, didn't really help that moment.

While avoiding work is covered with penalties, working too much for the wrong reason blinds us to the reality and robs us of many blessings, if not even our lives.

> *Don't work for food that spoils. Instead, work for the food that lasts into eternal life. (John 6:27a, GWORD)*

> *Whatever you do, work at it with all your heart, as working for the Lord, not for men. (Col 3:23)*

That's a straightforward statement, isn't it? In other words, God has to define the terms. He is our ultimate employer, even if He sends us to work for other people. If we try to enforce our own ways we shouldn't be surprised when God closes the tap of provision. If worldly employers have the right to caution employees for doing their own thing instead of adhering to the principles of the company and seeking the best for it, how much more God?

67. Relationships

The whole topic of 'personnel', i.e., the working relationship between employers, superiors, employees, workers, colleagues, etc., is relatively complex. While a full consideration would go beyond the scope of this book, some points must be mentioned here.

General Relationship Aspects

In a way, it's fairly easy for a Christian to fool others about his relationship with God. However, when it comes to interpersonal relationships you can't fool people for long. Because of the relative proximity to others in the workplace where we spend most of our wakefulness, unhealthy relationships will show pretty soon.

The Kingdom of God is based on relationships. It is therefore not surprising that God has established elementary principles of relationship for us. Sometimes they may be difficult to follow, but we cannot ignore them:

- We lie if we profess to love God yet hate fellow believers *(1John 4:20-21)*.
- Because Christians belong to the same (spiritual) body *(Rom 12:4-5; 1Cor 10:17; 12:12-13, 20; Eph 3:6; 4:25; Col 3:15)*, they must work together and complement each other instead of competing.
- The two fundamental principles of God's Kingdom are, (1) love God with all you are and have, and (2) love your neighbour as yourself *(Matt 22:37-39)*. It presupposes that we do love ourselves.
- Moreover, Jesus told us to even love our enemies and to do good to them *(Matt 5:44; Luke 6:27+35)*.
- Generally, we are expected to treat others the way we like to be treated *(Matt 7:12; Luke 6:31)*.
- Conversely, because bad company corrupts good character *(1Cor 15:33)*, we are warned to watch out with whom we associate.

These directives for a love-based altruistic conduct amongst each other stand in notable contrast to the secular climate of selfishness, unforgiveness, competition, ruthlessness, punishment and revenge.

> *Love is patient, love is kind. It does not envy, it does not boast, it is not proud. It is not rude, it is not self-seeking, it is not easily angered, it keeps no record of wrongs. Love does not delight in evil but rejoices with the truth. It always protects, always trusts, always hopes, always perseveres. Love never fails. (1Cor 13:4-8a)*

Work Relationships

Those general biblical guidelines for relationships must govern both private and work relationships. The latter one arguably even more so because we spend an average of 70% of our waking state at our jobs. Here is a, likely incomplete, list of statements and questions that may serve as a good starting point for reflection:

(A) Treatment/Handling Of Staff

REQUIREMENTS

- They are God's children, too, and not slaves to be exploited for financial gain.
- Do I allow constructive criticism?
- Am I open for suggestions, proposals, improvements, and things like that?
- Do they have the chance to correct shortcomings or make up for mishaps?

WORKING ATMOSPHERE

- Am I clear, leading, open, transparent, polite, reliable, encouraging, and willing to promote personal development?
- Am I sympathetic, accommodating and willing to make myself vulnerable (as far as appropriate)?
- Do I show proper respect *(Eph 6:5-9)*?
- Am I interested in their personal lives, families, challenges, etc. as far as that is possible and manageable?
- Am I willing to evaluate if their difficulties are a result of poor management?
- Do I blackmail, manipulate, suppress, oppress, mistreat those posing a threat to my position?
- Do I sacrifice others to save my own job?
- Do I treat them as a commodity as the name 'human resources' implies?

PAY/REMUNERATION

- Do I pay market-based salaries and wages or what is biblical just and fair?
- Would I be prepared to do this job for this payment?

EMPLOYMENT CRITERIA

- What's the criterion for filling a vacancy – theoretical, professional education, practical expertise, the applicant's character, untapped potential and skills?
- Do I seek the Lord's guidance on who the right person for the vacancy is?
- Would I give people a chance that the world considers failures, dropouts, poor, unpleasant, strange, neglected, etc.? (I might just encounter God in them – *Matt 25:36-40*)

RESPONSIBILITY

- Am I fostering the staff's development, training, character, abilities, education, etc.?

- Do I pray for the staff and their families and care for them as much as possible and manageable?

ECONIMICAL ASPECTS

- How do I go about retrenchment? Do I easily fire people to cut costs swiftly?
- Or do I ask the Lord what to do?
- Do I try to help those I have to release in finding a new job, vocation, etc.?
- Am I willing to keep people on the payroll at God's command, even when it looks economically unprofitable?

(B) Behaviour/Conduct Between Colleagues

- Colleagues aren't competitors. They need each other to fulfil their company duties.
- Am I willing to be a team player and pray for my colleagues?
- Do I respect them and treat them the way I want to be treated by them?
- Do I enjoy my colleagues having success or am I envious?
- Am I willing to go the extra mile to help and support them?
- Am I willing to lovingly point out wrongs instead of gossiping, and allow others also to correct me without becoming resentful?
- Am I reliable, honest with others, transparent and willing to be vulnerable? Do I keep my word and promises?
- Am I willing to contribute to a joyful, appreciative, caring and even loving work environment?

(C) Behaviour/Conduct Towards My Employer/Superior

- Am I submissive and acknowledge their role or am I constantly critical, envious and rebellious?
- Do I treat them with respect according to *Eph 6:5-9*?
- Do I pray for them?
- Am I willing to help them take their responsibilities by doing my job well and with the right attitude, or am I planning their demise?
- Am I prepared to make them look good?

- Am I reliable, honest with others, transparent and willing to be vulnerable? Do I keep my word and promises?
- Am I willing to give my very best for the salary/wage I receive or do I see my employer as a mere cash cow?
- How do I speak to others about the company/my employer?

In Closing

Especially due to the relative and close proximity to colleagues, it is easy to mess up work relations. From a secular point of view, work relationships are simply business transactions and are based on the benefits I can get from them. If you pay me I give you my expertise and workforce, and vice versa. You may not see it as negative, but strictly speaking, it's Satan's approach.

However, God wants us to approach relationships, even working relationships, differently. Not, 'how can you help me?', but 'how can I help you?'. That's biblical. The fact that there is an exchange of expertise and labor for payment does not mean we can neglect the general rules of relationships God imposes upon us.

Keeping the right balance between job requirements and godly relationships in the workplace can be quite difficult, but it's not impossible. If it was, God would not ask us to see to it.

Part G

Plan And Purpose

Reading this book has hopefully shed light on the great deception of the secular money system. It enslaves and ultimately destroys mankind. In response, I have described in detail the biblical foundation and approach to money, which results in (economic) freedom. A mere application of the financial principles of God will surely bring its results. But if this happens under God's guidance, born from an intimate relationship with Him *(John 15:4-8)*, it carries much more authority, dynamism, and transformative power.

The whole Bible is permeated with God's promises of blessings (divine favour and protection) and rewards for those who wholeheartedly follow and obey Him. In contrast, those who rebel against Him will have to deal with the consequences of the resultant curses (openness to injury and punishment).

The most compact and comprehensive list (relating to all spheres in life) of those blessings and curses are found in *Deut 28*. It is part of Moses' final words to the Israelites before they entered the Promised Land. Still, they are very relevant to us *(Rom 15:4; 1Cor 10:11)*. The possibly most striking comparison of blessing and curse in economic terms is the picture of acting as either head (freedom from financial slavery = blessed; *V12-13*) or tail (financially enslaved = cursed; *V44*).

Anyway, following God's ways with heart and soul, is about more than just the immediate effects on our earthly lives. We are fulfilling a specific purpose in His overarching plan. Let's end this book by looking at this.

Overarching Plan

Have you ever wondered why the Bible begins with creation *(Gen 1:6-31)*, which was good to very good in God's eyes, but then ends with everything created new *(Rev 21)*?

For this to make sense, we need to consider that before the first creation, God first separated the light from the darkness *(Gen 1:3-5)*, allowing us to distinguish between good and evil. The light revealed Satan's rebellion and the consequent corruption of creation *(Gen 3:1-7)*. Satan deceptively gained rule over earth.

Because God is righteous, the devil has to lose his rule over earth legally. So judgment and the destruction of Satan, all evil and corruption will precede the new creation *(Rev. 20:7-15)*. The event of new creation in turn allows us to enjoy the perfect light *(Rev 21:23)*.

Nestled in between those events are the narratives of Israel, Jesus Christ and the beginnings of the Body of Christ (Jew and Gentile believers). Whilst Israel, as God's chosen people, fought physical battles against God's enemies *(OT)*, the Son of God brought a new spiritual dimension and dynamism to those battles by introducing the Kingdom of God *(NT)*. Since then, the Body of Christ is engaged in a spiritual battle that eventually brings about the Final Judgment.

Light + darkness separated	*Gen 1:3-5*	
Creation	*Gen 1:6-31*	
Rebellion + corruption	*Gen 3:1-7*	Satan gains rule over earth deceptively
Israel	*Old Testam.*	physical battle
Jesus Christ	*New Testam.*	Kingdom of God
Body of Christ	*Ever since*	spiritual battle
Judgments + destruction	*Rev 20:7-15*	Satan loosing rule over earth legally
New creation	*Rev 21*	
Perfect Light	*Rev 21:23*	

The above table shows the highly summarised biblical flow of events in God's overarching plan. The reason for becoming a believer goes beyond our own mere salvation, as it were. Every Christian has a purpose in this plan of God.

Purpose

It is undisputed that Jesus Christ lived on this planet for a very specific purpose, too. The apostle John affirmed that the reason the Son of God appeared was to destroy the works of the devil *(1John 3:8)*.

> *Very truly I tell you, whoever believes in me* **will do** *the works I have been doing, and* **they will do** *even greater things than these, because I am going to the Father. (Jesus in John 14:12; emphasis added)*

> *[…] since that time* **he waits** *for his enemies* **to be made** *his footstool. (Heb 10:13; emphasis added)*

The two Bible verses above reveal two incredible facts: (1) Jesus leaves no doubt that those who believe in Him WILL surpass Him in the continuation of His work. This is not just a possibility but a given fact. (2) Since Jesus ascended to heaven and sat at the right hand of God, He is WAITING for us to fulfil our purpose here on earth. Our purpose, then, has obviously something to do with turning His enemies into His footstool.

> *For our struggle is not against flesh and blood, but against the rulers, against the authorities, against the powers of this dark world and against the spiritual forces of*

evil in the heavenly realms. (Eph 6:12)

However, since our fight is not against flesh and blood, making Jesus' enemies His footstool is not about a physical fight against Satan and anyone who rejects God. Rather, it's a spiritual battle that is fought and won by obedience to God's ways rather than following the world's.

Remember when in the desert Jesus finished His preparation for His ministry to destroy the works of the devil? Satan tried to tempt Him there, knowing that if his temptations were successful, he would render the Son of God useless for His ministry. For the devil, it was about life and death.

One of the three temptations was to offer Jesus all the riches of the world. As read elsewhere Satan was lawfully entitled to offer this. Interestingly, although Christ had all authority, power and ability to dispose of the devil then and there once and for all, He didn't. Instead, true to His righteous nature, He chose to resist all temptations and thereby create a platform on which Satan can in the end be legally judged and cast out of heaven *(Rev 12:7-13; Luke 10:17-18; Isa 14:12-17)* so that he no longer can accuse the faithful.

To make the enemies of Christ His footstool, we must follow Jesus' own example. This means resisting the temptations of Satan, for three good reasons: (1) To not harm and enslave ourselves; (2) To ensure that we do not become useless for our God-given purposes; (3) To add to the legal grounds for the devil to be judged (see e.g. the life story of *Job*) and in the fulness of time be disposed off for good *(Rev 20:7-10)*.

Ever since Satan tried to tempt Him, Jesus warned His followers that they can't serve both God and money *(Matt 6:24; Luke 16:13)*. They must also resist the lure of money for it brings with it a considerable danger of idolatry and bondage, something we have dealt with in this book.

Amid various financial messages Jesus once gave to His audience, the disciples asked Him how to pray correctly to avoid praying like the hypocrites, for they prayed prayers they didn't mean. He gave them a model prayer, which is still used today in the body of Christ. Part of it goes,

> *[…] your kingdom come, your will be done, on earth as it is in heaven. (Matt 6:10)*

This is in fact a declaration of intent to actively participate in God's amazing plans and establish His rule on earth to end the one of Satan. *'Your will be done'* **does definitely include the element of our active contribution. That also applies to all economic and financial matters. It conveys our willingness and determination to act in accordance with the righteous laws of God to expose the unrighteous laws of Satan's world system *(Eph 5:11)*. It brings judgement on Satan's rule.

The world's economic science teaches that in economies (the production and consumption of goods and services and the relating money supply) potential profits and losses determine what is feasible and what isn't. As a consequence everything and everyone is subservient to financial goals. People are reduced to either production factors or revenue streams. Their value rest entirely on the monetary benefit they provide.

But who, in all seriousness, would like to be reduced as a person to a mere factor of production or a source of income for mainly unscrupulous, exploitative and money-driven capitalist market economies? This is simply sickening in the eyes of our Creator, in whose image we are created and from whom we derive our value.

Speaking of obedience to God's laws, when Jesus was repeatedly challenged by the law teachers to name the most important law of God which man must follow, He quoted from *Deut 6:5* and *Lev 19:18*,

> *'Love the Lord your God with all your heart and with all your soul and with all your mind and with all your strength.' The second is this: 'Love your neighbour as yourself.' There is no commandment greater than these. (Mark 12:30-31; see also Matt 22:37-40; Luke 10:27)*

For the Israelites at that time, it was a written law that they had to obey on their own strength. NT believers have this law 'written' on their hearts *(Heb 10:16)*. The implementation of it is an expression of a personal relationship with Jesus Christ and the guidance of the Holy Spirit.

In one of his letters to the NT believers, Paul lists remarkable qualities of the very love Jesus was talking about:

> *Love is patient, love is kind. It does not envy, it does not boast, it is not proud. It does not dishonour others, it is not self-seeking, it is not easily angered, it keeps no record of wrongs. Love does not delight in evil but rejoices with the truth. It always protects, always trusts, always hopes, always perseveres. Love never fails. [...] (1Cor 13:4-8)*

In other words, these two greatest commandments of God that determine man's relation to Him and to each other, involve an amazing dimension and dynamism. Living by them is totally transformative, not only for oneself but also for one's neighbours. Think about it, when everyone gives this kind of love to God and his neighbours (incl. enemies), it must be like heaven on earth. It certainly brings judgement on the selfish, destructive ways of the world system.

Encouragement

Isn't it exciting that, rather than frustratingly submit to the slavery of the world money system, we can actually be part of God's transformation plan in which our life has real purpose? It will be truly awesome when we begin making healthy relationships with God and others, rather than money, the commanding currency of our economies. Imagine what life-changing effects that will have on man. The Lord is very passionate about this and totally encourages us to go for it. It will bear great results.

> *Do not conform to the pattern of this world, but be transformed by the renewing of your mind. Then you will be able to test and approve what God's will is – his good, pleasing and perfect will (Rom 12:2)*

Again, this will bring God's Kingdom rule to earth and His light will expose the darkness of the world system, so that its ruler, Satan, can legally be judged.

> *Have nothing to do with the fruitless deeds of darkness, but rather expose them. (Eph 5:11)*

The promises that God made to the Jews for the time after the Babylonian captivity are also valid for us today (see Paul's statement in *Rom 15:4; 1Cor 10:11*) when we leave Babylon.

> *"For I know the plans I have for you," declares the LORD, "plans to prosper you and not to harm you, plans to give you hope and a future." (Jer 29:11)*

Printed in Great Britain
by Amazon